The Digital Turn

How the Internet Transforms Our Existence

Wim Westera

authorHOUSE®

AuthorHouse™
1663 Liberty Drive
Bloomington, IN 47403
www.authorhouse.com
Phone: 1-800-839-8640

Published by AuthorHouse   2013

ISBN: 978-1-4772-5032-7 (sc)
ISBN: 978-1-4772-5033-4 (e)

The Digital Turn

CONTENTS

PREFACE

This book deals with the progressive virtualisation of the world and its boundless impact on human existence. It analyses the role of computers, smartphones, social media, and the Internet at large and how these contribute to our understanding of the world. It covers the fundamentally changing landscape of today's social interactions and our changing perceptions of space and time, knowledge, social relationships, citizenship, power and control, culture, and eventually, life.

Many thousands of years ago, we painted our first works of art on the walls of our caves. These were the first examples of our creation of a shared, mediated memory for consolidating and conveying messages. Thereafter, the invention of writing marked the birth of communication media. Individuals' valuable knowledge could now be recorded and preserved for future generations. Ever since, media have become more advanced and have helped to accumulate the knowledge and ideas that constitute our culture.

All media are essentially cognition amplifiers. Cave paintings, clay tablets, books, and computers enable us to extend our cognitive capacities. Hence, media operate on the defining feature of our species. Physically, we are not in the same league as lions, cheetahs, or crocodiles, but we compensate for our shortcomings with our superior cognitive abilities. We've managed to defeat predators with conscious thought, intelligent strategies, and planned behaviours. Our cognition has been the decisive element of our evolutionary success and has made our species the ruler of the world. Today, our cognitive abilities are greatly strengthened by the ever-growing flow of digital media, tools, and devices that pervade our daily lives and connect us to the news and the communities and culture we are part of. They help us to answer questions, to solve problems, and to connect to any resource or person on Earth. Media stretch our mental horizons and help us to better understand the world and ourselves.

Today we spend an ever larger portion of our lives in virtual spaces. But we easily go astray in the patchwork of media which is continually changing as new services and devices become available. The problem is that mediated communication fundamentally differs from the face-to-face communication that we are used to. The intermediate digital mechanisms restrict our opportunities for direct verification of the sincerity, reliability, and truth of messages. They make it hard for us to distinguish between appearance and reality, and from them we are likely to procure a distorted and truncated view of the world. The ongoing replacement of existing devices and software with newer and richer versions calls for a robust and sustainable approach to media literacy that breaks through superficial, volatile media features and uncovers the invariant key concepts of media and their interrelationships.

The premise of this book is that we should understand the basic determinants and mechanisms of media, meaning, and cognition rather than the particular attributes of them or devices they're carried on that happen to be in vogue. The book reveals the underlying machinery of mediated communication and the ways we attach meaning to it. It explains how media transform our natural habitat and influence the ways we arrange our lives—how the media are transforming us. Therefore, the book is mainly about ourselves, superior cognitive beings that have managed to subject all other species on Earth. It is a compact guide to media literacy and to coping with the flood of digital media that is yet to come, making it an indispensable aid for every twenty-first century citizen.

CHAPTER 1

The Unique Collection of Cells We Are

It is hard to fully understand who we are and why we exist at all. We seem to have a conscious mind that has a notion of self and of the self's interaction with the environment. We have come to know a lot about the world, its phenomena, and its processes, and we have created an abundance of ingenious tools that have helped us to improve our lives. Not without endearment and compassion, we may look at our helpless ancestors, prehistoric humans and their evolutionary precursors, who lived in the savannas, restlessly chasing food and ruthlessly being chased by beasts of prey. Precursors to *Homo sapiens* such as Java man and Lucy must have lived in ignorance, knowing very little—we suppose—about the world and the secrets of nature. If we could only see their faces as we showed them our skyscrapers, TVs, and aeroplanes! However, we should be modest, because what do we really understand about the world? What do we really understand about ourselves, our lives, our existence? To date, our conscious mind remains largely incomprehensible. We do not know whether humans will ever be capable of understanding what life is all about. At the same time, life is utterly fascinating because it's a mystery.

How long it took

Time is one of the most peculiar and intangible constructs. Any activity or event we experience is inevitably linked to this special singular point in time called "now". Whatever we do, we do it now, at this very moment, this steadily progressing point in time that relentlessly separates the future from the past. It is hard to fully capture and understand the significance of time. We may have a fair idea about the concepts of "yesterday", "next week", or "last month", but the longer durations of evolution or geology are simply beyond our imagination. But human life developed on exactly these time scales.

The Earth is calculated to have existed for about 4.5 billion years. It is hard to find a reference point that helps us grasp the significance of such a huge number, but here are some examples: 4.5 billion equals the number of seconds in one century, the earth's circumference in centimetres, and the number of words written in 100 copies of the *Encyclopaedia Britannica*. Not until 3.8 billion years ago did organic molecules form and group together to produce the first unicellular living creatures.

If we condense Earth's 4.5 billion years of age into one year, starting on 1 January, life would emerge on 26 February. From there, gradually more complex forms of life developed: algae, fungi, trilobites, fish. For a long period, only the seas were populated, but some 500 million years ago, plants and animals left the water and started colonising the land. On our one-year scale, this happened on 21 November. The dinosaurs appeared on 13 December (225 million years ago) and went extinct on 26 December (65 million years ago).

Still, we had to wait for *Homo erectus*, our direct ancestor with the peculiar habit of permanently balancing and moving upright on two legs. They arrived only on New Year's Eve at half past eight in the evening (1.8 million years ago). The brain of *Homo erectus* was remarkably large, up to 1,000 grams, twice the size of the brain of *Australopithecus*, the genus that preceded

Homo, three times that of a chimpanzee's brain, and four times that of a lion. Then, at 23 minutes to midnight (200,000 years ago), a new type of human showed up with even more brain volume, up to 1,500 grams. For obvious reasons, this new species was called *Homo sapiens*: wise human. These early ancestors were intelligent creatures that used tools, prepared food and clothes, and practiced hunting strategies, but with their short and stocky bodies and their flat and elongated skulls, they didn't quite look like today's humans. The famous Neanderthals belonged to this lineage. For unclear reasons, the species *Homo neanderthalensis* disappeared entirely. We had to wait until 12 minutes before midnight (100,000 years ago) for the earliest modern humans to appear: these are *Homo sapiens sapiens*, with the double label indicating the species of wise and thinking humans that we belong to. This species' physical appearance hardly differed from the average European's today: if they wore the right clothes and fashionable hairstyles, we wouldn't notice these ancient people walking our streets.

Altogether, the era of modern humans has been relatively short. We showed up on New Year's Eve, a few minutes before midnight. We've only just arrived.

How we made it

Looking back, it is miraculous that we've made it at all. On innumerable occasions, our bloodline nearly ended. First we had to wait for a planet to live on. Earth arose out of a large, rotating cloud of interstellar dust and gas and withstood the risk of being swallowed by the large mass in the centre of the cloud that formed the sun. Small fragments revolving around the sun collided and grouped together and gradually gained sufficient gravitational force to attract even larger fragments, eventually resulting in the stable planet we live on.

It has been suggested that in its early years, planet Earth collided with another proto-planet that happened to cross our trajectory. The giant impact ejected large amounts of material from Earth into space, where it grouped together under the influence of its own gravity to form our well-known satellite the moon. This collision was by far not a simple blast. It released enormous amounts of energy that would have caused Earth and the moon to become completely molten. Certainly, no living creature would have survived the extremely high temperatures. In addition, the collision tilted Earth's rotational axis. Without this axial tilt, Earth would be without seasons and its climate and ocean currents would be completely different: there would be no monsoons, no trade winds, and no bird migrations. Trees (if there were any) would blossom all the time or perhaps never. A year would be a useless unit of time.

From Earth's hot outer layers, steam escaped, gradually building the atmosphere. Violent volcanism added nitrogen, carbon dioxide, methane, and ammonia to it. Additional water vapour was supplied by the impacts of many small proto-planetary objects that populated the early solar system. As Earth gradually cooled, its crust solidified. Clouds formed, and rain filled the oceans. By accident, an ozone layer formed some dozens of kilometres above Earth's surface, absorbing up to 99 per cent of the sun's high-energy ultraviolet light. This layer turned out to be quite useful because ultraviolet light is extremely damaging to living cells.

Still, we had to wait until the primordial soup of organic molecules happened to produce amino acids, proteins, and enzymes, the main building blocks of life. Yet these were still just molecules, inanimate matter lacking brains, muscles, sex, digestion, and many more key characteristics of living things. During the next millions of years, life emerged by mere chance. Millions of millions of processes involving different molecules, temperatures, concentrations, and pressures failed to achieve this feat before this time. But then the unthinkable happened. Three basic conditions were needed to enable the transition from a mix of organic molecules to a coherent and stable entity that deserved to be called a living organism. First, the right mix of molecules needed a physical shelter to keep them together and to shield them from disruptive external influences. Such shelter was provided by polymer membranes of cells. Second, the molecules captured within the membrane required energy to keep their internal biological processes going. Inorganic compounds like hydrogen sulphide available in the environment rather than oxygen must have fuelled early cells. Later on, well-known aerobic metabolisms emerged, providing a striking similarity among species from unicellular bacteria to complex, multicellular organisms as human beings. Third, the cells required a mechanism for reproduction, including the coding of structural information and the transfer of this code to offspring. DNA proved capable of encoding the blueprints of life that could be passed on to the next generation. Other solutions may have also emerged, but as a consequence of the unrelenting laws of evolution, the most appropriate solution survived and weaker alternatives died out. Indeed, all life known to us now is characterised by DNA-based genes.

So, we had to wait for this glorious moment in which all pieces of the puzzle fitted together and the first living cell was born: a milestone in the evolution of the world. Probably a large number of different types of cells formed independently, but only one of these was destined to become the last universal ancestor, the one and only primal cell that all life descends from. This hypothesis is substantiated by the fundamental similarity of cellular processes across different species. Whatever living creature we analyse, we find that its cells use a fixed set of twenty amino acids for building proteins and nucleic acids for encoding genes. The universal ancestor is the very great-great-grandparent to horses, skunks, spiders, herrings, lobsters, trees, plants, fungi, bacteria, and us.

For billions of years, single-celled organisms were the only forms of life. They reproduced generation after generation without ever producing complex organisms. Then, some 1 billion years ago, a sudden change occurred: single cells managed to group together and form more complex creatures. Once this happened, cells specialised into nervous cells, muscle cells, retina cells, and so on. A flood of new creatures appeared and gradually became more complex: insects, amphibians, reptiles. Humans weren't around yet, but our genes were on their way if they could survive all the dangers of the prehistoric world. And they did.

Not too long ago, the first humans appeared. Conditions must have been tough in those days: the world was a mysterious and dangerous scene. Without appropriate knowledge, methods, and tools, procuring food, drink, clothing, and shelter was not straightforward. Humans had to cope with hunger, extreme weather conditions, diseases, injuries, and animals of prey. Our ancestors compensated for the greater strength, speed, and agility of bears, wolves, and other predators with our superior mental abilities, developing smart strategies for hiding and hunting. The human brain was capable of replacing instinctive impulses with well-considered anticipation, strategic thinking, and rational decision making. In the long run, these abilities worked out to be an unparalleled advantage. The human species has survived and even managed to rule the world, effectively subjecting all other species on Earth.

The genesis of humanity looks very much like a success story. To a great extent it is. One may wonder how on earth this was possible at all. Before producing us, life had to go through a series of odd developmental stages. It had to manage to replicate its cells; to differentiate those cells into scales, gills and fins, brains, eyes, limbs, fur, hands, fingers, genitals; and to learn how to move, climb, fly, growl, mate, and do many more things. We are the outcome of a long evolutionary process in which the qualities that provided the best fit to the conditions of life were preserved and those that didn't were doomed to fade. Slight deviations in the prevailing conditions would have made us look completely different. We might have had six arms, three eyes, a trunk, plumage, a split tongue, or even antlers. The fact that you are reading this means that you're lucky enough to be alive, which is the ultimate proof that you're part of the evolutionary line that has survived the last 3.8 billion years. All your ancestors, whether they were amoebas, fish, or mammals, proved strong and healthy enough to grow to adulthood, develop fertility, and reproduce while they avoided getting wounded, eaten, or starved before passing on their genes. After transferring their DNA they were prepared, capable, and available to protect and raise their offspring successfully. Every individual today is the outcome of an uninterrupted line of successful mating and gene replication with a proven record of withstanding all the dangers and challenges around.

So, if we truly are the best fit for the conditions of life, one might wonder why so many people need doctors, medications, surgery, and life-sustaining devices. The simple answer is that the very fact that we are capable of treating injuries and illnesses demonstrates our agility in adapting to external conditions. By defeating nature, we have proven to be the fittest indeed. We may regard ourselves as the crown of evolution, we may have survived and subjugated all our enemies, but this doesn't mean that we're invulnerable. Maybe one of our predators will finally find a way to defeat us. What about a pandemic caused by bacteria immune to any antibiotics, or by viruses? Alternatively, an asteroid impact similar to the one that wiped out the dinosaurs 65 million years ago may terminate our species. Our food supply or habitat may suffer the sweeping effects of climate change. Or suppose that we lose control of our nuclear arms and turn the world into an inferno? We have made it so far; we've survived myriad threats. Probably the major menace to humankind are humans themselves.

What is supposed to make us different

The self-proclaimed superiority of the human species inherently disqualifies other species from winning that title. We call each other animal names as popular forms of abuse. Nobody wants to be called a cow, worm, louse, insect, pig, chicken, beast, or animal. However, it is precarious to claim that the human species is the undisputed king of the universe. It is quite possible that superior extraterrestrial creatures exist out there in space that would look down their noses at our limited mental capabilities, just as we do for chickens or goldfish. Even compared to other species on Earth, our supposed superiority may be the result of flattery and distorted self-perception. The Neanderthals, our early cousins, may have had the same opinion about their unrivalled position in the hierarchy of life, but they nevertheless all became extinct. It is even hard to refute the idea that roundworms, *E. coli* bacteria, or dust mites consider themselves to be the one and only superior species on Earth. They may rightly claim that they have been around much longer than we have, that they exist in much larger numbers, or that they've successfully colonised humans and many other species.

Genetic differences between humans and other animals are not quite significant. Chimpanzees share up to 98 per cent of their genes with humans, cats 90 per cent, and mice up to 75 per cent. Even fruit flies (Drosophila) are 60 per cent similar to humans, the same as chickens. We share many of our features with other animals: we have heads, eyes, ears, limbs, toes. To a certain extent, we look like animals and we behave like animals. On a smaller scale, the similarities are likewise striking: we have blood, nerves, a metabolism, digestion, amino acids, hormones, and, last but not least, the living cell as the body's building block. Overall, our physique is unextraordinary. On many points, animals outperform us. Obviously, lions are much stronger than we are, cheetahs and horses are much faster, hawks have better sight, dogs have better hearing and smell, squirrels climb better, and so on. It is fair to say that many of our capabilities fail to exceed mediocrity.

There is this one particular feature, however, that seems to make us far superior to any other form of life: our unparalleled brain. The human brain is of matchless beauty and impenetrable complexity. It is much larger than any other mammal's brain, and its features differ mainly in the neocortex, the folded, grey top layer which enables higher-order mental functions like thought, language, consciousness, memory, and learning. The brain's disproportionate size causes severe problems at birth. Nature's solution is to move the timing of birth up and produce prematures compared to other animals—that's why newborns are so helpless. At birth, our skull isn't fused, allowing the brain to keep growing afterwards. It may take up to two years for the fontanelles to close.

Altogether, the brain is a huge parallel processor that outperforms all existing computer circuits. It provides us with mental powers that enable us to be reflective rather than reflexive, that is, to use considerate thought to control our instinctive impulses. Although we sometimes live by our impulses (by eating or shopping too much or acting out in anger), we often think, reason, evaluate, and plan our strategies and actions deliberately in order to master our environment. These powers make us excellent problem solvers, capable of achieving nearly inconceivable feats like defeating cholera, smallpox, and other deadly diseases; forecasting solar eclipses; and manipulating invisible molecules to create nano-scale computing units. Human beings are problem solvers by nature. We like to be challenged by quizzes and puzzles. That's probably why we're still here. In contrast, other mammals like cats, horses, and dogs get confused by minor problems. If you take your dog out for a walk and the lead happens to get twisted around a lamppost, it is quite unlikely that the dog will be able to work out the problem and solve it by making a reverse movement. Instead, the dog will pull and pull in the wrong direction, until you command him to sit and let you untwine the lead. Many animals do manage to solve problems, such as cracking nuts, stealing food, or opening doors, but most of these achievements are learned by trial and error rather than considerate thought.

Our unique neural architecture produces our conscious mind: the incomparable capability of experiencing, recognising, knowing, and reflecting about ourselves. We look upon the self as the unique identity that consciously experiences our sensory observations and controls our thoughts, choices, and actions. Although the self is bound to the body, we are capable of taking up an external perspective on ourselves and evaluating how we act and behave. Likewise, our conscious mind demonstrates the ability of empathy: we are capable of projecting ourselves into other individuals and understanding how others might feel, think, or look at the world. This is a favourable feature for building families, communities, and societies. Also, it demonstrates our imaginative powers. These are indispensible for creativity, solving problems, and developing effective strategies. Imagination allows us to escape from everyday worries. It makes us dream away in worlds of fantasy and to produce masterpieces of art and literature. Imagination makes us good survivors since it allows us to anticipate future events and threats.

Language is yet another feature that distinguishes us from other animals. Although many animals communicate with each other, they can only produce singular, predetermined sounds. Chimpanzees, dogs, and horses may learn to understand some human words, but they are unable to speak themselves. They simply lack the speech centre unique to human brains, Broca's area, which is responsible for controlling the multiple muscles involved in speech. Animals' brains simply cannot deal with words and grammar and cannot produce speech the way we do. Scientists analysing fossilised skulls of *Homo erectus* concluded that even brains this evolutionarily early must have included Broca's area. They also found that the anatomy of the bone anchoring the tongue and the structure of the head and neck in *Homo erectus* didn't differ much from ours. Therefore, it is quite likely that one million years ago, our early ancestors could speak like we do, albeit with limited vocabulary, perhaps simpler grammar, and less sophistication. This new attainment marks the beginning of human culture, because it allowed us to develop abstract concepts and ideas, describe relationships between objects, and explain mysterious phenomena. Language amplifies our thinking because it enables the manipulation of symbols and complex reasoning, and therefore it is strongly linked with other mental capabilities. Once language became available it also amplified itself, because the larger our vocabulary gets, the larger its expressive power will be as a result of increased combinatorial richness. It makes us discuss, suppose, assert, reason, judge, calculate, negotiate, trade, joke, plan, and many more things. In the end, language may be the basic condition for all of our achievements.

Apparently, a highly developed brain offers great evolutionary advantages. We have outperformed any predator not by physical strength but by thinking, talking, inventing the right tools, anticipating dangers, and undertaking the right actions. It must be frustrating for other animals to be confronted by these seemingly insignificant creatures that waddle on their hind legs so inconveniently and still manage to always come off best. We've managed to develop language, arts, science, and philosophy, components of our rich and venerable culture. We've invented new technologies that have radically changed the way we live. No longer do we have to stalk our prey on the savannas to get our daily meals. Admittedly, large numbers of people still suffer from poverty, hunger, wars, and diseases, but the average person in a developed country has no worries about basic needs like food, water, shelter, and safety. Recent technological breakthroughs like the Internet and mobile phones are completely changing our habitat by bringing a virtual world to our fingertips. Physical power is increasingly trivialised because we rule the world with our unequalled brain. The general picture of modern life is easily caricatured by a slightly overweight person sitting on a chair and indifferently staring at a screen while only making the minor movements to manipulate a mouse and keyboard. Indeed, the human body loses value. Today's men and women aren't brave fighters but committed knowledge workers exerting transactions from behind computers. Yes, we like sports, but most of us prefer watching sports to playing them. We admire athletes because they seem to reconfirm the latent but unreachable possibilities of our own bodies. Sporting events are like a site-show, a vanishing circus act that addresses our romanticism of bygone days when our physical capabilities were decisive for survival. Perhaps the human body is a relic of the past.

Our brains will probably grow larger still. It is the tragedy of humankind that our ever-increasing mental powers go with the decline of our bodies. Today's world of digital media doesn't seem to hinder this. It offers outstanding possibilities for transcending the body and entering a world completely controlled by the mind. To a large extent, we seem to like it. After all, it satisfies an intrinsic human obsession as spirituality, religion, and superstition do: the drive for immortality, the everlasting mind leaving the deteriorated body.

CHAPTER 2

How Far We Got

If prehistoric humans were to visit today's world, they certainly would be overwhelmed by the alien scene of our modern buildings, our congenial central heating and air conditioning, our well-structured farmlands, our buzzing factories, the wheels attached to our miraculously self-propelling vehicles, our power transmission lines stretching towards the horizon, and our aeroplanes insolently defying gravity. By no means does this look like the drudgery in desolate moorlands, disheartening hunting in endless savannas, or the fireless shelter during everlasting snowstorms that characterised prehistoric life. Naturally, today's humans would look a bit weird to our ancestors with our eye-catching clothes, dark sunglasses, styled hair, whitened teeth, and occasional earphones. Prehistoric humans would be struck by the abundance of white sheets covered with incomprehensible patterns of black strings and curls which seem to exert a hypnotising magic on people, freezing and sinking them into a daydream. Even more, they would be fascinated, if not frightened, by the full-scale phantoms appearing on walls, screens, and displays, appearing absolutely alive and talking to them. Also, it would be odd for our ancestors to notice people mumbling into little hand-held objects as if trying to overcome a curse. The perspective of ancient humans as naïve outsiders helps us to reflect about today's world and prevent us from taking it for granted. It makes us aware of the great impact of new technologies on our culture and the ways we arrange our lives.

The birth of writing

Like many social animals, early humans must have been deft at communication. Their early utterances may not have used proper sentences or even words, sounding like the growls of other animals. Nevertheless, humans' substantial cognitive powers enabled them to gradually develop a larger repertoire of communicative behaviours by combining sounds, gestures, and facial expressions. In turn, increased expressive power amplified cognition. The mutual stimulation of cognition and communication greatly accelerated human performance. Gradually, humans learned to make distinct sounds by moving the tongue against the palate. This allowed for more articulated utterances that could convey more details and subtleties. This was possibly far from what we consider speech today, but speech was clearly on its way.

Humans also learned to capture knowledge and ideas in pictorial representations. For a start, these may have been simple decorations on tools or adornments or easy sketches in the sand just like the art we make on a sunny day at the beach. Rock carvings and cave paintings date from some 30,000 years ago. These are the early attempts to capture and represent meaning visually. Of course, their impact was very limited because these messages were troublesome, if not impossible, to distribute. Little by little, pictorial codes were standardised and integrated in a shared framework for conveying meaning. Some 5,000 years ago, the first Babylonian clay tablets appeared. By then, spoken language had become highly sophisticated, but the increased complexity of labour and trade called for a detailed record of the arrangements. The early clay tablets recorded the administration of trade and work in graphical signs that represented commodities and the number of units concerned. They functioned as a shared memory for the parties involved. In the next millennium, Babylonian writing evolved into Sumerian cuneiform that used a grammar to deliver more complex messages. Slightly afterwards, the Egyptians developed their system of hieroglyphs, which also could convey detailed narratives.

The invention of writing marked the birth of communication media: now messages could be consolidated across time and location. The impact of this development can hardly be overestimated. Thanks to writing, human knowledge could now be accumulated in a collective recorded memory. In contrast with the preceding oral culture, which lasted over 100,000 years, valuable knowledge could now be codified on papyrus or another medium and preserved for generations. And that's what we did. We've created millions of writings since then. Any human achievement, be it in the sciences, arts, technology, literature, music, or politics, is one way or another rooted in writing. Indeed, our libraries carry the historic, creative, and intellectual inheritance of our species. The invention of writing marked a fundamental change in the way societies functioned. Its impact was larger than the impact of any other invention, such as gunpowder, penicillin, or motorcars, because writings are manifestations of thought, this unique human feature, and hence they are the cornerstones of human civilisation and human culture.

Although both Egyptian hieroglyphs and Babylonian clay messages were pictorial, deciphering these ancient writings was not as easy as reading a comic strip. Each ancient writing systems comprised up to a thousand different tokens and used a strict grammar, allowing a token to represent many different meanings dependent on context. Until the nineteenth century, attempts at deciphering the ancient codes failed. First it was nearly impossible to decide whether the characters were to be read from left to right or from right to left. Likewise, archaeologists had hardly any clues about what the tokens represented. Finally, through the combined efforts of many researchers, both codes were broken and the ancient messages were revealed.

In the course of time, cuneiform script gradually became more simplified. The number of characters decreased dramatically and pictorial dominance vanished as the characters became more abstract, thus marking the transition to symbolic representation. Some 3,000 years ago, various alphabetic systems emerged, including the Phoenician alphabet that used a very limited set of characters (up to twenty-two) representing phonemes, the elementary building blocks of spoken language. Because of its phonemic nature, the alphabet could support many different languages. The Phoenician alphabet is assumed to be the predecessor of the Roman alphabet, which the Romans spread across large parts of Europe. It became the basis for Western writing, and it gradually elbowed out cuneiform writing and hieroglyphs, extinguishing the ancient writing codes. In the early centuries AD, there was practically nobody left that could read these ancient texts.

Spreading the words

For many centuries, writing was reserved for very few because it required specialised skills and tools. The same holds for reading, not just because large parts of the population never were taught how to read, but also because hardly any written pieces or copies were available. Once books were invented, the making of a copy was a drudgery: each copy had to be written by hand, which required endless patience. This duty primarily fell to monks greatly devoted to copying the word of God. That's why at the time the Bible was one of the very few books around in Europe. This changed dramatically about the year 1450 by the invention of the printing press, which is generally attributed to the German goldsmith Johann Gutenberg. It seems that he was greatly inspired by the many wine presses spread about the fruitful borders of the river Rhine. Printing techniques were known in China and Japan as early as the third century, but Gutenberg's movable type technique provided superior printing quality against very low costs. This was not anymore about simple and laborious woodcarving but about typesetting with well-prepared metal character sets.

Naturally, one of the very first books to be printed was the Bible. In the first run, the nearly inconceivable number of 180 Bible copies were produced so that the word of God could now be spread across Europe at unprecedented speed. Such early adoption by a religious institution that altogether wasn't noted for its positive attitude towards innovation and change is remarkable. By contrast, Turkish Muslims rejected all this modernity and banned the printing of religious books because they considered it a sin. Hence, the Middle East was deprived of this innovation for many centuries. In Europe, however, the printing industry flourished, provoking a radical societal change. The number of book copies grew tremendously, in turn boosting the interest in reading and writing skills. After many centuries in which the alphabet had been an unreachable mystery except to nobles and clergymen, the printing press now made it a commodity accessible to almost everyone.

At the start, books were largely of religious nature and fully controlled by the church and monarchs who thereby established their power with greater intensity and reach. The impact of printing was far greater than these leaders could have ever imagined. The printing industry itself required new types of workers, like print compositors, print technicians, proofreaders, booksellers, and librarians, all of which needed to be proficient in reading and writing. Thus began the formation of a well-educated middle class in European cities. Circulation of texts exploded because of easy and inexpensive reproduction. The new invention was warmly welcomed, and the euphoria that went with it provoked utopian prospects about a future world in which knowledge was available to the common people, freed from any exclusion and oppression. Printing was regarded as a milestone, if not the major milestone, in the history of man. It was seen as fostering the democratisation of knowledge, just the way the Internet is viewed today. Criticism also surfaced, and it, too, bore a striking resemblance to the criticism of today's media. Many thought the flood of information was unhealthy or even a threat to peace. Church leaders perceived an affront to their authority now that laymen could study religious texts for themselves rather than relying on what they were told. The rise of newspapers amplified the anxiety even further. But the proliferation of printing was unstoppable.

Its overall impact on human culture is immense. Printing spread ideas at an unprecedented scale and paved the way for the Renaissance, the Reformation, the scientific revolution, and the technologies that built modern society. According to the English philosopher Francis Bacon, mechanical printing changed the whole face and state of things throughout the world.

Speeding up communication

Over the years, the world has become smaller. This is because communication became faster. In ancient days, the transfer of a message from one place to another might take weeks, if not months. Couriers had to walk or sail all the way or ride horses. Smoke signals and tom-toms could make announcements, but their reach was limited. From 1000 BC, carrier pigeons provided "high speed" distance communication. For centuries, this was the highest standard available, but unfortunately, senders never knew if their messages were properly delivered.

In the 1700s the Frenchman Claude Chappe introduced his optical telegraph. It transferred visual messages from one church tower to another a few miles distant. These messages were encoded by arranging a set of black and white panels in a particular order, similar to today's barcodes. A telescope on the receiving tower was used to read the code. A complete sentence could be transmitted by changing the codes. Of course, this encoding process took some time, but still, the system managed to transfer its first sentence, "If you succeed, you will bask in glory", in only 4 minutes across a distance of 10 miles, making its transmission at the staggering speed of 150 miles per hour. This is far better than any postal service could achieve today. To improve the optical telegraph, new lines were set up along a chain of multiple towers, for instance, one chain of 15 towers spanned 130 miles from Paris to Lille. It made the world a bit smaller. The system worked, but it was a bit clumsy and inaccurate, as any mistake in a single link in the chain would be forwarded to the next link. Within a few decades, the Chappe telegraph was outstripped by the wired telegraph, which was the first form of electrical telecommunication. The first messages used a code developed by Samuel Morse. This was inconvenient, but messages were transferred at almost the speed of light.

Half a century afterwards, in 1867, it must have been a moment of magic when Alexander Graham Bell first spoke through the telephone to his assistant, Thomas Augustus Watson, who was in the next room, saying: "Mr. Watson, come here. I want to see you." Although the two men were only a few metres apart and had to shout so loudly that they might have heard each other right through the walls, Bell's telephone had achieved what had been assumed nearly impossible: human speech communication over a distance.

Talking into a device may have looked a bit peculiar, and hearing a human voice coming out of a little box must have been like a hallucination. It was the very first example of telepresence, or extending a human presence to a remote location without moving. People had to get used to be speaking to someone who was not around. The magic was preserved, because conceptually, it was hard for people to understand how the trick worked. Previous inventions such as clockworks, the wheel, or the Chappe telegraph were easy to understand by their transparent, mechanical nature, but the mysterious, invisible powers of electromagnetism remained largely incomprehensible. Even today, the elementary electrostatic and electromagnetic experiments demonstrated in schools and museums arouse great excitement and amazement among spectators because of their weird and unexpected effects.

Soon after Bell's first demonstration, a number of cities in the United States and England installed local exchanges. The first long-distance line linking two major cities was established between New York and Boston in 1882. Selling telephones was good business at the time (and it still is). Consumers no longer wondered about the magic things that happened inside the device They could make do with a basic understanding based on the very simple metaphor of speaking through an elongated tube that transferred the sound without any losses to the remote location. They rashly accepted the new medium as a beneficial tool that enriched their lives.

The example of the telephone exactly explains the intermediary role of a communication medium between person A, who is sending a message, and person B, who is receiving it. It is the starting point for a whole range of new communication media that became available afterwards and that will continue to emerge in the future. These media all allow communication to flow across the world at enormous speed. When in 2009 Paul McCartney, former member of the Beatles, announced a concert in Las Vegas, all 4,000 tickets were gone within 7 seconds of the tickets' going on sale on the Internet. Likewise, all 250,000 tickets for Michael Jackson's planned 2009 concert series in London were sold out within a few days. Unfortunately, Michael Jackson didn't make it to London, but that's a different story. These examples demonstrate not only how incredibly fast the new media technologies are but also how easily people all over the world adopt these media and get engaged in worldwide communication. Today's phones may be more sophisticated than the early ones, but the basic idea didn't change much: they transfer human speech over a distance, thus effecting the real-time teleportation of a speaker's mental presence to some location other than where the body resides. It is quite a miracle that it all works and that we manage to deal with it.

Mediated mind

It may seem a cliché to say that media inventions like writing, printing, and the telephone have radically changed the ways individuals arrange their lives, but clichés are often true, as is the case here. Through our media, human communication is no longer restricted by direct, here-and-now face-to-face meetings. Instead, it has become invariant across location and time. In many cases, our physical presence is no longer a precondition for participation in events. We can address the whole world while sitting in an easy chair by watching a screen and pressing the right buttons. A simple phone call makes us engage in remote events as if we were really there. Our bodies may stay where they are while our minds effortlessly drop their thoughts and ideas at the remote event. To our other conversation partner, our mind is completely mediated, unhindered by physical constraints.

The idea of the mediated mind looks very much like the scene of control room operators of a chemical plant sitting behind their desks and sending out their messages to the far-off corners of the site. Near where I live is one of the largest chemical plants in the world. It is a sinister, hazy site which is loaded with chugging distilling systems, reservoirs, pipes, and chimneys. Every now and then it spews out huge flames to flare off waste, and large clouds of smoke linger in the sky above. At night, the abundance of lights makes it look like an friendly town. But it is a ghost town. Notwithstanding the evidence of bubbling activity, an onlooker will hardly detect any people on the site. Somewhere in the middle of the site, obscured by the labyrinth of pipes and installations, a small team of operations specialists run the plant from the control room. Here, surrounded by computers, displays, switchboards, and status indicators, the operators do their jobs. They are one mouse click away from turning off or adjusting one of the huge distillers at the other end of the site. Although physically stuck in the control room, their minds are everywhere.

The control room is a metaphor for the ways we use electronic media to interact with the world around us. An individual locked up in a small room and only able to interact with the outside world via electronic signals is close to being a mediated person. Unfortunately, the control room metaphor has been uselessly suggested as a theory for explaining the human mind. This faulty theory claims that the conscious mind can be represented by a little man in our head (the homunculus) who interprets and processes the signals received from the eyes, ears, and other sensory organs and responds to them by firing the appropriate motor nerves to activate the required muscle. The homunculus, the "conscious self", watches the representations of the external world on some kind of image projection screen, just like a control room operator, and tries to make sense of what he sees. The homunculus theory is a fallacy, however, because it still requires an explanation of the conscious mind of the homunculus, which, in turn, would require its own little homunculus in its own head. We are trapped in endless regression.

When we presuppose the existence of the human mind and try to explain its mediated interaction with the outside world, the control room metaphor can still be quite informative. Even when today most of us still rely upon physical mobility and direct inter-human communication, it would not be unreasonable to assume that electronic media will shortly become the dominant channel rather than an additional channel for our interactions with the world. The scene of individuals walking in the streets or sitting in a café mentally absorbed by their cell phones, laptops, or other devices and completely unaware of the physical environment around them is not rare. Even young kids that used to push their car toys through the sand now sit back in their chairs while carelessly operating the buttons of their remote controls. Unfortunately, modern diseases like obesity can be easily associated with such behaviour. In the extreme case, human life at large becomes virtualised, and we leave our bodies in a passive, vegetative state and use only digital media to interact with the world. So here we are, surrounded by our devices and linked to the Internet, the control room engineers of our lives, sitting in our easy chairs and ruling the world. Just like billions of others.

CHAPTER 3

Our Precious Mind

The mind is an intangible asset. It is the seat of thought, memory, imagination, and consciousness. It enables us to analyse problems, reason about possible solutions, and anticipate future events. Virtually any human achievement can essentially be traced back to our mental capabilities. The human mind is probably the most distinguishing result of evolution, even more than the body: it largely defines our humanness. Yet, despite all our mental powers, it is hard for us to fully understand what the mind is all about and how it relates to the body and to the physical world around us. By our intellect we have created artefacts like computers and other cognitive tools with some sort of intelligence of their own that, in turn, help to improve our intellectual performance. With the right tools, we can land a rocket on the moon within few centimetres of a target. Down on Earth, we use our cars' navigation devices to accurately predict at what time we will arrive at our destination (of course, provided that we don't run into some unforeseen traffic jam). It seems that some imbalance has arisen between our relatively fixed intellectual capabilities and the ever-improving cognitive tools we use. While computers are becoming more powerful and sophisticated day by day, the human brain as the seat of the mind is hopelessly constrained to the slow pace of biological evolution. Our brain hardly differs from the brain of our early ancestors that wandered through the fields 100,000 years ago. Inevitably, our being will be more and more determined by our technological artefacts. And exactly in the case of intelligent tools, which touch the core of our nature, we will not refrain from using them and integrating them into our daily activities. These artefacts signal the changing nature of our mind, of our existence.

Mind versus body

The French philosopher René Descartes described the human mind as a nonmaterial entity that is intrinsically bound to the body but that lacks any physical extension, mass, or movement and is averse to obeying any laws of physics. Because, evidently, there should be a close link between the mind and the body, Descartes suggested that somewhere in the middle of our head, our mind is connected to our brain. To be more precise, he suggested that this link was located in the pineal gland, a tiny organ about the size of a pea squeezed between the two brain hemispheres near the centre. His hypothesis was that mental signals arose from the pineal gland and were transferred by the surrounding brain liquids through the nerves to control the body. Today we know that the pineal gland produces melatonin, a hormone that is responsible for our biorhythm, which is undeniably a striking example of a mysterious effect that the mind may have on the body but is a mere coincidence.

No one takes Descartes's idea about the special role of the pineal gland in linking mind and body too seriously anymore because it can't be empirically verified. Even the very notion that mind and body are separate substances is highly questioned. Many researchers assume that mental states and processes will eventually be understood through physical theories. Neuroscientists use advanced imaging techniques like magnetic resonance imaging to reveal what happens inside our brains when we're exposed to certain stimuli. Supporters of this materialist view also point to the computer, a man-made physical machine that seems capable of arranging mental processes and displaying apparent intelligence. Opponents put forward, however, that computers can do amazing things, but in the end, they do no more than process available data without actually comprehending what they analyse. When you enter a simple word, let's say "house", in a search engine, the software will doubtlessly return a list of useful links, but it is very unlikely that it is aware of the idea that you're looking for a brick or wooden construct that people are apt to live in. Computers are supposedly mindless because they lack conscious thought. This touches on the philosophical debate about what conscious thought is. Would it be possible to construct a conscious computer, for instance, by teaching it to link the idea of a house to more detailed knowledge schemes including brick and wooden constructs that people live in? Or does this miss the point because it just extends the calculation but doesn't provide conscious thought at all? If so, what makes conscious thought of humans so special? Do we really consciously decide upon our actions or do we just experience such free will after our brain has computed its decisions? Aren't we overestimating the human mind? Couldn't it be of the same mechanical nature as a computer? These questions all need to be addressed in a theory of mind. So far, the debate is unresolved, and the mind remains one of the greatest mysteries in the world.

Enhancing our performance

Our mental capabilities are unrivalled among species. Nevertheless, we're often hindered by our mental limitations. For instance, it is quite tough for us to carry out complex calculations mentally, to precisely remember a long list of items, or to do two or more different things at the same time, such as reading a book while reciting a poem. As if it were an express proof of our intelligence, we have partly compensated for these flaws by inventing cognitive tools that support us: we've learned to use our fingers for counting, and we use a shopping list to compensate for memory failures. The computer in any of its manifestations is the most advanced cognitive tool we use today. Without computers, society would come to a standstill. This occasionally happens during power outages, which are apparently quite frequent: the Netherlands averages forty-five reports of power breakdowns per day, and these sometimes shut down computer systems so trains cannot move; flights have to be cancelled; traffic lights drop out; air-conditioning systems fail; telephone networks go down; medical services have to be suspended; factories stop operating; distribution of food, gas, and other products halt; and so on. Within a few hours, public life turns into chaos. This demonstrates our dependence on computers.

Computers don't just assist us anymore; for many tasks, they completely take over. Even today, we might feel kind of naked when deprived of our smartphones. On 1 January 2011, large parts of the world's population overslept because of a software bug in the iPhone's alarm clock. This dependence on technological artefacts is a strong argument for the externalist account of the mind, which says that the human mind is not contained within the boundaries of the skull but is the product of interactions with the environment. Our mind thus extends into the environment. Indeed, in many cases, external objects like computers or even pencil and paper play an important role in our cognitive processes. We can consider them external parts of our mind. This is where the difference between our mind and our brain becomes apparent: our mind includes objects that we use for our cognitive activities, while our brain is this 1.4 kilograms of nervous tissue, the physical substrate for our mental processes located within our skull. Hence, cognitive tools are literally extensions of our mind, enhancing our mental performance. Without these tools, our mind is truncated, incapable of performing to widely accepted standards. Without these tools, we are not who we really are.

The need for cognitive tools goes back many thousands of years. One of the earliest tools that helped us to make calculations was the abacus, used by traders in Africa and Asia. The abacus was a method rather than a device: the early versions were no more than beans or stones moved in grooves in the sand to aid in calculations. Different columns of the system indicated different orders of magnitude, so the value allocated to a bean depended on the column the bean was placed in. It reduced the mental effort for making calculations by offering a simple procedure that even worked for people that didn't quite understand the underlying principles of mathematics. The abacus wasn't just a mnemonic device that stored intermediate results, but because it enabled manipulation of different orders of magnitude, it also demonstrated some degree of processing power. Whatever interesting things the abacus was capable of, the important part of the story is that it helped us to achieve higher levels of performance. So the importance of the abacus is not that it is a tool but that it augmented our intelligence and greatly enhanced human processing power.

The advent of the computer

The first programmable machines arose in the nineteenth century's weaving mills. There, punched paper cards were used to produce complex weaving patterns automatically. These machines didn't do any calculations. The English inventor Charles Babbage is generally seen as the first person to design a computer. His "difference engine" could automatically generate numerical tables with an unequalled accuracy to 31 digits. Later on, he designed a more advanced general-purpose computer called the "analytical engine". Although the design was only partly made into a working machine, it is considered the blueprint of modern computer architecture. The machine was to be operated by a sort of programming language. The input, programming code or data to be processed, was recorded on punched cards fed into the machine. It had a processing unit for performing addition, subtraction, multiplication, and division and an internal memory for storing intermediate results of up to 1,000 numbers of 50 digits each. (Note that most of today's computers use at best only 18 digits.) Altogether, the analytical engine behaved pretty much like a modern computer, even though its operation was purely mechanical.

About a century later, the English mathematician Alan Turing described a formal model for a digital symbol-processing computer called the "Turing machine". Turing explained what functions a computer would be able to compute and also showed that there are functions that no machine would ever be able to compute, thereby identifying the fundamental limits of computation. While Babbage was the pioneer of practical computing, Turing explained the theoretical powers and constraints of any computing device we use today.

The invention of the first electromechanical computer is generally attributed to the German engineer Konrad Zuse in 1938. It was a simple binary calculator, but it had a memory and could be programmed for different purposes. The first fully digital computer was developed around 1940 by computer pioneer John Vincent Atanasoff and his student Clifford Berry at Iowa State College. The Atanasoff-Berry computer was designed for the single purpose of solving systems of linear equations. It couldn't be programmed for other tasks, which probably kept it from wide acceptance.

During the Second World War, more computers were developed, often with remarkable features. The Harvard Mark I computer was built by IBM in 1944. It used thousands of electromechanical relays and weighted almost 5,000 kilograms. It looked like a huge cupboard, stretching up to 16 metres long, 2.5 metres high, and 60 centimetres deep. Notwithstanding its weight and size, the Mark-I was by no means comparable with a modern computer or even a common modern calculator. A simple multiplication operation would take six seconds. It was quite impractical, and it seems that IBM president Thomas Watson estimated there was a world market for no more than about five of them.

The ENIAC, realised in 1946, was the first general-purpose computer that was completely electronic. Instead of electromechanical relays, it used vacuum tubes and diodes, which made it much faster: it could perform up to 385 multiplications per second. The machine was even larger than the Mark I; it weighed 27,000 kilograms. Unfortunately, it was a vulnerable machine: each day several of the 18,000 vacuum tubes burned out, breaking down the system. Nevertheless, the computer age had started, and more machines were to come. Progress was exponential. In the 1950s, the advent of the transistor was a major step in decreasing the size of computers while at the same time increasing their speed. Integrated circuits (chips) advanced this miniaturisation and enabled the production of the microcomputer in the 1980s, which marked the start of the domestic computer market. Miniaturisation still continues, yielding pin-head-sized computers with powers exceeding the Mark I and the ENIAC.

The end of this progression is nowhere near. Today's computers are impressively fast and intelligent. On many tasks, they outperform humans. This holds for bulky operations like calculations, administration, planning and scheduling, controlling processes, and searching but also for more sophisticated tasks like handwriting recognition, logistics, and weather forecasts. However, computers still demonstrate embarrassing shortcomings at simple human tasks like engaging in dialogue, dealing with emotions, or even understanding simple jokes. Although computers have achieved world-class skill in chess, in a similar strategy game called Go, the best computers are easily beaten by children. In many respects, the human mind is far more advanced and resilient. Still, computers are indispensable tools that in many respects help us to perform better and to arrive at states of augmented cognition. Without these cognitive tools, we would be thrown back many centuries.

Getting a hold on human cognition

In the late 1800s, the embryonic discipline of psychology started studying the human mind and conscious experience. Its prevailing research technique was introspection. By

29

careful analysis of one's own feelings, sensations, and mental pictures, psychologists assumed that the human mind would reveal its secrets. The basic idea of determining the nature of mental processes was commendable, but the approach was doomed to fail because the outcomes of introspection were fully subjective, unverifiable, and irreproducible. In the early twentieth century, psychologists tried to get rid of these dubious, unscientific methods. All subjectivism, including any vague issues like feelings and the human mind, was banned. Research took a behaviourist approach, relying only on individuals' observable behavioural responses to stimuli in the environment. Now it didn't matter anymore what individuals thought or felt but what they said or did. For researchers, the mind had become forbidden territory, a black box excluded from any scientific study. This approach certainly has improved the scientific soundness and reproducibility of psychological knowledge, but it also implied the neglect of any theorising about underlying mental processes.

The behaviourist approach was appropriate for understanding simple reflexive animal behaviours: indeed, we could teach impressive tricks to rats, goats, and pigeons simply by using rewards and punishments, that is, linking responses to controlled stimuli without the need for complex intermediate processes. For understanding the complex behaviours of humans and even advanced animals, however, the approach was inadequate. Humans don't simply respond in a reflexive way to external stimuli. Instead, we undertake deliberate actions based on extensive knowledge of the world. Increasingly, psychologists felt that any psychological theory was supposed to take into account the mental representations of knowledge like cognitive maps and spatial memories and should consider the role of memory and our evaluation and reasoning abilities. From a scientific point of view, the mind could no longer be neglected because it was regarded as the main source of our behaviours.

It was anything but a coincidence, then, that in the 1950s, psychologists adopted the information-processing model as the basis for their research. Those were the early days of the computer's amazing capabilities. Its apparent intelligence inspired psychologists to consider the human mind as an information-processing system. After many years of neglect, the study of the mind became acceptable again. Psychologists assumed that human cognitive architecture shared many features with the computer: it transfers sensory input data to a working memory that filters, transforms, and combines the data in a more or less intelligent process. We store new insights for future use in the long-term memory, our personal "hard disk" that acts as our permanent knowledge base. The cognitive system's outputs lead to a non-verbal unit that generates motor actions like walking, waving, playing the piano, and so on, or to a verbal unit that generates speech and writing. This revival of the mind signalled the beginning of cognitive psychology. The objective measurement of behaviour still was an important starting point, but research now extended to include studies of mind and brain. New instruments became available for the measurement of the brain's electrical activity, such as electroencephalography, or EEG. More recently, new imaging techniques like magnetic resonance imaging (MRI) even allowed clinicians to look into brains of living individuals. Studies revealed the different specialised components of the brain and the ways these components work together. New insights about the complex neural-network structure of the brain fostered the rise of cognitive sciences, a new multi-disciplinary approach bringing together cognitive psychology, neuroscience, artificial intelligence, physiology, linguistics, anatomy, and computational science. Without joining forces, these different scientific disciplines would never get a hold on the immense complexity of the human mind.

The brain as a supercomputer

Many people consider the computer to be the most sophisticated and influential invention ever. It probably is. Its complexity is striking. The amount of transistors that we're able to assemble and combine on a single silicon chip is hardly imaginable. Nevertheless, this all grows dull when compared with the human brain. The anatomy of the brain is impressive. The human brain contains up to 100 billion neurons. Each neuron is connected to some 10,000 other neurons, which makes up to 10^{15} inter-neuron connections (called axons). This is an immense number, about the number of grains of sand needed to turn London's Wembley football stadium into a giant sandbox. Although these interconnections may be relatively short, they produce a giant crisscross of wires with a total length of up to 1 million kilometres.

Various researchers have estimated the computational power of the brain. Roboticist Hans Moravec analysed the neural circuitry in the retina, which is the system in the eye that detects light, colours, and motion. He estimated that image detection by this neuron sample of only 0.02 grams would require 1 billion computing operations per second. By extrapolating this calculation to the 1,400 grams of nervous tissue in the brain, Moravec concluded that the human brain has the power to execute 10^{14} instructions per second. Others derived similar estimates from human audio processing capabilities. Even larger numbers up to 10^{15} instructions per second were found from computer simulations mimicking the processes in a specific region of the cerebellum. Computer scientist and philosopher Ray Kurzweil, looking for a conservative estimate of the upper limit of human computational power, posited a maximum figure of 10^{16} instructions per second. In comparison, Intel's Core i7 Extreme Edition i980EE, which is one of the most powerful commercially available processors, launched in 2010 achieves at best 10^{11} instructions per second. Although this is about 10,000 times better than the 1985 Intel 486DX processor (54 million instructions per second), it still is 100,000 times less powerful than the human brain.

So, if we were to use 100,000 of these processors in parallel, we would start to get close to the brain's power hardware-wise. In this comparison, another huge problem arises: power management. To run 100,000 computers, we would need a 10 megawatt power plant. The brain uses only 30 watts or less. So computer science could learn a lot from the way the brain works, especially with regard to power consumption. Electricity requirements are the most severe barrier for increasing processing capacities. Computers appear hopelessly inefficient. The faster they get, the more they resemble electric heaters. In the Netherlands, all the electrical power required by the country's computers for one year adds up to 8 per cent of the total national energy demand, which exceeds the requirements for the aviation sector, which is not particularly praised for its energy friendliness.

Green IT is a sympathetic movement using wind and solar energy and planting trees to compensate for carbon dioxide emissions, but it focuses on the symptoms rather than the causes. The real gains are in decreasing the energy consumption of processor chips. The human brain provides various hints of how to do this: neurons are very slow, about a billion times slower than a processor; they work massively in parallel; and when certain brain parts are not needed, they slow down their processing speed. This is what is done in today's supercomputers. In 2010, various supercomputers reached 10^{16} instructions per second, which is equal to the processing power of the human brain. This is a momentous milestone: computer power has caught up with human brain power. In any case, the limits if computer technology are nowhere near. On average, every two months a new supercomputer is launched that outperforms the existing leader. By the end of 2012, the leading system was the Titan Cray XK7 computer, which demonstrated a processing power of 17.6 petaflops, where the prefix "peta" means 10^{15} and "flops" are floating-point operations per second, comparable with "instructions per second" but more suitable for scientific purposes. The Titan Cray XK7 used 560,640 processors in parallel. Its processors throttle down when they are not needed. Still, its consumption of 8.2 megawatts is far too high, so there's still a lot to gain.

It's striking that at first the computer was used as a metaphor for the human brain, while now the human brain is used as the ultimate example for computers. By now computers are more powerful than the human brain, but we would still need the right software to emulate human thought.

Towards superhuman intelligence

The future of computing is driven by the costs of producing zeros and ones. Over the years, new technologies have achieved impressive reductions in scale and cost. At first, voluminous and vulnerable radio tubes were used for producing zeros and ones. Then the transistor, which used semiconducting materials to creating switchable electronic channels, was invented. These were thousand times smaller than radio tubes and used far less energy. Over the last 60 years, transistors have become smaller and smaller. Today's transistors are almost nano-structures, invisible to the naked eye and grouped together in huge numbers onto a single chip. Switching voltages also decreased, as did required currents and distances between transistors. Processing speeds went up and energy consumption continually diminished.

In the 1960s, Intel co-founder Gordon Moore noticed this steady pattern of improvement and pointed out that the number of transistors that could be placed on an integrated circuit (chip) doubled every two years. He prophesied that this pattern would continue for the next ten years. His prophecy proved accurate till beyond the turn of the twenty-first century, and it is now assumed to remain valid for the next decades. Moore's law has been reformulated to include power consumption, cost of hard-disk storage, pixels per dollar, memory space, and network capacity, but it still reflects the steady doubling within fixed time frames (which may vary for different indicators). It confirms the unstoppable exponential growth of computer technology. And more is still to come.

Futurist and computer scientist Ray Kurzweil cautiously analysed emerging technologies that will help to preserve the exponential growth rate of information technology in the next decades. Nano-science is on its way to take over in the next ten years, enabling structures composed of only one layer of atoms, or even better, tiny three-dimensional structures called nano-tubes for storing memory. For the decade afterwards, molecular computing is assumed to take over and to possibly be linked with DNA computing, which exploits the combinatorial power of replicated strands of DNA. Electron-spin computing would be a next candidate for storing and processing bits of information. After that, optical computing with laser light is supposed to steal the show with even smaller and faster technology. Eventually, quantum computing will outshine all previous approaches. While supercomputers have already reached the processing capacity of the human brain, Kurzweil soundly extrapolates on the basis of plain evidence that by 2020, the hardware for computational power equivalent to the human brain will cost around 1,000 dollars. By 2030, software emulating human brain processes will be available. By 2040, computational capacity will be a billion times larger than the capacity of the human brain. By 2050, emulation of the brains of all humans on Earth will cost no more than 1,000 dollars.

Somewhere during this continued increase in computational power, Kurzweil proposes the year 2045, we will pass a single point beyond which technological intelligence will structurally exceed biological intelligence—the singularity. From that point, the growth of computer intelligence will not be limited by human capabilities and will develop beyond any conceivable limits precisely because superhuman computer intelligence will continually augment itself. Superhuman intelligence will be able to design better, faster, and smaller computers, pervading our world with unequalled qualities. Kurzweil suggests that the differences between humans and machines will disappear. Current conceptions of being, thinking, knowing, learning, and communicating will be completely reframed. Our minds will become highly integrated with the environment as brain-computer interfaces will support direct interactions between our biological brain and its technological extensions.

Our thoughts might be outsourced to peripheral devices, and our knowledge and skills could be uploaded, duplicated, computationally enhanced, and downloaded rather than being transferred in time-consuming teaching and revising processes. The singularity will produce profound disruptive effects on human societies, while the integration of artificial intelligences and human creatures will irreversibly transform human life. Many people regard such an outlook with great scepticism and worry because it seems to affect and degrade what we consider to be the showpiece of evolution: our precious mind. But even the greatest techno-pessimist will have to agree that it is very unlikely that things will remain unchanged forever. Kurzweil explains that using new technologies is exactly what makes us human: our species inherently seeks to extend its physical and mental reach beyond current limitations. It seems inevitable that our mind will become largely mediated. In fact, we are nothing but our cognitive tools.

CHAPTER 4

Living with Technologies

The ancient world was entirely different from the world today. Our early ancestors were faced with a world full of dangers, magic, and mysteries ruled by the elements. Many things weren't understood. They had no clue about the moon, the seasons, diseases, volcanoes, or thunderstorms. There was so much still to be discovered. They may have dreamed and fantasised about ever-available food, effortless heating of their caves, or flying in the air, but they must have been quite convinced that none of these would ever come true. In those days, probably nothing seemed realisable. Today the opposite holds: it is hard to imagine anything that's impossible to achieve. Our lives are pervaded with technologies offering products early humans could only dream of. Food, clothes, housing, energy, vehicles, phones, TVs, hearing aids, coiled springs, even matches and paper clips are the result of the technologies we've created. Today, no single product, service, or human activity could exist without technology. Its complexity has become immense. We thoughtlessly use the stuff, and it's hard to understand how it all works. There is just so much to be learned. Technology seems to act as an autonomous power that rules our lives, offering us a world that is still full of magic and mysteries. It may be not so different from the ancient world after all.

Our innovation bent

It must have been more than 400,000 years ago when one of our ancient ancestors picked up a stone, sharpened and shaped it into an arrowhead, and then by accident discovered that it might be a useful tool for hunting, fishing, or chasing away intruders. One of the very first tools entered human culture. In those days, people developed and used a variety of new tools for building shelters, hunting, growing crops, painting, and many more things. They were made of stone, shell, bone, plants, or any other material that might seem appropriate. This early stage of technical development revealed our ceaseless diligence to improve and innovate which is inherently bound to our nature. As a product of evolution, our species searches for new insights, methods, and technologies that provide us a competitive advantage over our predators. It is our raison d'être to continuously create new ways to do things better, easier, or faster. Arrowheads, the wheel, the alphabet, mathematics, computers, these all are the fruitful results of our imagination. They helped us to survive in a predominantly dangerous and hostile world.

In the seventeenth century, after many centuries of steady but unrelentingly slow progress, the conditions for developing new technology changed favourably. The restrictive power of religion was fading, which enabled scientists to take a more independent stance. Most important, scientists and instrument builders found themselves in fruitful partnerships that led to an accelerated flow of new measurement tools like high quality lenses, microscopes, clockworks, balances, manometers. These in turn accelerated scientific development in an unequalled way. Over the last few hundred years, science prospered and, accordingly, the innovation achievements over the last centuries have been quite impressive: agricultural methods, medical cures, new modes of transport, communication media, computational power, and many more. Such achievements continued to foster optimism for prosperity and increasing standards of living, or, in a broader sense, better conditions of life.

The cradle of this optimism was the Enlightenment, an intellectual movement in the seventeenth and eighteenth centuries that strongly influenced the portrayal of mankind. It is the era of great scientists, philosophers, and writers like Descartes, Newton, Leibniz, Locke, Kant, Voltaire, and Diderot. They claimed that man is rational and good by nature. Darwin also deserves a mention. His theory of evolution magnified the conflict between science and religion while it rejected the idea of the creation of life found in the Bible book of Genesis. Rather than the creationist belief that every species was created individually by God and is not subject to change or progress, Darwin's evolutionary theory claimed that life has progressively developed from primitive forms to complex organisms. The Enlightenment marked the liberation from the medieval doctrines of magic, superstition, prejudice, and fear of God by replacing it with human rationality. The fear of God made way for a scientific description and explanation of the world. Beliefs were no longer accepted on the authority of priests, sacred texts, or tradition, but only on the basis of reason. Reinforced by the idea of natural regularity and material cause, the Scientific Revolution successfully proclaimed the ideology of upward development, progress, and improvement of the world through ever-increasing knowledge, understanding, and control of nature's processes. It asserted that the individual as well as humanity as a whole can progress to perfection. Indeed, tangible results of this are omnipresent, be they regrettably only for part of the world's population.

This innovative attitude is still reflected in the values and foundations of modern society such as economy of growth, capitalism, materialism, competition, techno-optimism, and scientific positivism to mention a few. The underlying premise of all of these is that innovation implies progress, which leads to a better world. It all fits well within the theory of evolution. For instance, the world economy is an unmistakable demonstration of survival of the fittest. The general pattern of economics is that the improvement of a company's production processes effects a competitive advantage. The outcome is either higher quality products at the same cost or the same quality at lower cost, or both. Companies that fail to innovate and instead rely on their fixed routines are doomed to bankruptcy, which is the business equivalent of becoming extinct. Technology, of course, is the main driver for this innovation. It furthers the creation of new products and services and the redesign of production processes, all of which lead to successful trade. In many respects, technology development has been a blessing for humanity, but, admittedly, in many respects, it hasn't been. Beyond any doubt, its influence radically changes our existence. It is quite likely that technology will become the defining factor of humanity.

Techno-pessimism

Enlightenment's rationalism has been subject of severe criticism. Opponents claim that the unconstrained belief in progress and its reliance on human reasoning isn't capable of describing the true nature of human emotions, feelings, morals, and ethics. The Enlightenment's strict depreciation of non-rational aspects of human behaviour disregards what probably are the predominant modes of human functioning. Consequently, the concept of progress is not applicable to happiness, compassion, and other states of mind. Put differently, progress does not imply that modern humans are happier or more compassionate than their ancestors were. Note that in recent years, the Organisation for Economic Co-operation and Development (OECD) introduced the "Better Life Index" for extending economic indices like gross national product with indicators of quality of life, happiness, and well-being.

Innovators are often accused of promoting decline rather than progress. Negative side effects like vanishing nature; depletion of fossil fuels; pollution of water, soil, and air; not to mention the threat of biological, chemical, and nuclear armament easily breed techno-pessimism and a glorification of the past. Some companies prefer to sell their industrial products by deliberately using the nostalgic image of traditional craftsmanship and avoiding any reference to technology, innovation, or improvement. Of course Grandma's Vegetable Soup tastes much better than Instant Vegetable Soup Powder, even when both are produced with the same large-scale industrial process. This is just marketing varnish, but it works. Since the 1960s, there has been a lot of opposition to large-scale food production, the use of pesticides, and the addition of chemical agents to enhance flavouring, colouring, and preservation. This opposition had a strong case since all these chemicals were known for their unwanted side effects. Those opposed to industrial agriculture argued that farming was supposed to use a small-scale, intensive, technology-avoiding approach to produce pure, natural food products. Of course, these "natural" methods were highly inefficient and for long time remained marginal. Not until the late 1990s was the value chain for organic food was professionalised and upgraded with the incorporation of new sustainable technologies in crop growth, trade, and distribution. Prices went down, quality went up, and market share exploded, which all made a splendid case for decreasing pesticides and additives. This demonstrates that some technologies do counteract the adverse effects of others. Organic foods are still often sold in greenish packaging as if they were directly harvested from nature without the use of any modern technologies.

Scepticism of new technologies as we know it now goes back to the nineteenth century, when the negative effects of the industrial revolution painfully became manifest. In a gloomy analysis, the German existentialist philosopher Karl Jaspers advocated his alienation thesis, that technology creates a totally new material environment that causes human beings to become alienated from the world. In this era of industrialisation, human craftsmen were increasingly replaced by machines that not only made production faster and cheaper but also allowed for the mass production of objects that met quality standards. In highly rationalised and controlled production processes, human workers were degraded from unique individuals to interchangeable tools, just cogs in the machine. In addition, highly bureaucratic organisational forms made people dissolve

41

into their functional roles rather than develop their unique identities and individuality. Through mass production, human individuals became more and more ignorant of the origins, composition, or functioning of industrial products, be they food, clothes, or consumer electronics. Prevailing values like frugality and sustainability lost ground because of the availability of many exchangeable duplicates: indeed, broken products could be easily replaced with new specimens. People were thus trapped in a pattern of passively fulfilling their material needs with ever-replaceable stuff that was abundantly available. In this view, inspired by the negative effects of the industrial revolution, technology seemed to have become a power in its own right, and it controlled society autonomously and alienated human individuals from the world and from themselves.

Many of these patterns can still be observed today: the inescapable way technology enters our lives and makes us dependent, our fixation on material needs, and the negative impact of technologies on our social and physical environments. Yet, Jaspers's alienation view doesn't quite come up to the mark to describe technology's role in the digital age: the idea of labourers in mass production differs significantly from the present situation of highly skilled and autonomous knowledge workers. Today, humans are no longer simple tool makers and tool users but empowered individuals that assimilate technology into their lives and largely decide upon their fates themselves. It is hard to contend that TV, the Internet, and cell phones alienate people from the world they're living in; in fact, people are now part of an irreversibly changing world that is made highly open and accessible by these new technologies.

Unlocking the world

In the twentieth century, the world changed radically under the influence of new technologies. It was the age of nuclear fission, DNA, plastics, skyscrapers, space travel, computers, and open heart surgery, to name a few. It was also the age of mass communication media. We witnessed the rise of film, radio, TV, and the Internet. Orbiting around Earth are a multitude of communication satellites that connect the farthest corners. A dense web of transmitters and cable networks enables an ever-increasing number of people to access an ever-increasing flow of information. Day in and day out, many thousands of radio and TV shows stream the news into our homes. War, hunger, incest, euthanasia, pets, gardening, any topic will be covered. New media's impact on our culture has been immense. New modes of expression such as documentaries, feature films, news shows, blogs, and tweets developed and enriched our culture. Along with them, new behavioural patterns arose. The simple fact that people spend many hours per day watching television and surfing the Internet instead of visiting their neighbours or reading books signifies a radical change. Cultural patterns could now be widely exchanged, and this exchange fostered a transnational awareness of the varieties of human culture. The change is not without its adverse effects, however. For instance, the Western dominance in film and TV pushed back local stories and habits: a modern type of colonialism that replaces local heroes with James Bond and Mr. Bean. However, the principal claim about mass media is political in kind: a free press and easy access to information promote democracy. Since knowledge is power, the spread of knowledge brings power to the people, at least theoretically. Many a regime has seen how difficult it is to control the trans-border nature of modern news services. The collapse of communism, with the fall of the Berlin wall in 1989 as one of its peaks, is largely attributed to the role of mass media. So far, mass media are a mighty weapon against dictatorship and oppression.

Lost in apathy

Some scholars are sceptical about the effects of mass media on freedom and democracy. As early as 1941, even before the rise of TV, the German philosopher Erich Fromm concluded that mass media paralysed human thought. He pointed at the catastrophic effect of radio and film newsreels bombarding people with an endless flow of dispersed and incoherent facts that fail to offer a comprehensible view of the world. The advent of TV didn't improve the situation. Perception of the world through mass media is a truncated and distorted perception; individuals aren't personally connected, involved, and touched anymore. They are restricted in their feelings and their critical judgement, and life loses its structure and coherence. They get hopelessly lost amidst the abundance of disconnected facts and thereby fail to act as responsible, independent, critical citizens. According to Fromm, mass media create the impression that the world is of such discouraging complexity that only specialists can comprehend and explain it. This is what happens when radio and TV present an endless series of specialists explaining their cases. The audience switches off their own thinking and patiently adopts these experts' views as their own. Consequently, the correctness of an opinion is determined not by the power of argumentation or the depth of analysis but by the tasteful way it is dished out. Outstanding examples can be found in politics, where the pre-election phase is dominated by the biggest smiles, the funniest one-liners, and the most resolute and reassuring attitudes. In the 1960 US presidential elections, John F. Kennedy beat his opponent, Richard Nixon, after a famous public debate on radio and TV. Although the radio audience slightly favoured Nixon, TV viewers unrelentingly understood that this weary, hollow-eyed, nervous, sweating man was certainly not the one to lead the nation for the next couple of years.

The rash adoption of the opinions of experts who tell us what to do and what to think endangers the democratic power of society. It reflects a childish belief in anything that is put forth with authority. American media theorist Neil Postman came to negative conclusions about mass media similar to Fromm's. He denounced the entertainment culture of TV and executives' one-sided orientation on viewing figures and audience ratings. Even news shows are positioned as entertainment, dishing up

44

insignificant lightweight topics while avoiding any profundity, complexity, and length because these deter viewers rather than keeping them tuned in. Any significant exchange of thoughts seems impossible because hesitation or circumspection wouldn't work with the required TV formats. Dutch writer Gerrit Komrij puts it this way: "whatever ominous tidings the anchorman informs us of, viewers will massively phone up only when a greasy stain is on his tie". The German writer Hans Magnus Enzenberger calls television the most corrupt of all media.

According to Postman, the attractive power of TV is in the easy consumption of the fascinating spectacle of thousands and thousands of images intended solely for our emotional satisfaction that demand no intellectual effort. The French philosopher Jean Baudrillard suggests that such a technological innovation is only material in nature and supports the loss of human capabilities like commitment, reflectivity, and profundity. Such criticisms are quite likely to be applicable to current media on the Internet and mobile phones. By using social media services like Twitter and Facebook, we open ourselves to the same risks: fragmentation, shallowness, and alienation lie in wait.

In accordance with the objections against mass media, critics argue that hyperlinks as presented on the web often lead to unwanted disorientations, which makes in-depth and coherent study of online texts problematic. With all the answers in the world within reach, it is tempting to switch off thinking: answering questions with the Internet may easily lead to the random and impulsive collection of data which at face value seem appropriate but lack significance. This would promote unconcerned citation of sources but would hamper the acquisition of insights and understanding. Erich Fromm died in 1980 and didn't witness the coming of the Internet. Almost certainly he would have noticed the pattern of confusing mass media that promote decline rather than progress repeating.

Us and our devices

The huge impact of mass media demonstrates that the simple nineteenth century conception of technologies as industrial productivity tools is no longer tenable. Technology's role is much more complex in today's world. Technology makes up an integral part of life and fundamentally alters the ways individuals perceive and experience the world. Both communication theorists Marshall McLuhan and Neil Postman argued that TV is not just an information channel in addition to books, newspapers, or lectures but that it deeply changes our interactions with the world. Indeed, TV creates new ways to open up reality. The same holds for any new medium that appears. Technology in its widest sense mediates and gives form to the relationship that individuals have with the world they experience. The important part of technology is not its technical or functional characteristics but in its ability to change the context of life.

German philosopher Albert Borgmann successfully broke through the one-sided gloomy evaluation of technology by analysing the very causes of alienation. His starting point is the positivist notion that technology promises a lightening and enrichment of human existence. It liberates humans from burdens by making a multitude of goods like heat, light, water, food, and information available without any effort whatsoever. In ancient times, our ancestors needed to work a full day to find enough food, gather wood, make fire, and so on, while today, we dish up a ready-to-eat meal within a few minutes. Bygone days were tough times: lighting the stove required knowledge but also dedication, perseverance, orientation towards a goal, and involvement with the tools available. Today, the availability of goods is straightforward, omnipresent, easy, safe, and immediate. Heat, light, and information come to us by simply switching on technical devices like central heating, electric lighting, and TV sets. What used to be an achievement has become a simple commodity which demands no commitment, proficiency, or skill acquired by effort, discipline, and involvement with the world.

The efforts that people formerly put forth for these tasks are now taken care of by a device's machinery. In most devices, this machinery, its technology, is deliberately kept out of sight. A person who needs light only needs to flick a switch to turn it on. The machinery of electric wires and connectors is hidden in the ceiling and walls. The general idea is that only by hiding the machinery and separating it from the commodity are commodities made straightforward and effortless to use, that is, their use requires no commitment or technical skill. No knowledge about the device's interior is required to use it. Why should we bother to learn about the wiring? According to Borgmann, however, this pattern of separating the commodity from the machinery leads to apathetic consumption, consumption detached from any social or material context that removes us from the world. Blindfolded, we locate and operate the switches that provide us with what we need without wondering a single moment where this all comes from. We're spoiled by the convenience of services. Like Jaspers, Borgmann observes that people are becoming alienated from the world as they become more and more ignorant of the origin, composition, or inner workings of the products they consume. However, Borgmann argues not that mass production itself is the cause, as in Jaspers's view, but that humans have no access to the machinery of products and thus are forced to accept them as magical accomplished facts. Maybe our world doesn't differ so much from the magical and mysterious world of our ancestors.

In his devices theory, Borgmann calls on us to break out of this technological consumerism not by simply rejecting technology but by restoring the relationship between the commodity and the machinery. Users of technological artefacts should be given the opportunity to develop a commitment to it. Devices should preferably be transparent to reveal the secrets of their machinery. To amplify the users' involvement, devices should also be adjustable to personal preferences. By making a device's machinery accessible, users are able to maintain, repair, and adapt it. Such involvement with the device's machinery will further insight into its workings and satisfaction with it. Borgmann

47

suggests that devices be offered that support "focal practices", that is, activities that demand high degrees of involvement; that require discipline, perseverance, concentration, and skill to use; that are physically and mentally challenging and are difficult to master; that provide satisfaction and pleasure; that stimulate rather than discourage our ties with the world; and that serve no particular goal other than being a focal practice. Examples of focal practices would be walking (instead of taking the bus), cooking (instead of ordering a pizza), repairing an old bicycle (instead of buying a new one), or engaging in any other activity that demands intrinsic involvement and hence serves our existential relationship with our world.

Besides the commodity and the machinery level, a third level of analysis is applicable to devices: the level of symbolic meaning. We attach a symbolic meaning to the ownership of a device that we communicate to others. This meaning allows devices' owners to express and distinguish themselves and to become part of a specific subculture. Cars, watches, spectacles, music, these are all means of showing others and ourselves who we are. Driving an oversized four-wheel drive indicates a different lifestyle or status than riding a bicycle. New digital devices like tablets and smartphones are excellent means to display one's modernity. Some people are even prepared to camp out on a cold night outside the gadget shop to be the first one to buy the newest thingies in the morning. Of course, this is all caused by cautious brand marketing and the creation of artificial scarcity. The effects are impressive. In many cases, the outward appearance of products has become its decisive asset at the expense of functionality. Wearing sunglasses in the dark might be an example, and so would wearing shoes with heels so high that nobody could ever walk in them. In all cases, these artefacts signal "This is me." This exactly demonstrates Marshall McLuhan's famous quote: "We shape our tools and thereafter our tools shape us." Exactly: we are our devices.

CHAPTER 5

Conveying Meaning

For those who believe in the supernatural, a medium is a person capable of communication with invisible and not scientifically explainable agents like ghosts, spirits, devils, or gods. Basically, this type of medium doesn't differ very much from radio, TV, telephone, and many more topical media because this person likewise transfers messages from one remote agent to the other. One of the best-known spiritual media in history was the Oracle at Delphi in ancient Greece. The oracle, a priestess named the Pythia, passed on divine messages from the god Apollo to the worshippers. She sat on a tripod over an opening in the earth which produced intoxicating vapours. When the Pythia fell into trance, she made incoherent, unintelligible sounds that priests interpreted to reproduce the prophecies of Apollo. Now, this may seem a bit naïve or even primitive, but such oral mediation of an occult and spiritualistic nature continues even today. Over 60 per cent of Americans believe in paranormal phenomena. Astrology calendars are among the most popular sections of newspapers and magazines. Many get upset by broken mirrors and black cats or avoid any risk on Friday the Thirteenth. One in four Americans believe in witchcraft. This belief is also held by professionals: many psychiatric nursing professionals presume a direct relationship between the lunar phase and weird human behaviour, often referred to as lunacy. In the medical domain, magical rituals like faith healing, magnetisation, therapeutic touch, bio-resonance, and homeopathy are practiced quite commonly, even though any scientific evidence for their effectiveness is lacking. Whether this all makes sense or not, the issue is that the Pythia acted as a medium between the metaphysical world of the gods and the real world. This exemplifies very well what a medium is supposed to do: be a third-party element between some remote sender of a message and an audience. It captures the sender's message and uses a distortive, noisy channel to transferring the messages to the audience, which finally tries to make sense of it. The concept doesn't really differ much from TV or any other communication device. Similar to the Pythia, TV may readily be considered a noisy channel producing incoherent, unintelligible sounds that the audience unthinkingly accepts as the true stories of the world and beyond.

Different roles of media

The story of the Pythia offers an informative metaphor for the role of modern communication media. A medium is literally something intermediate: it captures and transfers messages between one party (the sender of a message) and another (the receiver). In daily parlance, the term "media" refers to mass media like newspapers, magazines, TV, and radio, especially in connection with the social and political forces that exert influence on public opinion. Technically, the term "medium" is a container that applies to various communication-related artefacts ranging from simple pencil and paper to hard disks, smartphones, and high-definition cinema. Confusingly, it applies to both hardware (technical facilities) and software (content). For instance, a book is the collection of paper sheets covered with patterns of ink (hardware), but a book is also the story (software) it conveys. People may like books because of the smell of ink or the tactile sensations they have when browsing through the pages; they also may like books because of their exciting stories or interesting styles of writing. Notably, many people buy a book because of its hardware (its cover, its typeface, its paper), assuming a direct relationship between the quality of hardware and the quality of software. This, of course, need not be the case.

Most media, including radio, TV, and the Internet, aren't just simple devices. Instead, they denote composite concepts that cover the whole communication value chain: message creation, message storage, message transfer, and message display. A clay tablet, a goose quill with parchment, but also a camera, a microphone, a typewriter, and a telegraph serve message creation; they all capture human utterances or ideas into codified signals. The same holds for productivity tools like word processors, video editing software, graphic design programs, and software development platforms. In addition, media can store recorded messages for retrieval at a later stage. Examples of storage media are hard disks and the associated data files, blackboards, videocassettes, and even the tree bark which contains the inscriptions of a loving couple. Distribution media transfer the messages to the receivers. Telephone lines, satellites, and Bluetooth radio waves are examples of distribution media. Even though they're no longer common, homing pigeons, stagecoaches, or human couriers may also act as media of distribution. To display the original message in front of the receiver, the distributed data require presentation media. Examples are the film projector, a video screen, headphones, and a Dolby surround-sound system. So mediated communication usually involves a chain of different media for creation, storage, distribution, and presentation.

Our unrivalled expressive power

The human capability to compose informative messages is outstanding. We are capable of expressing our thoughts, feelings, and intentions in great detail. For this we have at our disposal a rich repertoire of utterances and behaviours ranging from well-composed and well-articulated sentences to heartfelt cries, gestures, and facial expressions and, in many cases, a combination of all of these. Even a simple message requires a complex and subtle communication process. Ordering a cup of coffee in a bar starts with some mental considerations about what to order. Then you attract the attention of the waiter with beckoning gestures and subtle nodding followed by some polite sentences expressing your wishes according to the sociocultural code of the catering domain. The waiter in turn listens patiently while (preferably) avoiding any signs of disapproval and evaluates the request against the reference of available services before politely answering.

In principle, any achievement of human culture, be it in science, arts, architecture, technology, literature, music, or politics, is the result of human expression. Civilisation indeed is the cumulative result of communication. Without the alphabet, musical notation, mathematics, and other systems of expression we would be deprived of the 4,000-year-old Sumerian clay tablets, Mozart's *Requiem*, Einstein's theory of relativity, Da Vinci's *Mona Lisa*, and of modern popular culture. Meaningful expression requires systems of signs. These are coherent collections of conventions about which signs to use and what they mean. Sign systems include languages like French, English, and Chinese; musical notation; and Morse code. Mime and gestures also constitute sign systems with great expressive power, even though no one can make explicit their precise rules and conventions because the production and interpretation of mime and gestures are largely subconscious processes.

The incompatibility of channels

Many people may have the naïve view that media are interchangeable carriers of information, but it is not too difficult to demonstrate this idea's incorrectness. There are fundamental limitations to the translation of a message from one sign system into the other. Different sign systems convey different types of information. They may use different modalities (e.g. sound, images), address different senses (sight, hearing, even smell or touch), and undergo processing in different parts of the brain. It's clear that the auditory and visual channels are quite different. In the auditory channel, messages are sequential: time and timing are relevant parameters, and meaning is expressed by the sequence of signals such as words or musical tones. In contrast, visual messages such as still pictures, are holistic in nature: they provide a direct, overall impression. This is why telling a joke is so different from showing a cartoon. Telling a joke requires a step-by-step construction of a narrative. In each step, a well-considered amount of new information is given to gradually build up tension until its final release in the joke's punchline. A cartoon, however, can do without story, climax, and punchline since its message is based on the immediate overall impression of the scene. Conversion of a cartoon into a spoken joke is highly impractical: the humour would be gone and would leave the joke teller in the embarrassing situation where no one appreciates the gag. The sign systems are just too different for lossless conversion.

This holds for many other examples. It is impossible to explain the colour yellow to a blind person. It is impossible to properly visualise or describe the sound of a saxophone to a deaf person. Language is inadequate for describing the taste of wine, although some connoisseurs would disagree and claim mastery of a dedicated vocabulary. It is very difficult to learn to dance by using a carpet printed with footsteps, instructional arrows, and other graphical symbols. The cinema version of a novel tends to be remarkably different from the original work. It produces a whole new instance of the story. Readers are frequently disappointed after having watched the film version because of translation losses in the narrative and conflicts between the explicit *mise en scène* with the images readers have imagined themselves of the setting and the leading characters. Indeed, the film version of a book uses completely different means of expression (sound and images), conforms to different conventions of style and tempo, and addresses different senses and parts of the brain. If the script and the film were exactly equal, there would be no need to produce the film at all.

Even the conversion of spoken texts to written texts is not without losses. The human voice loads language with emotional connotations. Written texts go without intonation, pitch, timbre, accent, and other voice attributes that could enhance expressive power. Spoken texts simply offer more opportunities for manipulating the audience. Moreover, sounds are inescapable, since a listener must process the full signal to hear. This is exactly why disturbances from neighbours are a top annoyance. Images, in contrast, allow us to filter and to focus on the relevant details. Eventually, we might even close our eyes if we don't want to see the image. Sounds, however, remain irresistible. In *Instructional Message Design*, psychologists Malcolm Fleming and Howard Levie rightly point out that spoken texts have more influence than written texts. All great world leaders in history excelled at verbally playing to crowds, while none of the world's greatest writers or thinkers ever managed to obtain a comparably powerful position. If Hitler, Mao, Stalin, or Napoleon had been writers instead of orators, history would have taken a different turn.

Media as self-establishing means of expression

Since different sign systems enable different types of messages, their combination produces greater expressive power. Therefore film is one of the richest media. In it, sound and moving images combine a whole range of different sign systems. By the end of the nineteenth century, Thomas Alva Edison was the first to create the technology for recording and displaying moving images. His kinetograph, patented in 1892, marked the birth of the silent movie. In those early days, film was simply used to register images. Events were recorded with a fixed camera angle and camera position. This all changed over time. Filmmakers learned to combine different shots and camera movements to create drama. Film transformed into image-based storytelling, neatly adopting Aristotle's structural notion that every story should have a beginning, a middle, and an end. Synchronous sound then became available, enabling recorded dialogues to create a deceptive realism. The expressive power of the combined linearity of language systems and the immediacy of visual cues in film was unequalled. Musical scores increased dramatic impact. New genres of film developed by challenging prevailing conventions. In the 1960s, avant-garde movie maker Jean-Luc Godard was one of the leaders of a new film genre called "nouvelle vague" (new wave) based on the motto that every film should have a beginning, a middle, and an end, but not necessarily in that order. Later on, computer graphics and 3D-projection helped viewers to visualise any spectacular scene. Over the last century, film has outgrown the instrumental level of simple message transfer. It has developed its own conventions, grammar, codes, and genres that transformed it into a medium of expression in its own right. It exemplifies the common pattern that in the course of time, any new medium produces its own conventions for conveying meaning. This is what Marshall McLuhan meant when he coined the phrase "the medium is the message": the nature of the medium strongly influences the message that it puts across. When a new medium arises, new modes of expression will appear. For instance, in today's chat channels and SMS services, users employ "chat speech", which is a spontaneous new convention of abbreviated writing like "CU L8R"(see you later) and "GTG" (got to go), to optimise the quality of communication under the limitations of the channel.

This all underscores once again that the idea of media as neutral transmitters of messages is a fallacy. It doesn't make sense to regard messages and their carriers as separate entities. How could a message ever exist without any mediating substrate? What is a message supposed to be when it is not understandably expressed in any sign system, code, or convention? Indeed, messages only arise when media come into play. Media are the self-establishing means that enable us to express ourselves.

The encoding challenge

The essence of communication is not the transfer of messages as such but the transfer of meaning. Whatever message is being transferred, it will be useless if it is misunderstood. And to be fair, so many things can cause misunderstanding.

Newborn babies are known for their loud but unclear messages of discomfort. We interpret their crying as an urgent notification of hunger or thirst, which is easily verified when the crying stops for a while after feeding. At about nine months of age, babies learn to use meaningful gestures to express their needs. When they reach for or point to an object outside their range, sometimes along with a whine or moan, parents can hardly misinterpret their wishes: "I want to have that thing!" It is an unmistakable sign of the desire for possession. Pointing at an object to direct attention to it is one of the simplest ways for adults to express a message as well. However, this strategy is only feasible when the indicated objects are more or less within sight. This is rarely the case. Suppose that you vaguely wave your hand southwards while you are standing in the middle of Amsterdam. How could anyone ever understand that you are calling attention to the Eiffel Tower, some 400 kilometres distant? Moreover, abstract concepts like "love", "poverty", or "euro crisis" lack a material counterpart to point at.

This is where sign coding comes into play. According to Ferdinand de Saussure's theory of meaning, each sign that we use to convey meaning is composed of two inherently connected components: the signifier of the sign (the designation, the form, the representation) and its meaning (the referent, the signified). We use signifiers (e.g. words, arrows, pictures) as a replacement for the real thing. The word "house" is the signifier that refers to the meaningful construct that people can live in. It is no more than an arbitrary label that we have agreed upon. It allows us to talk about houses even in the middle of the Sahara, where no houses are around to point to. The approach also allows us to deal with abstract concepts which lack any material referent. This theory of signs goes far beyond language. Pointing out an object sends a clear message without using any words. Practically, all our behaviours, gestures, and even our hairstyles and clothes are subjected to cultural codes and help to express messages to our social environment. They reveal our preferences, our lifestyle, our values. They reveal who we are, or, in many cases, who we want others to believe we are, which, in the end, doesn't make a big difference. Even apparent commodities like smartphones, glasses, watches, or cars are important signs of expressing our status, cultural profile, and lifestyle. It is quite naïve to suppose that our car is only for travelling from point A to point B because, indeed, quite a few alternatives achieve that result better, faster, and cheaper (e.g. bus, train, metro, cab). Probably the main function of our car is a symbolic one: it expresses our lifestyle. That's why we always fall for buying a specific type, dressed up with accessories that we don't really need but that satisfy our urge to express our identities.

In language systems, most signifiers are of a symbolic nature, which means that the signifier doesn't look very much like the signified object. It's easy to see that the word "house" is a symbolic signifier since it looks very different from a real house. To understanding the meaning of the word, you would have to know the agreed code: "house" means a building to live in. In contrast, a painting of a house is an example of an icon. This displays some similarity to the signified object (provided that the painting isn't too expressionistic). Hence, understanding an iconic message is a matter of recognising rather than knowing. The secret of good pictograms is the strong resemblance between signifier and signified, which allows for easy recognition. Surprisingly, quite a few words, such as those that replicate sounds, are iconic in nature: "bang", "flash", "grumble", "cough", "clap", "mumble", "whinny", "sneeze", and so on. Such examples display some (acoustic) resemblance to the phenomena they signify.

Philosopher Charles Sanders Peirce defined a third type of signifier, the index, which is intermediate between the symbol and the icon. The index is neither an arbitrary indicator like the symbol nor is it based on resemblance like the icon. Instead, the index requires a different type of relationship. In linguistics, this is known as metonymy: using an attribute of an idea to refer to the whole idea. The message "I'm reading Shakespeare" is metonymy, where the word "Shakespeare" doesn't refer to the great writer but to his body of work. Other examples are "9/11 changed the world", "the trains are on strike", and "she lost her tongue". The index is particularly valuable, if not indispensible, in pictorial media. For instance, because of the denotative nature of film, it is very difficult to visualise abstract concepts like society, ideology, eternity, or freedom. Over the years, filmmakers and TV reporters have established idioms for these which are largely based on such metonymic indices. You may have noticed TV news shows and documentaries visualising the world's economy with shots of industrial sites crowded with fuming chimneys. Society at large is commonly depicted by a-specific long-focus footage of modern city buildings and lots of people bustling about on the pavement. Scientific progress is easily demonstrated by incomprehensible shots of bubbling test tubes, laboratory equipment, and blinking computer lights, possibly operated by bespectacled staff in white coats. The Hollywood clichés of the hero beyond reproach and the relentless villain are metonymies for good and evil, respectively. Sheets of a tear-off calendar coming loose and falling down one after the other is an index for the idea "as time goes by". A clock with fast moving hands conveys the same idea. These examples demonstrate that the index can be a valuable stylistic device for visualising abstract concepts. The life span of such idiom is quite limited, however. Since filmmakers consider themselves to be arty, creative persons, they tend to avoid any clichés—who wants to be accused of using clichés?—and continually try to create new indices and stylistic devices. From a communication perspective, the avoidance of established idiom doesn't favour comprehensibility, as the audience may not directly understand the new signifiers.

Extracting the right meaning from a film may thus look very much like solving a puzzle. Paradoxically, such ambiguity and lack of precision yield attractive content that challenges the receivers to establish their own truths according to their personal preferences and needs. This may sound a bit weird, but this is exactly the essence of literature, poetry, sculpture, music, opera, and the arts at large. In language, words are loaded with connotations that create delicate distinctions and allow us to depict multicoloured, ambiguous narratives. Reading a novel requires active extraction of meaning from the subtle interplay of wording, syntax, and storyline. Experienced readers inevitably will profit more from this richness than inexperienced ones. The same holds for viewers of film or TV. The naïve viewer may easily fail to catch the connotation of the tear-off calendar sheets and may wonder if something is wrong with the glue keeping it all together, whereas a skilled viewer would be able to see through to the message. In his seminal work *How to Read a Film*, James Monaco describes a subtle scene from Godard's *La Chinoise* in which the radical-left-wing leading actress takes cover behind a pile of Mao's red books: covered by Maoist theory, she is about to attack the establishment. This is a latent indexical clue that addresses deeper levels of communication that are easily overlooked. On the other hand, subtle, implicit messages like this allow a lot of room for interpretation for the viewer. It is exactly this room for interpretation, this ability for the viewer to construct his or her own truth, that makes film attractive as a communication medium.

In the 1980s, media scientist Neil Postman rightly argued that we should teach our children how to watch TV, just like we teach them how to read texts. Watching TV seems deceptively simple when looking only at manifest contents and neglecting indexical connotations, the main carriers of meaning. He strongly criticised this new mass medium for delivering an incoherent flow of trivialities to reinforce a primitive and fragmented view of the world (the "zap" culture) and effecting apathetic and indifferent consumption of visual stimuli and thus causing viewers to lose original human capabilities like commitment, reflectivity, and profundity. In recent years, the ubiquity of the web, social networking, and mobile devices has raised similar concerns. Both nationally and internationally, the encouragement of media literacy has gained high priority, prompting consumers to answer the crucial question for any message: "What does it mean?"

Message distortion

Each medium has its own limitations in representing the world's reality. Phones only provide an audio channel, email provides no acoustic information, and SMS is even more limited. It is naïve to think that a camera just captures and reproduces reality. Images and sounds are affected by technology's limitations. Sources of technical distortion include limited image resolution of the video camera, inferior contrast ratio, sharpness problems, poor reproduction of colours, and clipped audio because of bandwidth limitations. So far, even the most advanced high-definition cameras cannot cope with the sensory richness of the real-life thing. Notwithstanding the digital nature of many storage formats, technical encoding processes inherently require simplifications and approximations of the real image. Technical conversions during signal processing result in conversion losses and the lowering of signal-noise ratios.

Even more important are the conceptual truncations that result from the characteristics of the chosen media. In audiovisual media like film, TV, and video, the fundamental issue is the apparent denotative nature of the images (and sounds). A shot of a house can hardly be misinterpreted; it is just what it is. Such a shot simply says: "Look, here is a house; not just any house, but this particular one." All important details of the house are displayed with great fidelity. Stills and moving images are markedly denotative with respect to concrete objects, phenomena, and persons from our physical reality. According to film analyst James Monaco, it is exactly this denotative nature of film that causes big problems because it pretends to show the world as it is, but it really doesn't. Moving images are seen to dictate the absolute truth about reality. In fact, they show a distorted, biased reality. Any film, video, or TV programme is a selective, tendentious representation of reality, a personal interpretation of reality rather than an objective reproduction. Indeed, for each shot, filmmakers decide what viewers will see and what they will not. They choose the camera position, camera angle, and camera movements like a zoom, pan, track, or roll along with the staging, composition, and duration of a shot. They also decide about the assembly of separate shots into a story-based sequence. They add music and sound effects to make things more dramatic or cheerful, or they add a laugh track to make it seem funny. Each of these decisions has an impact on the meaning that is presented to the audience.

The richness of expression that most sign systems offer provides a solid foundation for manipulating readers, listeners, and viewers. This holds for mass media in general. Newspapers and TV news shows are likely to represent established powers and institutions rather than independent journalism. The manipulations of images in the former Russian republic were disreputable. Propagandists retouched photographs by replacing images of unwelcome opponents in photographs with bushes, plants, or other neutral objects to preserve the assumed purity of the message. In the 1930s, the German film director Leni Riefenstahl developed a new promotional film genre that unconditionally glorified the political ideology of the Nazis through such films as *Triumph des Willens* in 1934 and *Olympia* in 1936. Such deliberate manipulation is not a relic of the past, though. To become a leading politician today, candidates cannot do without modern mass media promoting them as the ideal, sympathetic, cheerful, reasonable, reliable, and competent candidates to vote for. Competence and expertise are outshined by the biggest smile, the nicest stunts, and the most self-assured attitude, cautiously orchestrated and controlled by spin doctors. In the summer of 2008, newspapers reported that a photograph of Italian prime minister Silvio Berlusconi had been retouched to mask a woman's breast that appeared in a painting in the background. Berlusconi's advisors had decided to simply cover the breast with an extra fold to preserve Berlusconi's image as an honourable and decent leader. Ironically, the painting by eighteenth century master Giovanni Tiepolo was titled *Time Reveals Truth* [*La verità svelata dal tempo*], which indeed happened.

Besides politics, commercial advertising is concerned with wittingly promoting untruths. The cleaning power of detergents, the seductive qualities of perfume, the aromatic taste of coffee, the whitening effect of toothpaste, the defining characteristics of any product are advertised with the sophisticated use of attractive images to create the right connotations and bypass viewers' cognitive systems. It targets irrational, primitive, subconscious mental activity so that we are receptive to the message. Even though we may be well aware of the one-sided, seductive, Photoshopped nonsense, we're defenceless and cannot do anything but accept it. Indeed, every company knows that sales increase proportionally with advertising efforts. It seems we want to be fooled.

Such bias and distortion appears in any mediated communication. Unlike window glass, whose transparency offers an (almost) unperturbed view at the world behind it, communication media inevitably deform messages. Any message that is created, stored, transmitted, or displayed is subjected to noise, distortion, truncation, and manipulation. Viewers should protect themselves against the suggested reality by learning to be sensitive to the underlying connotations and distortions.

Our truncated perception

Human perception is largely a matter of information reduction. In our continuous effort to making sense of the world, we have to selectively reduce the amount of information to process. An ancient man in the wilderness, taken by surprise by a bear or a lion, could only survive because of a quick judgement of the overall situation that neglected irrelevant details like an account of the different types of plants that were crushed by the swiftly approaching monster. Taking such details into account would require too much processing power and, regrettably, too much time. Evolution has made us powerful information reducers. We need only very few clues to know what's going on. According to Gestalt theory, we use templates—a circle, square, house, tree—to quickly recognise patterns. If we sense a rough pattern that more or less matches a template, we swiftly recognise the pattern and identify its source. Roaring sounds and the rough shape of something big quickly approaching gives us enough clues to identify a predator and run away without hesitation. Template matching isn't a sufficient model for explaining human perception as a whole because it would require us to hold an immense number of templates in our memory to cover all the objects and processes of the world. There is more to it.

Perception cannot do without our knowledge of the world. Therefore, perception is driven by our theories of the world. We use our knowledge and previous experiences to hypothesise about the external world and use the information we receive from our senses to deciding whether to accept or adjust our hypotheses. So, we continually subject our observances to a hypothesis-testing procedure. According to this view, perception is a highly subjective experience because personal meaning is constructed based on available personal knowledge. Since we are constrained to a limited set of perceptual data, the process of perception is highly driven by probabilities and expectations. We take chances based on conclusions from little empirical evidence. This makes our judgements faster. We know the risks remain low since it's highly probable that what we expect to happen will happen. Consequently, we are taken by surprise when something unexpected happens and refutes our hypotheses. This is what conjurers exploit. They are the masters of deceit. With sleight of hand, they painfully demonstrate the limitations of human perception by first cautiously helping us to develop obvious (but invalid) theories and then disprove these by showing a conflicting outcome. They first make us believe that the magic hat is empty, and then they suddenly pull out a rabbit so that in the most literal way, we cannot believe our own eyes. In daily life, our perception may fail dramatically when our theories about the world prove to be inadequate. The simple action of walking down the stairs requires the complex interplay of visual cues, our balance mechanism, muscular tension, and feedback about the position, angle, and speed of our body, legs, and feet. We rely on our knowledge about gravity, our assumptions about the regularities of stairs, and our previous experiences with loose carpets and continuously test hypotheses about this particular staircase against our sensory inputs. Since perception is so highly practiced, the hypothesis-testing process is automatic and outside of our conscious awareness. The whole action is performed with a limited set of sensory data and, in most cases, it works out well. In the worst case, we are confronted with the dramatic consequences of using a staircase theory that turns out to be invalid, even when nothing is wrong with our eyes.

Neuroscientist Henri Markram takes this idea one step further. He says the human brain is an imaginarion, a machine that has learned to imagine the world on the basis of rough, partial clues. We don't need complete and explicit information. We can do with vague hints. Our brain will make sense of them. This idea is supported by experiments in which subjects with cochlear, retinal, and brain implants that restrict sensory information understood a full picture. Our brain fools us by making us think that we perceive the world, when, in fact, we're imagining it.

The subjective nature of perception means that the things we see and hear are not necessarily the things that other people see and hear. Some people adhere the theory that gnomes exist: little people about 15 centimetres tall who wear peaked red caps and live happily in the woods. Since perception is driven by theory, these people may happen to detect a gnome every now and then, particularly in partial darkness. Such detections in turn reconfirm and strengthen these people's theory and increase the likelihood that they will perceive gnomes. A similar self-establishing mechanism can be found in superstition, obscure therapies, religion, and even in science. Many people seem to be prepared to accept supernatural theories about the world that lack any empirical or scientific foundation such as homoeopathy, magic, earth rays, ghosts, heaven, witchcraft, spells, UFOs, canals on Mars, occultism, the paranormal, magnetisers, spiritualism, aromatherapy, faith healing, and many more. When you believe that a disproportionate percentage of the cars on the street are blue pickups, you are likely to notice a lot of blue pickups. In all cases, these theories drive perception and thus effect their self-confirmation.

In serious domains, perception is also biased by theoretical premises. Xenophobia is fostered by selective indignation towards immigrants. Those who are obsessed by the fallacy of foreigners' spite and inferiority tend to magnify evidence that supports that theory while neglecting any that refutes it. Likewise, scientists, desperately searching for evidence supporting their groundbreaking theory are likely to see the evidence even if it is not there. In 1988, physicists Martin Fleischmann and Stanley Pons believed that they observed cold fusion, which many consider to be the holy grail of energy production. For decades scientists have been working on nuclear fusion research in order to solve the world's energy problem. They are trying to create a stable and controlled mini sun, which would be a cheap and abundant source of energy because it requires only water as fuel. The fusion process, however, typically requires temperatures up to one billion kelvins, which makes it very difficult to produce in a laboratory. Fleischmann and Pons, two leading and well-respected scientists in their field, claimed to have realised nuclear fusion at room temperature in a simple tabletop experiment. After the first wave of excitement about this breakthrough (there were already rumours that they would be awarded the Nobel Prize), problems arose when no one else managed to reproduce the original experiment. To date, cold fusion has not been achieved. The researchers strongly chasing their theory of cold fusion perceived things that weren't really there. Altogether, this doesn't differ much from the gnome case. Essentially, the idea that perception is about the processing of sensory stimuli is naïve because is unjustly neglects the often overwhelming influence of the prejudices we have about the world.

Failing communication

One may wonder if the case of the Pythia reflects successful communication. It is difficult to check if the meaning extracted by the priests exactly corresponds with the original prophecies of Apollo. In general, the problem of communication is that it is apt to fail. There are many examples of miscommunication with a dramatic impact. In 1977, two passenger aircrafts collided on the runway of Los Rodeos Airport in Tenerife after the crew of one of the planes misunderstood the instructions from the tower. They thought they were cleared for take-off, but the tower only specified what route to follow after take-off. In the crash, 583 people died.

All along the communication pipeline, many things can go wrong. Syntactic errors infringe on the rules of spelling and grammar and are likely to produce unclear, ambiguous messages that cannot be deciphered very well. A sentence like "the swiffle horqe be runninged" doesn't seem to make much sense. Using our imagination, we might speculate that the message is about a horse, possibly a fast-running horse. The context of communication may be of help here: being at the horse races would provide some extra reassurance that the interpretation was correct. If we were at a flower shop or at a pop concert, we would certainly be lost. In film and TV, the syntax is less strict, yet there are some conventions for framing, moving the camera, and preserving orientation. The latter, for instance, is about preserving the actors' sight lines or action lines across subsequent shots in order to maintain the overall geometry of the scene. A close-up of actor 1 looking to the left, followed by a close-up of actor 2 looking to the right along the same angle suggests a scene where the two are facing each other. When instead both actors look in the same direction, the spatial relationship fails and no dialogue is conveyed. Nevertheless, wittingly breaking this grammar rule is a useful way to deliberately disorientate the viewer. Such a technique can be observed in many music videos, TV programmes, and feature films. When it occurs accidentally, though, for instance, during the transmission of a football match, viewers are not able to construct a mental map of spatial conditions in the scene and may find themselves mistakenly jubilant at the opponent's goal.

Miscommunication can also be a perception problem. In a noisy environment, we might have difficulty picking up spoken words appropriately. Generally this need not be a problem since our mental process of hypothesis testing compensates for this. In extreme cases of sparse or incomplete information, however, this process fails and we start reading into the message with the wrong theories without being able to check the correctness of the derived meaning. So we think we understand, but we don't.

Another category of failure is semantic complexity. Well-formed messages may still be difficult to understand. Messages can be so complex or detailed that the receivers easily lose the thread. Only very few people will be able to fully understand an explanation of Einstein's general theory of relativity, which requires deep insights into the physical concepts of space, time, mass, and energy and sufficient proficiency in the mathematics involved. In general, the sender of a message should take into account the knowledge and expertise of the receiving party. If this is overestimated, the communication will fail. Logical propositions are yet another source of problems. How to answer a simple question such as "Don't you like coffee?" Saying no could mean that indeed you don't like coffee, but because this implies a confirmation, you could have answered yes instead. Multiple negations arouse even more confusion: "Why should I deny that I'm not the one who couldn't wait his turn?" Our cognitive system is just not quite suited to cascaded logical reasoning. It is not that easy to see that you are the grandchild of the father of your brother's mother. Likewise, the illogical sign attached to the wall that says, "Forbidden to hang up signs" is confusing. Is it a joke or what? Occasionally speakers may mistakenly use the wrong words. The text "I speak Spinach" refers neither to one's foreign language skills nor to one's meal. Sometimes one may suspect a Freudian slip: mixing speech actions with private thoughts or subconscious feelings that had better not surface. For instance, intrigued by the really giant nose of Mr. Jones, you might inadvertently say, "Hello, Mr. Nose!"

In addition, a complex mix of style components like proverbs, wordplay, and humour challenge the audience to get wise to the meaning. It often includes eponyms (words that have multiple meanings), metaphors (similarities), hyperboles (extreme exaggeration), irony (using words to express the opposite of literal meaning), or understatements (downplaying a big issue), all of which require some intelligence and knowledge of the world to understand. That's why it is so difficult for computers to understand a text like "Of course I will go to London", when spoken with irony (try it out by extending the text with something like "Pfff, do you think I'm crazy?", while slightly shaking your head). So, similar to visual media, texts are loaded with index signifiers, challenging the receiver to capture the connotations rather than the denotations.

Politicians are apt to use very unclear, inconclusive phrasing, leaving much room for interpretation. The strategy is as simple as it is effective: first reassure the people with an attractive promise, then make the opposite decision and finally get away with it by unconcernedly referring to the original message. Especially when they are in trouble, politicians seem to deliberately pursue miscommunication by creating confusion or using veiled language. Unclear statements like "The economy is growing, productivity is high, trade is up, people are working. It's not as good as we'd like, but . . . and to the extent that we find weakness, we'll move" and "I just want you to know that, when we talk about war, we're really talking about peace" were made by former US governor and president George W. Bush. It is likely that these peculiar statements were made on purpose to disguise problems. Admittedly, some believe they were made by accident.

Messages cannot be evaluated in a vacuum. They always refer to aspects of the world and serve a particular purpose, are directed to a particular audience, and located within a sociocultural context. Meaning is not just an invariant attribute of the message but is largely determined by the context of use. A signifier may effect a different understanding in different communities depending on different languages, different rituals, different etiquettes, different clothing, different attitudes, different lifestyles, and so on. Two street gangs violently fighting each other with baseball bats, knuckledusters, and knives will probably take no notice of a police officer politely asking, "Excuse me, excuse me, do you have a moment please? My name is constable Jim Brown, and if you don't mind, I have an urgent request for you: please, would you be so kind as to . . ." The tone simply doesn't match the situation: the message is in the wrong tone, wrong style, and wrong wording at the wrong place. Another situational error would be neglecting a dress code because this violates people's expectations. This is not limited to parties or official occasions. Every situation requires its own code. It is okay to wear a swimming suit on the beach, but it puts forward a different message when worn at a funeral. Cross-cultural differences are yet another source of contextual misunderstanding. Hilarious mistakes have been made in international advertising. An international advertising campaign for "Schweppes Tonic Water" translated in Italy into "Schweppes Toilet Water". After the introduction in South America of the Chevy Nova, a new General Motors car, the company found out that in Spanish "no va" means "it won't go". Now they understood why sales fell short! Tourists and businessmen should always take care when dealing with other cultures. Common Western European gestures like shaking hands, waving, or shrugging the shoulders can have completely different meanings in other parts of the world. A thumbs up, which signifies satisfaction or approval in Europe and America, is very impolite in Australia.

Sometimes, most peculiarly, the communication can be perfect and the receiver may fully understand the message the sender means, but nevertheless, the receiver's response appears opposite to the sender's intentions. This is the case when the message is understood but ignored because it conflicts with the receiver's other ideas, beliefs, or behaviours. For example, smokers have to deal with two opposing truths: "I like smoking" and "smoking is dangerous". By mentally eliminating one of these truths, the inconsistency is removed. The process is highly irrational. That's why it is so difficult to change our behaviour. Even when we're convinced that we'd better stop smoking, we ignore the arguments and stick to the habit. In psychology, this is called "cognitive dissonance": the idea that we want to preserve the consistency of our beliefs and our behaviours. We hear and understand the message but ignore it. A second example of a response that seems to conflict with the message has to do with smart reasoning. Sometimes, smart evaluation of the message provides new insights that call for a different response than the one asked for. In the Netherlands every now and then, the authorities announce a "rush hour alarm", which aims to discourage people from using their cars. However, quite a few drivers conclude that this will be an excellent opportunity to take the car because the streets will be nearly empty because of the message.

Indeed, communication is a delicate process. Effective communication will never be easy. Mistakes lie in wait, either on the sender's side or the receiver's side or in the middle as messages are transferred. It is quite likely that many of these misunderstandings are hardly noticed, thus suggesting a pseudo common ground while they accumulate a series of hidden differences that could eventually lead to hostile outbursts by individuals, groups, or even nations.

CHAPTER 6
The Mystery of True Knowledge

If animals could consciously notice the way we humans communicate, they would be astounded by the incredible amount and variety of conversations we engage in. The verbal repertoire of cows is well known to be quite limited, and the same holds for their body language. Human languages comprise up to many hundreds of thousands of different words, if not well over a million, many of which have different meanings in different contexts. We read, listen, watch, and talk all day using a wide range of channels like books, billboards, traffic signs, TV, newspapers, email, phone, and SMS, occasionally interrupted by a good old face-to-face dialogue. We engage in an avalanche of messages loaded with significance. An alien civilisation out there in outer space searching for signs of extragalactic life might suddenly come across a mysterious and persistent electro-acoustic buzz surrounding our blue planet. Without claiming that all of these messages reflect the profoundest intellectual qualities of our species, it is fair to say that they are the key to acquiring and sharing knowledge. Messages help us to express, to judge, and to extend our knowledge. Today we capitalise on the knowledge accumulated over many thousands of years in clay tablets, books, and computer files that constitute our ever-extending collective memory. Today's digital media technologies are indispensable for this since they are the prevailing carriers of our messages. We use them for the creation, storage, and transfer of our knowledge, be it about medical treatments, building skyscrapers, or simply cooking a meal. They connect us to the culture, the news, and the people of our communities. Media are the cognitive tools that help us to extend our knowledge of the world. In many cases, they stretch our mental horizons and help us to achieve a better understanding of the world and ourselves

The power of knowledge

Over the last two decades it has become fashionable to conceive of our economy as a knowledge economy. Stressing the importance of knowledge is not new, however. The adage "knowledge is power" is commonly attributed to sixteenth century philosopher Francis Bacon or sometimes to his colleague Thomas Hobbes. Similar statements even date back to the great Persian empire 3,000 years ago. Bacon represented a new scientific movement that promoted the search for true knowledge through observation and that condemned simply accepting fallacies and prejudices imposed by authority or tradition. "Knowledge is power" expresses the enabling qualities of knowledge, encouraging people to study because it helps them to go far in the world. So, knowledge had been valued for many centuries, but a new era favouring knowledge as the key element of life was yet to come. At the end of the twentieth century the emergence of digital technologies created a disruptive and irreversible change in society, putting knowledge at the core of economic activity. After many thousands of years of steady farming and over 200 years of industrial development, the recent digitisation of society has completely changed the economical landscape. The focus of economic activity shifted from material products and their associated industrial processes, smoking chimneys or blue-collar workers, to virtual products and services: content, software, connectivity, consultancy, banking, social networking, online advertising, online shopping, and so on. Among the world's leading companies are Google, Facebook, Microsoft, and Twitter, which all became multi-billion-dollar businesses using knowledge as their core asset. Nicholas Negroponte, founder of the famous MIT Medialab, aptly explained this change as a shift in the economy from processing atoms to processing bits. In many respects, the traditional economy cannot compete with the speed, bandwidth, memory capacity, and intelligence of the digital economy. People have achieved success in online banking, stock trade, hotel bookings, electronic mail, e-publishing, gaming, video conferencing, tax declarations, online ordering, traffic control, parcel tracking, and, unfortunately, also cyber crime.

Material products are still being manufactured, but their most important component now is the knowledge embedded in them. TV sets, smartphones, and tablet computers use the latest technologies for signal processing, noise reduction, and image resolution. The knowledge about how to produce a product is more valuable than all the materials used to make it. The chip inside a car is more valuable than all the materials used for the coachwork, windows, and wheels. In any profession, workers raise their knowledge and skills to bring them up to the latest standards. Low-skilled jobs are about to disappear. Bench fitters have to be able to use the latest computer-driven machines. Nurses have to continually update their knowledge about diagnostic tools, medications, and treatment methods. Today's farmers are less active inspecting their crops outside and instead monitor and control their businesses with computers. Less romantic, that's for sure. From an economic perspective, knowledge is the driving force for the development of new products and increased production efficiency, which provide an economic actor an advantage over its competitors. This is why governments and industries keep investing in education, research, and innovation. In the end, knowledge is the key to economic power.

The nature of knowledge

The ironic thing about knowledge is that our lives are imbued with knowledge, but we don't quite know what knowledge is. Knowledge is a difficult thing to grasp. Apparently it is something we can acquire, we can share, and we can transfer through messages. Knowledge is not the same as the messages we compose—it is certainly not the equivalent of the words or the characters that make up the messages. Transferring knowledge is not simply sending a message. Teachers explaining to their pupils how to add 6 and 8 will always try to find out if their pupils got the message. Even if the pupils say, "Yes, I see," they still could be dull. Transferring knowledge involves a sense-making process. This suggests that knowledge is of a subjective nature. On the other hand, the ability to add two numbers is easily tested as an objective fact of the world. So, to what extent is knowledge something very personal, located inside our heads, and to what extent is knowledge something objective that exists independent of ourselves?

In the objectivist view, knowledge of the world exists independent of the individual. Objectivism regards knowledge as the set of natural entities, rules, and principles that govern the world. We can get to know them through experience and observation. We can reason about the observations and develop theories about the world that we can test empirically. For this we use scientific methods rather than any subjective ones like imagination, feelings, or dogmas. The more evidence we collect, the closer our knowledge will approach the reality of the world. Basically, it means that we are engaged in discovering the world as it is. Objectivism reflects the premise that "reality constructs the person": we adapt our understanding of the world as much as possible to the way reality manifests itself. The rules and principles that govern the world are independent of our understanding, even independent of our existence. If life on Earth were suddenly wiped out, for instance, by a lethal virus or a nuclear disaster, the rules and principles of the solar system would still apply and the planets would unconcernedly continue orbiting around the sun.

In the subjectivist view, there is no such thing as an external reality that we get to know through discovery. Subjectivism says that the observer and the observed cannot be separated. Reality is the result of our personal interpretation. We create our own knowledge of the world and our own truths. We are active makers of meaning and heavily rely on our background, feelings, emotions, and prior experiences to do so. As opposed to the objectivist idea that "reality constructs the person", subjectivists claim that "the person constructs reality". However, this doesn't mean that anything goes. Individual meaning is tested against the meaning of others, and through this process of social negotiation, a common understanding can be attained. In the end, knowledge is a social artefact.

Even till today, philosophers have argued about these different approaches without ever solving the issue. It is commonly accepted now that knowledge has both subjective and objective traits. Only very few subjectivists today deny the existence of a true reality out there. These so-called solipsists claim that life is only a dream, a proposition that is interesting but hard to verify or refute. By far the majority of subjectivists recognise that reality is bigger than themselves and that the solar system will outlive them. At the same time, objectivism displays severe weaknesses. American Philosopher Thomas Kuhn explained that the objectivist approach is not capable of providing objective, absolute truths because the justification of theories is overshadowed by the process of social negotiation. Brilliant new theories have a hard time getting accepted because they challenge existing theories, which are likely to be defended tenaciously by the scientific establishment. The work of Albert Einstein is a revealing case because it remained controversial for many years. In 1921, he was awarded the Nobel Prize for his early work on the photo-electric effect, which was outstanding but was not what is generally considered his masterpiece, the general theory of relativity that enervated Newton's laws of motion and gravitation by demonstrating that space and time are no longer absolute and stable quantities but are distorted under the influence of mass. The scientific community just needed more time to accept and appreciate this new approach.

Although these different views on the nature and origin of knowledge seem to make mutually exclusive claims, in practice, they overlap quite a bit. The shared motto could be "reality and the person constitute each other". Thousands years ago, Plato defined knowledge as "justified true belief", which covers both the personal aspect ("I believe") and the external verification ("justified and true"). We should have listened to Plato because he proposed a fine and appropriate compromise long ago.

Between noise and understanding

It is said that a lot of our knowledge is stored in books and journal papers. This is probably correct: written texts allow us to enjoy the extraordinary lines of reasoning of great thinkers from the past. We can directly access the groundbreaking works of Plato, Newton, and Einstein or enjoy the great expressive powers of Shakespeare and Goethe. This is only one side of the coin. The other side is the difficulty of getting the knowledge out of the documents and reconstructing it correctly in the reader's brain. The effectiveness of this reconstruction is not straightforward. To fully grasp the significance of the work of, say, Einstein, the reader should possess quite some expertise already. Many people will be able to literally read the words and sentences that Einstein wrote and may notice that the text is in English (or perhaps German) about some difficult topic regarding light, time, and velocity but will not understand what it says. Primary school children will probably gain no new insights from the text. They will be able to recognise the characters and to read them out, but they will have no clue whatsoever of their significance. An illiterate person wouldn't even get that far, at best guessing that these strange black patterns on the white paper sheets must be characters.

Cats and dogs are certainly able to perceive the black spots, but after casual inspection (if inspection is made at all), they will classify these as irrelevant background noise: hard to eat, unnecessary to hide from or to chase away. So, ignorance only allows for the perception of noise. Likewise, illiterates will only see noise, albeit that they will understand that they must be looking at a text. Schoolchildren perceive the text as plain data: they will read the arbitrary characters and words as unorganised facts without any meaning. They use their knowledge for recognising the characters and maybe some words, but they don't see the coherence that produces the well-articulated sentences and the underlying meaning. The vast majority of people will likely see some informative interconnections or even understand that this sentence, "during continued acceleration of the particle its mass will increase, whereby it will not be able to exceed the speed of light", reflects information about the relationship between one parameter (acceleration) and another (mass). They may learn the sentence by heart as an organised fact and replicate it at a party to impress the guests (I suppose this sort of showing off false expertise happens a lot). Still, they wouldn't quite know what they're talking about. Understanding the writings of Einstein requires detailed knowledge of the concepts of matter and energy and the underlying mathematical procedures. Science students and physicists are likely to get the most out of it. They will be able to internalise the knowledge and integrate it within their existing conceptions and experiences. They will go through the texts and extract the hidden logic and principles that need to be understood and captured in order to achieve mastery in using the knowledge for specific purposes. This knowledge will not be an exact copy of the original work: the reader will modify and personalise the knowledge to meaningfully integrate it into his or her internal cognitive structure. Nevertheless, chances are high that he or she gets the right picture.

These examples demonstrate that whatever is captured in a book, the thing that we get out of it can be either knowledge, information, data, or noise, dependent on our pre-existing knowledge and understanding. This is what makes knowledge a knowledge amplifier: the more you know, the more you will learn and understand.

The hidden treasure

British philosopher Gilbert Ryle published an anecdote that explains the limitations of learning from written or spoken texts quite well. Medieval knights, he says, are well known for their tendency to save desperate maidens locked up in castle towers. They possess the moral and formal attitude that produces the behavioural style of engaging in various rescue operations. The knowledge required for these is hard to describe and will comprise only very few explicit behavioural instructions and rules, like, "If the castle is surrounded by a canal, if the guards don't notice me, then . . ." Most of the required knowledge cannot be made explicit. It is subtle, context dependent, intuitive, creative, and instinctive, and it is directly linked to action. Hence, teaching young aspirant knights cannot be done very well through books or lectures. Instead, the aspirants should be involved somehow in situations where they are confronted with the required behaviours. According to Ryle, it is a huge misconception to assert that all knowledge can be taught with written or spoken words. In many cases, knowledge cannot be captured in explicit rules and instructions because it is directly embedded in practical actions and behaviours.

Unthinkingly lifting a suitcase that turns out to be empty will make you look like an idiot, but it shows how your knowledge about suitcases and their expected weights and the muscle power that usually is required for lifting these is seamlessly intertwined with the action of lifting. Physical chemist Michel Polanyi was the first to introduce the term "tacit knowledge", which he explained with the example of riding a bicycle. It is quite unlikely that you will be able to learn how to ride a bicycle by just reading an instructional text. Please try it out: "Stand upright with the bicycle between your legs, your feet on each side of the bike. Place your right foot on the right pedal and carefully transfer your weight onto it. When the bicycle starts to move forwards, quickly place your left foot on the left pedal, which is just in opposition to the right pedal. Keep the handlebars straight so that you don't go off the road. When your left foot has slightly passed its uppermost position, shift your weight onto it. To steer to the left, turn the handlebars to the right (note: this is counterintuitive), and lean slightly in the direction you want to go. If necessary, turn the handlebars again. Practice with wide turns before trying sharp ones." These instructions may look quite precise (and they are), but they will not be very helpful because they lack the essential subtleties of timing, balancing, and responding to sudden disturbances that can only be learned from practical experience. To describe this implicit, procedural, or tacit knowledge, Gilbert Ryle used the phrase "knowing how": you know how to do it, but you cannot explain it. It is the opposite of "knowing that": the declarative, articulate, or codified knowledge that is captured in written or spoken words. Books and web pages are splendid for covering codified knowledge, but they fail dramatically when it comes to tacit knowledge. Radio, TV, and film are known for their engaging narratives and dramatic impact. Nevertheless, these are all one-way media that compel the receiver to remain an outsider without taking any active role or controlling power in the story. Games, simulations, and virtual worlds could make a difference here because these exactly put the user at the centre of the action, thus enabling him or her to express tacit knowledge. These media increasingly encourage intelligent, adaptive responses and sometimes even literally offer artificial characters for users to interact with. Hence, media are becoming the platform for our interaction with the world, enabling us to exert tacit knowledge, as is already the case for computer-assisted turning lathes, stock trading, tools for data manipulation, productivity software, and many more.

Taking a completely different perspective, we come across a peculiar type of knowledge generally referred to as "meta-knowledge" or "meta-cognition": the ability for people to have knowledge about their own knowledge. If you possess certain knowledge, you will also know that you know it. Interestingly, we also know that we don't know about certain things: "I know that I don't know how to do heart surgery." Likewise, we may have forgotten that we have certain knowledge: we don't know that we know. The worst thing that could happen is not knowing that we don't know: it reflects ignorance, generally articulated as stupidity. Unfortunately, it is abundantly present. Meta-cognition allows us to evaluate and regulate our own thinking and thereby improve our strategies of thinking and learning. It is directly linked with self-awareness and conscious thought. It makes us the self-aware, conscious individuals we are. Meta-cognition is generally assumed to be a unique human capacity, although there is some evidence that monkeys and dolphins also display cognitive self-awareness and are capable of monitoring and regulating their own states of mind. However, consciousness is hard to replicate in a machine. Computers are great at data processing, but they don't seem to have a clue (yet) about what they are doing.

Limits to truth

As Plato wisely noted, knowledge is justified true belief. Interestingly, not all knowledge is justified to the same extent. At one side of the spectrum is scientific knowledge: by its method, it requires extensive justification, thus obtaining a status of high validity. For instance, our knowledge of planetary motion is outstanding because it has been the object of empirical checking and double-checking over many centuries. The predictive power and precision of Newton's theories are matchless: we can foresee all eclipses in the next few centuries with unbelievable precision. At the other end of the spectrum, we see people who emphasise their belief instead of justifying its truth. Some people have the true belief that gnomes exist, and they easily but indirectly justify it by the fact that one morning they found their messy garden mysteriously raked up. Their criteria for truth are not intellectual but emotional or spiritual. They have developed an intense, personal conviction about the state of the world and see empirical evidence of it everywhere without taking into account its plausibility or likelihood. It is hard to refute their claims because of the fundamental impossibility of demonstrating the nonexistence of things. Although their knowledge lacks any empirical substantiation and looks very much like imagination, it is indelicate to disqualify it because similar considerations apply for religion, which commonly commands considerable respect.

But even scientific knowledge has its weak spots. It is tempting to believe that science is the route to absolute truth. After the work of Newton, who managed to capture the complex movements of bodies in simple mathematical equations, scientists strongly believed that mathematics could describe all the world's processes. In the early 1900s, the French physicist Pierre-Simon Laplace claimed that if only we would know all the forces in nature, we would be able to use mathematics to calculate how today's world transforms into tomorrow's world and nothing would be uncertain. This "determination theory"—the past completely determines the future—would mean that everything would be knowable beforehand. Uncertainty, chance, and even free will would be just illusions. The church strongly opposed this idea because if everything was known beforehand and nothing could be influenced, what would be the point of trying to be good, pious, or repentant? Why should we blame criminals for the crimes they committed when they couldn't influence the course of events?

Science itself demonstrated that Laplace was wrong. In the 1930s, Austrian mathematician Kurt Gödel proved that many problems can never be solved with mathematics. He also demonstrated that mathematics was not capable of proving anything about mathematics itself, for instance, it could not prove its own validity. So, for fundamental reasons, it is impossible to calculate the world. At the same time, quantum mechanics arose, starting from the very idea that reality expresses itself by chance. Quantum theorists Erwin Schrödinger and Werner Heisenberg showed that observations are loaded with probabilities and that uncertainty is an inherent characteristic of the world. Somewhat later, chaos theory demonstrated the limits of predictability. Weather forecasts are the infamous example of the limited reliability of calculations largely because small inaccuracies in input variables may produce huge differences in the calculated results. Philosopher of science Karl Popper explained the temporary nature of true knowledge by pointing at the fact that the starting points of science can never be validated: there is no rock bottom of knowledge that grounds all other knowledge. A scientific theory is the best theory available until it is refuted or until a better theory becomes available. Hence, scientific knowledge is inherently uncertain and temporary. Theories are regularly replaced with new theories that produce better descriptions of the world. Even the solid Newtonian laws that describe planetary motion were replaced with a new theory to include relativistic effects. When you browse through a scientific paper, you will be surprised to see how often the authors use disclaiming wordings like "we assume", "we suggest", "we suppose", "we believe", and "we hope". Most knowledge will probably appear improper in the long run.

Nevertheless, knowledge is the most distinguishing asset of our species. It holds the key to money, fame, and power, all of which are greatly compelling. Pretending to have knowledge is a natural human tendency: indeed, nobody wants to be regarded as a nitwit. Showing off your supposed expertise is a social phenomenon, the cognitive analogue of the physical intimidation that animals display to gain status, recognition, and respect. It is complemented with witty statements and persuasiveness. Successfully disguising your ignorance may easily help you to become a well-respected consultant, politician, or even president. Lying can be quite profitable.

Media and truth

Google, Twitter, Facebook, Wikipedia, and TV networks are becoming the mainstream sources of our knowledge. Such media also are the appropriate channels for amplifying falsehoods. First, a great deal of the knowledge available is incorrect. Second, the distortive properties of these media can easily be used to manipulating messages, which further affects the validity of the knowledge.

Often both problems co-occur. Commercial advertising is the ultimate example, even if we know beforehand that we'll be taken in. We know this genre, we know that what they are saying is all untrue. We understand that the enthusiastic presenter praising the revolutionary cleansing power of product X speaks on behalf of the washing powder company that just wants to increase its sales. It is quite unlikely that after viewing the commercial you would excitedly run outside and exclaim that finally, the problem of washing is solved! It could make a difference if this breakthrough in washing power were communicated by an independent scientist—that is, a real scientist, not an actor in a white lab coat portraying a scientist. Indeed, the person who is speaking makes quite a difference. The identity of the sender is of utter importance for the interpretation and judgement of the message's truth. If someone says that the weather will get cloudy and rainy in the afternoon, it makes quite a difference if the person is an official representative of a meteorological station or my chatty neighbour. The problem with media is that it is often unclear who the sender is. While in a common conversation we will be able to discern the sender as the person who performs the speech act, this doesn't hold for media like film, TV, or even websites. It is hard to see "who says". In fact, the grammar of these media dictates the concealment of any symptoms of the speech act's equivalent: the message production process. We seldom see cameras, microphones, tripods, stage lights, or any other clues about production in movies, news shows, or documentaries. Everything is set up to enhance the impression that what we're looking at is all real. This is amplified by the manifest denotative nature of (moving) images: the images tell what they show. Thus, the mediated story seems an autonomic process whereby the images apparently narrate themselves.

Concealing the message-production process also occurs in written texts. Linguist Emile Benveniste distinguished between "histoire" and "discours". A "histoire" uses a descriptive, detached, objective writing style. All characteristics of human speech production are lacking: "I", "you", "mine", "yours", and so on are not used. In contrast, "discours" directly addresses the reader in a personal way, as is common in letters, speeches, and some fiction. Moving images often present histoire because message production is deliberately kept out of sight. The style of TV newsreaders' speaking is histoire: traditionally, newsreaders are trained to read their texts flawlessly from autocue, mimicking robot-like neutrality. Presenters that would display any natural symptoms of human speech production like stuttering, mistakes, words like "I" and "you", poor grammar, or incomplete sentences are likely to be fired instantly. It all fits in trying to avoid discours in favour of histoire. Images as well as words are no longer expressed as opinions but presented anonymously with such great detachedness, determination, and perfection that they pretend to reflect reality. Thus, the world is depicted in the way it would be perceived by the all-seeing eye of God. The viewers easily adopt a vision like that.

CHAPTER 7

Getting Wiser Every Minute

Newborn babies are the most helpless creatures in the universe. When they come into the world, they do nothing but sleep, drink, and cry. They're not able to look, listen, point, walk, or talk. Probably they cannot even think. Right from the start, they learn to do new things, and they do so at a tremendous pace. Within a few months, they recognise their parents, they smile, and they are able to follow objects with their eyes. After half a year, they know their own name, they take objects in their hands, and they make a variety of sounds in preparation for speech. After one year, they understand quite a few words and they learned to use meaningful gestures, like waving goodbye or pointing at things. Soon after, they stand up and manage—not without some painful failures—to perform the complex bipedal balancing act of walking upright that is so characteristic of our species. They start using single words to express themselves and soon after combine those into short sentences. At school or even before, they learn to read and to write, and they learn about math, history, science, music, social behaviour, and all these things that make life worth living. Altogether, it takes twenty years or even more to prepare young people for the complexities and challenges of adulthood. Yet after their graduation as a plumber, musician, doctor, or mechanic, they are no more than novices in the field beginning the sustained extension of their knowledge and skills for the rest of their lives. This may seem a burden, but it is the inevitable and ultimate consequence of the course of evolution, which made us surpass the reflexive and instinctive behaviours of other animals and become the cognition-driven beings we are now. Curiosity, creativity, and eagerness to understand and to master new things are the inherent and unavoidable drivers of our behaviour. Our cognition is both the cause and the effect of our drive to learn new things. It brought us language, music, numbers, writing, print, and all the other assets that support the self-amplification of our cognition.

One might want to object that many pupils hate school and hate to do their homework, so they seem to hate learning. This may be the case, but what does it prove? It is questionable to attribute such reluctance to an intrinsic lack of curiosity and eagerness to learn. Instead, it is likely the effect of the inadequate ways our school systems and their lessons are arranged, offering many mandatory activities and only very few opportunities for pupils to take ownership of their own long-term strategies. But even though learning is sometimes boring as compared to taking a walk or going to the pub, we are prepared to accept this and still make the effort. It is the inherent characteristic of our cognition to engage in strategic thinking and plan long-term goals while controlling the distracting impulses for short-term satisfaction. In many cases, we are prepared to abstain from short-term fulfilment in favour of long-term goals. Endurance sports are a good illustration of this: long-distance runners may sometimes have a hard time during their races, but they are prepared to accept this because of the long-term reward they aim for: a personal best, a glittering medal, or even the glory of passing the finishing line. This is a unique human trait. We are prone to invest in enhancing our knowledge and skills for long-term gains. This is the basic attitude we display from early childhood. Engaging in new things is our second nature.

Our precious memory

Learning new things requires a memory for their retention. Without a memory, we wouldn't be able to consolidate any experience. We wouldn't know who we are and where we are, and we wouldn't be able to explain what we did a few seconds before. Various people who have sustained severe brain damage after an injury or surgery have experienced a permanent loss of memory function. This is especially the case when the damage is done to the hippocampus, the part of the brain known for its role in memory. The brains of patients displaying certain early symptoms of Alzheimer's disease also show severe damage to the hippocampus. Life without a memory proves to be very complex. These people are unable to remember anything for a period longer than a few dozens of seconds. They don't know their past and they cannot record the present. Without the memories of the past and the experiences of the present, it is impossible for them to anticipate the future. They cannot recollect the most trivial facts: they don't know if they had breakfast already, they don't know what food they like, they don't know if they're married, and if so, they don't know whether they have any children or what their names are. They are prepared to answer the same question over and over again because they don't remember that they already did. Remarkably, they are able to walk around or ride a bicycle without problems. Only the conscious part of memory, the declarative memory, is affected, while the non-declarative memory, which stores the things we do without thinking, like walking and eating, remains intact. Sometimes they can even play the piano, like the British former musician Clive Wearing, who was portrayed in the 2006 BBC documentary *The Man Without a Memory*. They don't know what ever happened to them. It must feel like being in a permanent state of awakening from lifelong unconsciousness. They cannot even remember the very notion of suffering from a memory injury. A lacking memory implies ignorance.

At the opposite end of the spectrum are people gifted with an almost perfect memory. For many of them, this gift comes at a price: while they may display superior skills in one specific area such as mathematics or history, they often completely dysfunction in other areas such as social skills. If so, they are called "idiots savants", which means "knowledgeable idiots". One of the best documented cases is of the Russian journalist Solomon Shereshevsky, who lived in the first half of the twentieth century. Neuropsychologist Aleksander Luria, who wrote a book about his findings, studied him for many years. Shereshevsky memorised everything he came across. He could effortlessly memorise poems, scientific formulas, extensive tables of meaningless numbers, or lists of nonsense syllables or words in any foreign language, even in reverse order. The man was a living computer. He was unable to forget, which seemed to be more or less a tragedy. Due to his superior memory function, Shereshevsky had difficulty enjoying simple everyday activities like taking a walk or reading a book because he was unable to avoid the intense and confusing rush of associations aroused by his memory when he noticed an object or a text. He experienced problems recognising the faces of people he knew because he had imprinted their images in so much detail that he wasn't able to link these images to the same people when their facial expressions changed. He had to give up his job as a journalist. Spanish writer Jorge Louis Borges describes a similar tragedy in his 1942 short story "Funes el memorioso". The main character likewise suffers from an infallible memory. With his mind permanently showered by all the details of his life, he is not capable of distinguishing between important issues and trivialities. His perfect memory seems to make life impossible. Borges suggests in the story that the ability to forget is more important for a human than the ability to remember. Superior memory confuses the mind.

Most people stay far away from these extremes. The distribution of memory capability is best depicted as a bell-shaped curve, showing that the fewest people fall both at the extreme low and high ends and that most people fall in the middle. The average human memory still is an excellent one, although it may be less impressive than the memories of idiots savants. It enables us to achieve high levels of cognition to perform beyond instinctual and reflexive behaviours. Remembering something means we know it. We rely on memory every single second of our lives. We use it to record simple but convenient facts like where we live, where we put our keys, or what the names of our children are and also to demonstrate complex cognitive processes linked with improving understanding, argumentation, and reasoning about the world. It also includes the implicit information that enables us to control our body, to stand upright, and to run away, duck, or jump when we need to do. Our memory helps us to interpret events in the present on the basis of our knowledge and previous experiences and to anticipate what will happen in the future. It is exactly these interpretive and predictive abilities that have enabled the success of our species in a world full of dangers. However, the average memory is not without its flaws. We may not like it very much that it displays the ability to forget. Some forgetfulness is quite useful, though, provided that it doesn't compare with the cases of severe brain defects. If we stored everything we saw, heard, smelled, or touched, our memory would be a mess. The majority of things that pass through our brain don't deserve to be stored any longer than the blink of an eye. Swiftly forgetting irrelevant information safeguards the memory from overloading and creates some order in the chaos of memories. Admittedly, forgetfulness is sometimes inconvenient, for instance, when you cannot find your coat, but in the end, the delicate balance between remembering and forgetting is highly beneficial. Our memory helps us to recall what is relevant and helps us to forget what is trivial. It preserves us from both ignorance and confusion.

The mystery of brain functioning

How this all functions inside the brain is still a big mystery. The complexity of thought remains hidden inside the skull. Even though we understand a bit about the physiology of the brain, the structure of nerve cells, the interconnections they make with other cells, and the process of electrical conduction along the elongated, slender projections of the cells, the mind remains inaccessible and incomprehensible. Since modern electromagnetic imaging techniques have provided us with a live view of the brain in action, we know more or less what parts of the brain are in charge of particular functions like seeing, hearing, sexual arousal, motor action, and emotions and how different parts of the brain communicate with each other. But the key question of how we are able to think, to process, to store and recall information, and to make sense of it all remains unanswered. We have no idea whatsoever where we store memories, how they are arranged, and how we are able to retrieve them. On occasion, it may take us a while to produce the right information, but interestingly, we still know for sure that it is somewhere in our head: "Let's see, hmm. I know; wait a minute. What was it again?" We're certain that we know it, even while we're busy finding it. It is as if we're consulting a registry of the brain to discover where to find the information we require. But there is no registry in the brain; there is no such thing for looking up where to find what we've stored in the past. Likewise, we know for sure that we don't know. For instance, there is a pretty good chance that you've never heard of "Tsamblak". Without any registry available and without having the time to check all your memories, you will still be able to reply instantly and with absolute certainty that you've never heard the term before. All in all, this is miraculous. (By the way, "Tsamblak" is the name of a medieval Bulgarian writer.)

Over the years, emerging media have served as helpful metaphors for the ways human memory was believed to function. Ancient Greek philosopher Plato compared human memory to a wax tablet. This was a quite common piece of equipment composed of two little wooden blocks that could be covered with wax on which a user could inscribe notes or sketches. Like a wax tablet, human memory was seen to function as an imprinting device that captured impressions obtained from our senses. Notably, the words "imprinting" and "impressions" are still being used to refer to memory. Unlike clay tablets that hardened, the wax tablets could be reused once the wax layer was evened out. So, forgetting could be understood as the erasure of recorded information. New technologies inspired new metaphors of memory. After the advent of print, human memory was compared to a textbook that was continually extended with new paragraphs as a result of new experiences. Some centuries later, the camera obscura and photography provided a model for visual memory; the phonograph did the same for sounds. In more recent years, film, magnetic tape, holograms, optical devices, computer disks, and neural networks inspired new metaphors, all of which reflect the idea that human memory is a tool for storing and recalling sensory stimuli.

But these media metaphors can be quite deceptive. To a large extent, we know that our memory is very different from a wax tablet or a computer database. It lacks the mechanical precision and reliability of modern media that excel in the meticulous recording of data and their errorless reproduction time after time. Also, human memory isn't merely an inventory of facts. It has nothing like an alphabetically or chronologically categorised index. Instead, it is believed that storage is based on semantic relationships between the new information to be stored and the existing recordings of previous experiences. We can only interpret new knowledge in a meaningful way based on our existing knowledge. That is, we connect new things with the things we know already and thus assimilate those new things in a meaningful way into our existing mental structure. So when we notice that our neighbour has bought a new red car, we create a new information node connected to the existing information nodes that cover the concepts "car", "red", and "my neighbour". The result of this assimilation process is an extended network of meaningful relationships among different nodes of information. This semantic network should not to be confused with the underlying physical network of interconnected nerve cells. One single nerve cell would not be capable of storing any meaningful information. Instead, each information item requires a networked pattern of millions and millions of nerve cells. In turn, such a pattern is semantically connected with other information patterns, thus constituting a network of patterns. Our memory is simply a network of networks.

Getting it all into our heads

Learning something new is not straightforward. Getting it all into our heads can be quite a hard job. Cramming a few pages of Latin vocabulary or the anatomy of the human eye requires considerable concentration, drive, and perseverance. It takes a lot of time too. Becoming a mechanic will take you twenty years of your life; becoming a doctor or a lawyer can take up to twenty-five years. Couldn't we just directly intervene in our brain to enhance our cognitive capabilities?

Driven by research into Alzheimer's disease and dementia, pharmaceutical companies have sought to create new drugs for preserving and improving the brain's ability to record and retrieve information. Some psychostimulants like Ritalin and Adderall that are officially allowed for the treatment of ADHD are being used by students as "learning pills". Similar to food supplements enhancing physical power and endurance in sports, brain supplements for enhancing cognitive functioning seem about to become big business. This is a very dubious development, though, since, like performance-enhancing drugs in sports, the efficacy of these learning pills is questionable and adverse effects like dependency, long-term damage, abuse, and illegal trade cannot be neglected. Likewise, brain surgery for enhancing our cognitive structure has its shortcomings. Although there have been many advances in micro-neurosurgery, these have mainly been used to treat severe brain disorders like epilepsy, intractable psychiatric disorders, or Parkinson's disease and to remove tumours from the brain and to stop bleeding after brain injuries. Many patients may benefit from such surgery, but the damage it can cause, including loss of affective skills, identity problems, memory problems, and problems co-ordinating the left and the right brain hemispheres, is considerable. Even in the absence of all these side effects, it is highly unlikely that surgical incisions in the physical substrate of nervous tissue could ever have any positive impact on the semantic relationships stored in the brain. For the same reason, electroshock therapy is inappropriate. In electroshock, a technician applies a pulse of considerable electrical tension (up to several hundred volts) to the brain of an anaesthetised patient. Although this treatment is less popular than it was some decades ago, it is still used in extreme cases of major depression combined with psychosis that have failed to respond to medications. Electroshock is a kill-or-cure remedy that is widely disputed because of its uncertain outcomes. A few patients may benefit from it, but its side effects, including generalised cognitive dysfunction, bleeding in brain tissue, and cell death, are destructive. It is a bit like reformatting one's hard disk: in extreme cases it may be a win, but it generally comes with severe information losses.

All these direct interventions in the brain are inappropriate for enhancing our cognitive capabilities. The only thing we can do to get it all smoothly into our heads is to influence the brain from the outside by exposing ourselves to favourable external conditions. This is what parents and teachers try to do (or at least what they are expected to do): create the best external conditions for learning to occur. Teaching is like inviting an orchestra to play music outside a house and hoping that the people inside the house sing and dance. It is also what producers of media, be it print, TV, film, radio, or web, try to do: produce the right tone that triggers the audience to internalise information and extend their knowledge.

The mind as an association machine

It is not too difficult to teach animals amazing new behaviours. Dogs can learn to give a paw, to lie still even when a cheeky cat is challenging them, or to howl along with a radio song. Circus lions and elephants effortlessly pirouette and stand on their hind legs as if it were their natural behaviour. Dolphins will cheerfully jump through a hoop and dance on the surface of the water, possibly in synch with three or more congeners, while gracefully waving at the audience. Dressage horses seem to parody Michael Jackson's moonwalk, doing funny steps exactly to the beat of the background music. Similarly, pigeons, rabbits, mice, and many other species can be taught astounding tricks. The basic mechanism for this is to provide rewards for wanted behaviours and punishments for the opposite. Circus lions only do their trick because they have learned to associate the behaviour with the reward of receiving fresh meat or the punishment of a whiplash (or even the sound of the whiplash). This idea of association is basically the same as in Pavlov's famous experiment in which dogs produced saliva (digestive fluid) whenever a white-coated laboratory assistant entered the room: the dogs responded to the white-coated assistant, whom they had learned to associate with food provision (the reward). This is a primitive, reflexive way of knowing, without too much active thinking, but still it is a powerful mechanism for learning new things.

Although we tend to consider ourselves advanced, conscious, and rational beings with cognitive capacities far superior to those of animals, a great deal of our learning involves just these simple mechanisms of association, reward, and punishment. Toddlers can be encouraged to pee on the potty by receiving positive attention from their parents for successful efforts. Likewise, we could teach them not to touch a lighted candle either by giving a reward when they stay at a distance or a punishment when they don't. Touching the flame also provides a quite informative experience that provides a punishment, teaching a toddler to stay away from lighted candles in the future. It is just simple conditioning without too much thinking involved. These examples show that this model of learning requires an authority, someone who decides on the rewards and the punishments meted out for correct and incorrect responses. Clearly this type of learning is highly appreciated in the army, since generals wouldn't appreciate too much discussion with their recruits when they are under attack. The downside of using this successful learning mechanism in the army is that unthinkingly obeying orders ("Fire!", "Bomb!", "Torture!") while neglecting any individual responsibility has been the cause of numerous crimes against humanity. Most of our school systems are also based on the presence of an authority, which is embodied by the teacher acting as the source of knowledge. Direct instruction, the assumption of a passive, receptive role by learners, and other methods like drill and practice and learning by rote employ the principles of associative learning and reduced thinking. They reflect the objectivist viewpoint that the knowledge can be acquired by the simple transfer of information.

The same principles apply to the apprenticeship model that is used in many professional fields: a master transfers his or her expertise to a novice by explaining and demonstrating how to act. A major mechanism underlying this is imitation: human beings have the natural tendency to imitate the behaviours they see. This is obvious in the case of young children, as they try to replicate all the things their parents do: walk, talk, wave, sing, laugh, and many more. Observation and imitation remain a major learning mechanism throughout our lives. Research in neuroscience has demonstrated the existence of "mirror neurons" in the human brain. These mirror neurons not only fire when we carry out a certain task but also when we're just observing someone carrying it out. When we observe an action carried out by someone else, our brain mentally rehearses the activity as if we were doing the action ourselves. This is why we experience pain and anxiety when a movie hero gets beaten up. Imitation enables us to adopt and conform to prevailing sociocultural codes. Mass media like radio, TV, film, the web, and games are inexhaustible sources of demonstrations of how to behave, and we're happy to imitate them by adapting our language, manners, fashion, and lifestyle to those of public role models and by adopting the underlying attitudes, morals, and premises for how to live. When a pop star introduces a new jacket, we cannot wait to buy one. Unfortunately, we are likely to imitate adverse behaviours too. There are many clues that violent incidents like the Columbine High School massacre or the Oslo mass shooting are inspired by manifest violence in films and shooter games. Many people have called for restrictions on the presentation and glorification of violence in these media.

Another special case is commercial advertising, which also isn't very different from teaching in the Pavlovian way. Those advertising guys will do anything to condition us to imitate their role models and buy their products. Their ads are entirely directed to establish positive associations between two distinct concepts: a new beer and having fun, a new car and discovering the world, washing powder and a colourful life. When we enter a department store, we will be rewarded by a pleasant temperature and relaxing background music. When we buy a product, our kid will receive a balloon, and if we're a regular customer, we will be pampered with savings stamps and discounts. Of course, we know we're fooled. Still, the power of advertisement is that we're doomed to imitate and that we cannot withstand the primitive attraction of short-term rewards. So we behave accordingly.

Promoting associations between concepts is an outstanding teaching mechanism. It comes close to manipulation. The danger of it lies in the elimination of thought and in the dominance of authority promoting absolute truth, which is exactly what happens in the army, in religion, and in dictatorships. It brings teaching close to propaganda, brainwashing, and indoctrination, providing thoughtless fanatics unthinkingly repeating predefined mantras.

The mind as an information processor

In the 1950s, a new vision of human learning emerged under the influence of the advent of the computer. Now that computer scientists had constructed intelligent machines that apparently could think, psychologists adopted the computer as metaphor for describing the human cognitive system. They believed that the existing theory of association and the mechanisms of reward and punishment needed to be extended with models that covered the process of thinking. Human intelligence was assumed to be far more advanced than the intelligence of animals that only produced primitive responses to environmental stimuli. Humans were now viewed as creatures whose responses were the outcome of thinking. The process of human thinking was to be understood through the mechanisms of a computer: In our mind, our processing unit is continually checking inputs from our senses. It combines new information with existing information retrieved from memory and provides the appropriate output of speech or motor action in the external world. This was really a great advancement because over centuries, the human mind had been treated as an inconceivable, supernatural phenomenon, a divine gift, impenetrable and inaccessible even to itself.

The computer metaphor was a new impetus to open up the black box and study the mechanisms of cognition. New insights were gained in the physiology of the brain and in the roles that different brain parts played. New models were developed for describing human memory, perception, visual attention, problem solving, spatial skills, language, and many more. Various insights in cognitive psychology suggested how learning might be improved, or at least produced scientific evidence for common practices. Learning was now equated with the creation of a mental model, which is a coherent knowledge structure in the mind that links together diverse contents in a meaningful and understandable way. This means that learning new things requires the activation of existing knowledge so that it can be integrated meaningfully. When the mind receives and deciphers messages, different symbol systems and modalities may interfere with each other and hinder our understanding. Research in brain neurophysiology demonstrated which parts of the brain processed sounds and images. Learning is best performed in cases of high contiguity and coherence of words and images. This means that words and pictures should be closely connected to each other rather than in conflict with each other. Like any computer, the human mind has only a limited capacity for processing, which means that high information loads are likely to affect the quality of learning. Consequently, doing two or more things at the same time causes performance problems. This observation seems to conflict with the popular idea that young people who grew up immersed in a world full of smartphones, games, Twitter, and Facebook are good at multitasking. These so-called digital natives may have developed excellent skill with ICT that help them to outperform their parents or grandparents when using these media, but it is a fallacy to assume that a few years of using modern media produces fundamental changes in their brain architecture, which is the robust result of many thousands of years of evolution. Overall, our brains are very similar to the brains of ancient humans. Multitasking is more likely to be just quick switching between different loci of attention, inevitably resulting in fragmentation, weakened concentration, and reduced performance.

The computer metaphor has radically extended our view on human thinking. Learning new things was no longer a matter of simple conditioning to reproduce new tricks but a thinking process for achieving a better understanding. Humans were now perceived as intelligent problem solvers driven by curiosity, motivation, and concentration. Learning as a thinking process, however, wouldn't fully replace learning by conditioning. Much of our learning is still no more than the unthinking imitation of observed behaviours.

The mind as a subjective truth producer

The computer metaphor described above has one major drawback: it considers learning to be the mechanical process of handling external inputs without taking into account the unique, individual achievement of making sense of these inputs. We may be impressed by the speed with which a computer processes information, but altogether, the computer understands none of the information it receives. It just tirelessly processes the streams of ones and zeroes according to strict, preset routines laid out in the software. Feeding one signal to different computers produces identical outcomes in each computer. Doing the same with human minds would never elicit identical responses since each mind tends to make its own meaningful interpretation based on prior knowledge and experiences, which tend to be very different for different individuals. Apparently, human thinking is just very different from the way a computer works. For this reason, a new learning paradigm called "constructivism" emerged because of its claim that people construct their own personal knowledge and understanding rather than just receive and absorb information from outside.

So, the mind is viewed as a subjective truth producer, constructing its knowledge by making meaningful interpretations of the world. The main sources of our thinking are the interactions we have with other people and with the environment we live in. This means that knowledge is not something isolated inside our heads but something situated and naturally tied to the social and cultural context of our activities. Therefore, the principles for effective learning emphasise the importance of immersing the learner in real-life situations because this helps the learner to achieve a deeper understanding, to improve motivation, and to better intertwine theory and practice. The things we learn are not disconnected facts, concepts, and theories that we store in our heads separate from the things we know already, our beliefs, our experiences, and our preferences. Instead, they are directly related to this pre-existing knowledge and form an intrinsic part of the life we live. A second learning principle is to stimulate exploration and active inquiry, to foster learning by experience, discovery, and reflection. Another principle says that learning is the result of engaging in social practices and the associated culture, that is, engaging with a group of people that share the same concern or interest, and exchanging knowledge through discussion, inquiry, and mutual evaluations. Much of this type of learning is not deliberate. We probably highly underestimate how much we learn on the streets, in shops, at work, or even at home without noticing it. Most of our learning is an incidental and unintended side effect of social interactions.

The different metaphors of mind, namely as an association machine, information processor, and subjective truth producer, reflect fundamentally different starting points for understanding learning. Nevertheless, separate learning models may well apply when used together. We may learn simple tricks just the way animals do, and at the same time we may process new information and integrate the results in a cognitive pattern or communicate them to the outside world, or we may engage in the subjective process of attaching meaning to the outcomes of interactions with our social environment. We can pragmatically knit together different theories to capture the wide range of phenomena associated with our mental performances. The range of different principles marks the richness and versatility of human cognition, as well as the limits of theories of mind. It is hard to say which learning principle is best: the only thing we know is that with each principle, we learn differently and we learn different things.

As digital media are becoming our primary sources of knowledge, what can we say about how they influence these learning models? Because of their pictorial and one-way nature, TV and film can in many cases be channels for Pavlovian conditioning. This certainly holds for commercial advertising, from which we simply link together a product and a (positive) emotion. Likewise, TV also offers exposure to social practices, cultural codes, and role models, allowing for both conditioning and meaningful interpretation. However, some critics question the potential of TV for learning because watching TV precludes any personal contribution and interaction: it constrains viewers in a receptive mode of absorbing visual stimuli and prevents the active engagement that would be required by constructivism. In its early stages, the World Wide Web was very focused on presenting information on web pages. It offered some freedom of movement for users as they navigated through the information according to their personal needs, but it didn't allow productive interactions. This has radically changed in recent years with the advent of social spaces and social-network services like Facebook and Twitter. Now we are able to actively engage in social practices and produce meaningful knowledge about the world, even though this world is largely a digital one.

CHAPTER 8
Media as Cognitive Prostheses

Tedious cramming in order to get knowledge into our heads is not the only way to get wise. Search engines like Google, Bing, and Yahoo provide us with the right answers within seconds. Why should we bother trying to memorise what the capital of the Kiribati Republic is, what song was number one in the Hit Parade in December 1983, or how much water the withering begonia on the windowsill needs if the answers are just one click away? When connected to the Internet, young children are likely to outperform experts at answering questions like these. It is hard to deny that these tools radically enhance performance. The same holds for other technical services like route navigation systems, which help us to effortlessly find our way to unknown locations in the maze of lanes in an old city centre. A simple pocket calculator turns us into infallible mathematical geniuses. All these tools enhance our cognitive performance.

Some sceptics, however, claim the opposite. A calculator reduces complex mathematical concepts like a logarithm or a power law to a single button push that requires no knowledge or understanding of the underlying logic to produce answers. Navigation systems are likely to affect our spatial orientation skills since we only have to follow the instructions that the system provides. Similar ignorance can be observed among tourists excitedly flying to their holiday destinations while assuming that Turkey is near Denmark or that Bulgaria is near Lithuania. The

Internet supposedly produces these negative effects because of the abundance and speed of information. We restlessly click from link to link as superficial information browsers rather than cautious readers. Browsing deprives us of exercising our true cognitive abilities like concentration, abstraction, coherent reasoning, imagination, and reflection if not of our intellectual capacity. The web is inherently volatile and fragmented. It lacks the stable, linear structure of books, which provide consistency and allow for deep reading. Who reads books these days, anyway? So, these sceptics claim that new media promote ignorance.

Those who glorify the book as a more informative medium than the Internet may not be aware of the fact that in ancient times, the book was also the subject of suspicion. Plato's renowned work *Phaedrus* covers Socrates' story of Theuth, the Egyptian inventor of writing. When Theuth presents his invention to the Egyptian King Thamus, he claims that the written word will improve the knowledge and wisdom of all Egyptians. But King Thamus is sceptical and rejects the invention by arguing that a written text will do exactly the opposite. He suggests that written texts will create forgetfulness in the learners' souls because they will not use their own memories and will instead rely on the external writings, which don't reflect truth but only the semblance of truth. He claims that "the people will hear of many things but will have learned nothing; they will appear to be omniscient, but will generally know nothing; they will be tiresome company, having to show off wisdom without the reality". Plato's 2,400-year-old text perfectly matches the criticism of the Internet. We know today that the argument fails.

Although human culture is the accumulated outcome of persistent innovation and improvement, individuals tend to be conservative, preferably preserving what they have attained without risking its loss. It seems a natural human response to reject any new technology. Indeed, trains, cars, planes, printing presses, and telephones were widely rejected and approached with distrust when first introduced. But in the long run, all these artefacts have effected tremendous advances in science, music, literature, travel, and wealth. Today's digital media offer almost unlimited access to worldwide resources of information and are unmistakably becoming the main drivers for enhancing our cognition.

Exploiting our environment

Even though human cognition has been the decisive element of our evolutionary success, it has severe limitations. We suffer from limited attention spans, losses of concentration, and forgetfulness. We're not very good at doing more than one thing at a time. The mastery of new skills is ponderous, and sometimes we find ourselves hearing explanations without understanding what they mean. If we're good at one thing, it is likely that we're weak at another: we may be brilliant at quantum physics but dramatically fail at writing a text or cooking a meal. Learning or simply staying up to date puts a heavy load on our cognitive system. To reduce this load, we're happy to rely on external aids. We support our memory by using pocket diaries, electronic calendars, shopping lists, or a nut in our handkerchief. We even use our fingers for counting. The continuous and smart exploitation of our environment to improve our performance must be a product of our evolution. We used caves for shelter, we used sticks to cultivate the soil, we domesticated horses for transport and dogs for surveillance—like parasites, we take advantage of our environment to make things easier and reduce the load on our body and soul. Today we're hooked on our computers, tablets, and smartphones. It seems we're hardwired for this pursuit of efficiency. It helped us to get where we are now.

Using a search engine is quite favourable. It overcomes the limitations of our knowledge and memory. It has liberated us from storing all the answers in our heads; digesting all the books in the world is quite impractical anyway. It puts the digital memory of the whole world at our disposal. We instantly search when we need to do. It helps us to unmask idle medical doctors who lean on their social status rather than their medical expertise. It helps us to become legal experts and overrule any unlawful tricks or offerings. It essentially helps us to deepen our knowledge of the world. Because of the ease of clicking a mouse, it may seem that scholarship and erudition are less valued these days: what's the point of being knowledgeable if all knowledge is at our fingertips? The answer is counterintuitive: knowledgeable people will get more out of digital information. They use their knowledge to frame their information needs, to ask the right questions and to adjust their strategies based on the results they obtain from the web. Knowing that your dried-up plant on the windowsill is a begonia makes it much easier to find the right treatment for it than not knowing what it is. Knowledge is a search amplifier, whereas ignorance will make people drown in a sea of facts.

There is nothing new about using media as external memory stores. Clay tablets were early examples of consolidating human thought outside the brain. They marked the birth of human civilisation. Today's world is loaded with applications of media as external memory stores, helping us to recall the things we might forget and directing us to new things worth knowing. But the role of media goes even beyond external memory. Media also resemble a looking glass or a telescope, showing us things that are literally out of sight, beyond the limits of our perception. TV connects us to the hotbeds of the world many thousands of miles away. In the middle of town, our smartphones show us where to find the best shops and restaurants. They augment our cognition by projecting relevant data from memory on top of the visual field of the phone's camera: "Chinese restaurant, rating 8/10, 60 metres away". This looks pretty much like the way Arnold "Terminator" Schwarzenegger's robot character recalls information from memory, which in his case is instantly displayed in his visual field. The successes of smartphones are largely based on the enormous sets of geo-connected data available for recall. Finally, media are also synthesisers of new data sets that enable us to foretell and visualise possible futures. The renovation of your house or the installation of a new kitchen are easily created and displayed as full 3D environments that allow you to explore and inspect the alterations before demolishing anything. Detailed weather forecasts are almost too common for us to be amazed by them. Likewise, meticulously planning the best route to a remote location with satnav is a common practice. It still provides us with new insights and thus augments our cognition. All these media overcome fundamental limitations of the human mind. They afford the achievement of amazing intelligent things that ancient humans could only dream of. Media turn us into a different type of creatures.

The boundaries of mind

Body augmentation is a well-established practice. When they malfunction, body parts are easily replaced with prostheses that compensate for our shortcomings and enhance our performance. Artificial teeth replace our affected originals and allow us to bite into any firm, leathery, hot, or cold substance without problems. Artificial legs offer disabled people new opportunities to stand, walk, and even run. Implanted pacemakers are common devices for overcoming heart rate irregularities to extend the owner's range of physical activities. The options for bodily improvement are endless and useful.

Likewise, digital media act as prostheses that enhance our cognition. Web search, GPS, and pocket calculators are artificial entities that replace or extend the processing capabilities of our brain. They extend our memory capacity, our spatial orientation skills, and arithmetic agility, respectively. Consequently, our cognition is inextricably bound to these media. Removing such a medium is like removing a prosthesis; it will throw us back to lower levels of performance just the way a crippled person who is deprived of his artificial leg is forced to limp. It would be like removing part of our cognition, which suggests that our cognition is not restricted to the chunks of nervous tissue inside our heads but includes the interplay of the brain and the external media we use. This would mean that our mind is not confined within the boundaries of our skull and skin but extends into the outside world. This somewhat peculiar suggestion was first made in 1998 by Andy Clark and David Chalmers in their active externalism theory.

Consider the following hypothetical example, which is an adaptation from Clark and Chalmers: Anna and Bridget are identical twins raised under exactly the same conditions who have perfectly identical behaviours and performances. They do all the same things, have the same hobbies, and obtain the same scores at school. When they occasionally make mistakes, even their mistakes are identical. Unfortunately, one of the twins, let's say Anna, is severely injured in a car accident. Afterwards, she suffers from major memory failure. But she learns to cope with it by using a pen and a notepad and making notes about everything worth remembering and looking up old information when she needs it. This works so well that Anna and Bridget continue to display the same behaviours and performances. Everything Bridget can do, Anna can also do with the same accuracy and speed. Anna's pen and notepad act as external prostheses that fully replace her malfunctioning biological memory. Her cognition is completely restored by the delegation of some of its operations to external artefacts. Her mind includes these artefacts effortlessly in the cognitive loop, and its quality is not affected. Sometimes when Bridget has difficulty recalling the right information due to fatigue or concentration loss, Anna even manages to outperform Bridget. Taking away Anna's pen and notepad, however, would certainly reduce her capabilities. To do so would be like having a neurosurgeon cut out the corresponding parts of Bridget's brain. Apparently there is no difference between using innate brain parts for cognition and using external media for this.

Our cognitive capacity

Taking away Anna's pen and notepad for a while would certainly affect the quality of her performances. She wouldn't be able to memorise anything. But would it affect her cognition? After returning the pen and notepad to her, she would instantly demonstrate the same level of cognition as before, without the need to go through any tedious learning process. It seems that her cognition has remained intact during the short period of deprivation. Apparently, her brain knows exactly what to do but just wasn't able to demonstrate it in the temporary absence of memory. Anna temporarily couldn't express her cognition. This is nothing special, though, since it also occurs for Bridget. When Bridget is asleep, when she is tired, or when she has a fever, her cognitive performance will be well below her normal level. And like it was for Anna, this is only temporary. So cognition is something different from performance. Cognition is a sustained individual capability that reflects a potential rather than the actual performance. This means that although Anna uses external peripherals, the core of her cognition is in her head. It is clear that she has certain potential abilities whether or not she has her pen and notepad around. She has the potential but may not be able to demonstrate her skills at a particular moment. The same holds for Bridget and any other individual.

According to this analysis, the human mind is like a bubbling collection of cognitive potential waiting for the right conditions to come to the surface. Cognition itself doesn't depend on the availability or absence of media, such as a pen and notepad or any other medium. Nevertheless, media enhance our cognition. Our mind tends to exploit objects in the environment to amplify its cognitive processes. Because of this, our interaction with the environment is an important mechanism, if not the only one, for learning new things. It means that our cognition potential is inextricably bound to objects in the environment. Pen and notepad, as well as web search, GPS, and pocket calculators, help us to develop the promise of future performance.

Connecting computers to our nervous system

In science fiction books and movies, advanced machines are used for mind transfer. In the *Star Trek* series, the minds of Captain Kirk and Dr. Janice Lester are successfully swapped. Her mind shows up in his body, and his mind in hers. The underlying idea very well meshes with the computer metaphor of the brain: the physiology of the brain is the hardware which can emulate the human mind by running the right software. In another movie, *The Matrix*, the characters are directly connected to a computer with a huge wire that plugs deeply into their spinal cords (it remains unclear why they didn't use a wireless connection). Through this connection, programs of a simulated reality are downloaded to the characters' brains. The main goal is to subdue the human population. The process suggests that human thinking and perception can be tuned by downloading the right software. If this download really worked, learning new things would be simply a matter of loading new files into our brain. This will remain science fiction for a while, yet successful progress has been achieved in linking external computing devices directly to the human nervous system. Well-established examples are cochlear implants, which are small electronic devices used for solving hearing problems. They capture sounds from the environment and, using a few dozen electrodes inside the ear, transfer the resulting electrical signals directly to the auditory nerve cells. Likewise, retinal implants have successfully helped people who suffer from degenerative eye diseases. The implants convert light into electrical signals that stimulate retinal cells. Likewise, pacemakers use electrical pulses to synchronise the heart rate.

In the psycho-motor domain, artificial limbs have been used for many centuries. Until recently, these were no more than static mechanical aids, unable to actively bend joints and execute delicate motor functions. In 2004, Matt Nagle was the first person to control a robotic hand through a brain-computer interface. He was paralysed after a stabbing incident that caused a lesion of his spinal cord. The implant comprised a set of antennae placed directly under the skull on Nagle's brain's motor cortex area, which is responsible for arm and hand movements. The electrical signals from the antennae were fed into a computer that was connected to the robotic hand. He was able to control the robotic hand and pick up things just by thinking of moving his own (paralysed) hand. In 2011, fourteen-year-old Matthew James, who was born without left hand, received a dedicated bionic hand sponsored by the Mercedes Formula 1 racing team. The hand was made of high-grade plastic and had a small computer and electric motors inside that controlled detailed movements of the fingers. Interestingly, it uses a non-invasive interface of electrodes that pick up the electrical signals from the muscles in James's lower arm, so no surgery was needed. In this case, James controls the prosthesis not by thinking of moving his non-existent fingers but by tightening his lower arm muscles (which, admittedly, is also controlled by thinking). The subtlety of control is impressive. James can now catch a ball, tie his shoelaces, and draw pictures as if the robot hand were a biological hand.

We are cyborgs already. We have been replacing and improving our biological bodies with artificial components for a long time. But today, our focus is shifting from physical to cognitive enhancement. The linking of digital technologies directly to the brain and the rest of our nervous system is a matter of fact. Computational intelligence will augment our cognitive functioning. In the near future we may be able to plug in extra modules for special purposes like memory capacity, translations, or arithmetic skills. As James's bionic hand demonstrates, wireless connections reduce the need for implants. We don't need to undergo surgery to enhance our cognition.

These new technologies may have far-reaching philosophical, ethical, legal, and psychological consequences. What does it mean to enhance your cognition by downloading new knowledge and skills? Will this only be possible for the wealthy? Does it replace our personal knowledge? What if we all download the same modules; isn't that uniform brainwashing? What happens to individual performance and identity? Will we also be able to download happiness and satisfaction? Aren't we just talking about a new type of drug? What about software errors? And what about modules for aggression, violence, and suppression?

The location of self

In his famous essay "Where Am I?", Daniel Dennett explores the complex relationship between the body, the brain, the mind, and the self-concept. His elaboration was subsequently extended by David Sanford. These works demonstrate how the notion of human identity becomes unclear when we extend our body or mind with technical artefacts.

In his essay, Dennett describes a hypothetical experiment about separating the brain from the body while preserving the communications between the two. Dennett presents himself as a secret agent who is charged with dismantling a radioactive warhead located deep underground in an old mine. The nuclear radiation of the warhead is extremely harmful to brain tissue but is supposed to leave other cells intact. In order to survive this mission, Dennett agrees to the temporary removal of his brain, which will be preserved under full operational conditions in a laboratory. An ingenious system of electromagnetic transmitters and receivers is used to preserve all the connections between the brain and the nerve endings of the brainless body so that no information is lost. When Dennett wakes after the surgery, he finds himself in a hospital room. Little antennae are popping out of his skull. With his brain safely stored in the lab, his body sets to work underground dismantling the warhead. He thinks it is quite amazing that he can do all this hard work in the mine while his brain is communicating from a distance, far away from the hazardous radiation. Practically speaking, he is in two locations at once. But it confuses him that he feels like he's with his body rather than with his brain because he's always assumed that his thinking and his mind were located somewhere in the brain.

Unfortunately, some technical problems occur with the antennae. First, the sound breaks down. Soon after, he loses sight and other sensations. Finally, the whole connection to his brain breaks down, leaving his body lifeless in the underground mine. He panics, but at the same time he gratefully realises that he still exists, thanks to his perfectly functioning brain in the lab. It is reassuring thought for him to know that he's not deep down in this dangerous mine: he really feels that he is in the lab where his brain is. Unable to talk, to smile, or to wave his hand, he now suffers from genuine locked-in syndrome. Fortunately, the doctors manage to talk to him by connecting a cochlear prosthesis directly to his brain. They explain to him that his body could not be retrieved but that they will provide him with a new one. He's put to sleep for almost a year. When Dennett wakes, he finds himself equipped with a new body slightly different from his original one but likewise equipped with antennae to communicate with the remote brain.

Everything seems to be okay, but while he slept, the technicians in the lab managed to create a computer copy of his brain, backing up his full memory structure and cognitive capacity. The technicians extensively tested this electronic replica and proved that it produced exactly the same responses as the original brain stored in the lab. The technicians could switch the antennae to communicate with the biological brain and the computer program and back. The responses were so fully identical that Dennett can't tell any differences between them. It doesn't matter whether he uses the original system or the backup. Dennett now has two identical brains and one body, each of which can be switched off without destroying the self. This would suggest that the self is located neither in the body nor in the brain but is of a supernatural nature. Dennett now indulges in fantasies about what could happen if one of his brains were connected to a new body: would this create a new individual with perceptions and values distinct from the original, and if so, who would be the true Dennett? Finally, Dennett demonstrates the problems that occur when he switches from one brain to the other. As soon as he switches, Dennett's ego, highly relieved to be back in control of his body after a dreadful period of forced passivity, takes over his personality.

David Sanford continues the story by explaining that the nuclear radiation deep down in the mine proves to be more harmful than expected. It destroys not only brain tissue, but it also appears to affect Dennett's brainless body. Soon, his eyes and ears are burned off by the radiation, and gradually his sense of touch and ability to speak disappear as well. The authorities feel sorry for their initial decision to remove only the brain. They might have done better to remove his eyeballs and ears too and replace these with advanced eye video cameras and microphones that produce the same perceptual signals. But it is too late.

Sanford assists the technicians in dismantling the warhead. For this, they use a robot that looks identical to Sanford. The robot is equipped with eye video cameras and microphones, and its exterior is fully covered with a thin film of touch transmitters that fully replicate human tactile sense. Sanford controls the robot by wearing a special membrane-like suit that tracks all his movements and directly transmits the data to the robot, which makes perfectly synchronised movements. The robot's perceptions are directly fed into Sanford's brain through a mechanism that didn't require any surgery. Sanford can make the robot move, observe, speak, and act as an intelligent man. When the robot starts work underground, Sanford, just like Dennett, cannot avoid a sense of telepresence, of being underground himself, although his brain and the rest of his body are safely in the remote laboratory. It's confusing when he, that is, the robot, can observe Sanford without having the conviction that he is looking at himself. This gets even worse when scientists manage to bypass Sanford's motor system and tap the motor-system transmitters directly onto his nervous system, allowing the robot to move independent of the original living body. Additional complications arise when it turns out that the team alternately uses three robots. Upon switching between different robots, Sanford feels teleported from one location to the other. He assumes that the technicians could easily replace the connection with his brain to a connection with an identical computer brain, just as in Dennett's story. In that case, Sanford would be a robot completely disconnected from the organic Sanford, who would be safely in the lab drinking a cup of coffee. He would be separated from his original self without knowing it.

So far, the stories of Dennett and Sanford are quite hypothetical. Despite recent advances in brain-computer interfacing, the physical separation of the brain and the body while maintaining their electrical interconnections is still in the future. Dennett and Sanford demonstrate the inconceivable complexities that arise when technology would make a few more steps. The notion of mind transfer challenges the fundamental concept of the human individual, the unique self, the unique identity. Adding artificial intelligence and robotics would remove the differences between humans and machines, and transform us into cyborgs. Eventually, we would all be part of distributed intelligent organism, composed of interconnected intelligent programs, sensors, actuators, robots and possibly human components. This is an idea that greatly conflicts with the way we understand the world and ourselves. New technologies incite us to a deep reflection on the complex relationship between the individual's mind and body.

CHAPTER 9

The Educational Battlefield

It is amazing that schools have proved to be more or less immune to the endless flow of cognitive amplifiers like TV, video, and computers that have effected such disruptive changes in society. Whatever new media became available during the last century, schools managed to neglect them or reject them and to maintain their long-standing oral tradition supplemented with "old" technologies like blackboards and books.

The loss of our inquisitive mind

Curiosity is one of the evolutionary traits that helped us to become the cognitive creatures we are now. Our natural attitude is to explore new things. At birth we start to explore our environment and try to understand it. Guided by our parents, we learn to walk, talk, sing, and do many more things. When we're four years old, school takes over from our parents, and for 20,000 hours afterwards, school will be the most influential factor in our cognitive development. For many children, the transition to school is a tough one. They have to get acquainted with a very strict organisational system that is quite different from the family life they're used to. Of course, they like being a part of this new social community and have fun with their classmates and most of their teachers are highly committed to working with children and teaching them as much as possible, but the overall context of school is a restrictive one governed by regulations, schedules, discipline, standards, demands, and sometimes even punishments. Although the elevating potential of all this should be recognised and respected, no one will fail to notice the dramatic attitudinal changes that learners undergo during their school careers. Young children are so eager to learn new things that they can hardly wait until the first day that they're allowed to go to school. It is striking to see that the educational system gradually transforms them into disinterested, bored, and passive individuals full of negative attitudes towards school and learning. Adults seldom have sweet memories about their school years. Most of them will give you scathing judgements while looking back with contempt. Their inquisitive minds have gone and they think spending time learning new things is pathetic waste. It seems that school destroys our natural curiosity.

The school film fiasco

The school film case is a good example of a whole series of school reform failures. By the end of the nineteenth century, Thomas Alva Edison was the first to create the technology for recording and displaying (silent) moving images. His kinetograph, patented in 1892, was a new type of camera that recorded images on film rolls rather than single plates. His invention marked the beginning of motion pictures. Edison had high hopes for the instructional value of this new medium. He claimed that film would revolutionise education by enabling a new modality of learning, bringing recorded realities into the classroom. He proclaimed the death of the book because learners no longer needed to read texts about how things worked in practice and instead could just watch the recordings. Like Edison, many other innovators had high expectations for the educational potential of film, but history took a different turn. Admittedly, film had some practical problems linked to the size and reliability of projectors: standard thirty-five-millimetre film required bulky, noisy, and expensive equipment that failed frequently. Early film composed of cellulose nitrate could easily break and was highly flammable. Also, the number of available instructional films was quite limited and licenses to show them were expensive. And even though I myself retain good memories of watching films in darkened classrooms, the whole practice must have been a kind of nightmare for the teachers who were supposed to keep track of their pupils.

Two additional circumstances created problems for the adoption of film by teachers. First, the swift successes of the motion picture as an entertainment medium made it suspect as an instructional medium. Second, when sound film was gradually replacing silent movies, teachers opposed their use in their classrooms because they claimed to be the only ones responsible for narration: as teachers, they should do the talking themselves! They saw the built-in narration in films as interfering with their teaching duties. It wasn't until the late 1950s that instructional film saw a modest revival when eight-millimetre loop films were distributed as "single concept cartridges". In those years, sixteen-millimetre films also became available at affordable prices. At the same time, the rise of television as a new medium for sounds and moving images hampered the worldwide adoption of film as an instructional medium. Despite Edison's enthusiasm, film never lived up to its lofty promises for education.

Over the last hundred years, various other new media were proudly announced as great improvements for teaching and learning, but only few of these turned out to be successful. Besides film, the parade of failures include school radio, school TV, videocassettes, the laser videodisc, intelligent tutoring systems, and computers. Thirty years after their advent, personal computers still aren't well integrated into school curricula. It is difficult for schools to keep their hardware up to date, so students have to work with computers far inferior to what they have at home. Institutional Internet locks aren't very helpful either. Smartphones and PDAs are often banned from the classroom in spite of their potential as cognition amplifiers. Schools miss an opportunity for enhancing learners' performance with these cognitive tools. The only new media that seem to have been successfully adopted by schools are digital blackboards, a technology that matches old teaching models. Digital blackboards simply preserve the prevailing educational model.

School's tyranny

Today's school system dates back to the 1800s, when new advances in steam power production, iron production, and cotton spinning effected worldwide industrialisation. Traditional handcrafting was replaced with mechanisation. In factories, products could be produced cheaper, faster, and to set quality standards. Like raw materials, labour was considered just an input to production. In this climate, school was meant to prepare workers for factory jobs and even conceived as an industry in itself dedicated to the conversion of ignorant learners into qualified workers that met standards of knowledge and skills. The similarities between schools and factories can hardly be overlooked: the fixed time schedules, the predefined tasks, the uniform treatments, the uniform products, the fixed classroom model, the quality standards, even the sound of the bell to indicate lunchtime were borrowed from the factory model. Relics of the industrial revolution pervade school culture. But it is beyond any dispute that today's children are not helped by the approaches and standards of days long gone and that they need to learn the knowledge and skills required for our modern information-based society.

Although there is nothing wrong with discipline and time schedules, school is not fit for its purpose anymore. School offers a ready-made education package tuned to the average child. But the average child doesn't exist. School fails to offer personalised programmes tuned to individual needs. One thing that children will learn at school is that they don't need to think for themselves about what to learn. At school you have to learn what others want you to and can't learn things because of your own interests. School is based on discipline and obedience. It kills initiative. It deprives children of autonomy, responsibility, and ownership. It kills their curiosity and eagerness to learn and produces anxiety, aversion, and boredom instead.

One might object that this is all necessary since children simply will not be able to decide what is beneficial for them. This is at most partly true. Children may have dreams about their future such as becoming an astronaut. We should respect these dreams rather than destroy them because they are important drivers for cognitive development. Even though they won't be able to achieve most of their dreams, it is important for them to take responsibility and find this out for themselves. It is also tempting to blame today's youth for the failures of schools. It is said that today's young people are spoilt materialists, growing up with their PlayStations and smartphones, that they are lazy and lack any discipline, used to the instant fulfilment of their desires, and completely unfamiliar with the idea that satisfying their needs may require patience, effort, and persistence. "Children today are tyrants. They contradict their parents, gobble their food, and tyrannise their teachers." Before you agree with this and think that youth these days are intractable, it is good to realise that the quote above, from Socrates, dates back to 400 BC. Complaining about youth is a persistent issue. Youth shouldn't adjust to school; school should adjust to youth.

Conservatism explained

Schools are apt to disqualify new promising technologies as temporary fads that will soon die out. Such an excuse may be valid every now and then, but as a standard response, it is inappropriate. The school system reflects intrinsic conservatism because its main task is restricted to consolidating existing knowledge and transferring it from one generation to the next. Through that task, it establishes society's role models, traditions, and power relationships. It serves the status quo. All school staff members are inevitably the products of the school system itself and are probably likewise pervaded with its mental legacy.

Today's education has very much in common with agriculture in days gone by. Like farmers, teachers try to create the perfect conditions for young organisms to grow and to flourish. Farmers as well as teachers are endowed with a built-in conservatism, a result of the never-changing cycle of sowing and harvesting year after year. Just like farming, teaching is more than a profession, it is a vocation, a passion, a way of life, a mixture of art and skill aimed at personal care and attention for maturing organisms. New technologies which might undermine the way of life can, of course, expect to be met with scepticism. The devoted, humanist teacher rarely agrees with the industrial vision of policymakers, managers, and politicians who aim to transform schools into efficient, large-scale diploma factories that treat their pupils as mere numbers. Of course, teachers are fighting for a good cause because those who study are not products. It is common knowledge that behind the gigantic facades of the schools, small-scale craftsmanship in which caring teachers take pity on their plots like crofters remains hidden. The school building is the educational equivalent of the greenhouse that protects vulnerable seedlings against hail, wind, cold, and other influences that could interfere with their growth. This conservatism explains to a great extent why school is so disconnected from the rest of the world.

While agriculture started modernising its methods and tools two centuries ago, education is just beginning to do so. In agriculture, new machines and methods yielded profits of scale. Land consolidations straightened the landscape and enlarged the farmlands and made them more uniform. The all-round farm labourer gave way to specialised and well-trained agricultural contractors such as tractor drivers, potato harvesters, and drainage technicians. This all is absent in education. According to educational researcher Tony Bates, school is rooted too much in the traditional methods of the medieval apprenticeship model, featuring an omniscient master and a naive pupil. Teaching has not been professionalised. Instruction rarely uses a design and doesn't favour required susceptibility to scientific evidence. It has hardly been influenced by research into instructional design, psychology of learning, or other topics concerning human functioning. Teaching remains largely a craft, preserving the oral tradition with almost religious persistence. As a consequence, it hardly allows for any division of labour to increase efficiency. Indeed, educational institutions fairly well resemble a collection of distinct one-man shops. Because they rarely consider other organisational models, efforts to innovate are just add-ons to regular work and readily lead to increased unit costs. School reforms are easily blocked whenever they might affect the power or position of teachers, even when teachers just believe they might.

However, it is unthinkable that education can stay the way it is now since the outside world is changing at such a rapid pace. Today's learners grow up immersed in new digital communication technologies and may wonder in amazement why they cannot use the tools at school that they use at home. Because of the pervasion of new media as cognitive tools not only in everyday life but also in work settings, they must be swiftly integrated into school curricula. Media aren't just simple tools; they disruptively alter life. Parents, employers, and possibly pupils themselves will raise the pressure on schools to innovate their models. Education will not be able to resist the new technologies that saturate the market and are eagerly used by target consumers as cognitive amplifiers. This pattern of market pull will force innovation for education.

In the beginning, farmers did not like trading in their shire horses for tractors. Today's farmers, however, spend more time at their computers than in the fields inspecting the crop. From a romantic viewpoint, this may seem a disgrace, but agricultural productivity and quality have reached unparalleled levels. It seems school is still trapped in habitual patterns. It is very hard to get rid of these.

The need for reform

The domain of education is severely challenged by the vital and substantive impact of new technologies on society at large. In today's digital economy, products derive value not from their materials but from the knowledge put into them. Producing cars or buildings is no longer about steel, plastic, and bricks. It requires detailed knowledge from many disciplines. Growing tulips and brewing beer are now pretty much bio-chemical industries. Producing and distributing all these products in a cost-effective way requires highly skilled people: computer programmers, mechanics, process engineers, biologists, logistical experts, chemists, and many more. While today's schools provide standardised curricula, teaching standard tasks and standard content according to standard qualifications for assumed standard pupils, professional workers do anything but standard tasks. Instead they work with complex, multi-faceted, non-standard problems and provide creative solutions by stretching the boundaries of their expertise through inquiry, experimentation, and collaboration in a cross-disciplinary context.

Education shouldn't prepare students for nineteenth century factories anymore; standard tasks are performed by machines and computers these days. In the past, the skills acquired at school were sufficient for one's whole working life until retirement. But the knowledge life cycle has shortened dramatically: the things we learn today will be obsolete tomorrow. Learning doesn't end at graduation but is a lifelong necessity. We should realise that we need to prepare children for professions and technologies that don't yet exist. Ten years ago there were no e-books, smartphones, mobile apps, social networks, or virtual worlds. Even a whole branch of e-business was still to be invented, requiring expertise that couldn't be taught at schools. For dealing with new knowledge, meta-learning skills—the ability to identify one's own knowledge gaps, to search for and evaluate new knowledge sources, and to arrange and assess one's own learning, will be of paramount importance not only for a small elite of doctors, lawyers, and engineers but for almost anyone in any profession.

Education has to respond to these changes by adapting its business models, its technologies, and its modes of delivery. It has to anticipate and explore new modes of knowledge creation and representation and to create new patterns of learning and teaching for twenty-first century education. School should get rid of the standard curriculum and include opportunities for students to engage in stimulating new initiatives, responsibility, creativity, and imagination. It should prepare new generations of learners capable of and willing to deal with new knowledge and take charge of their own cognitive development. Instead of destroying children's innate curiosity, school should preserve and amplify it and support their positive attitude towards learning new things.

School must use the cognitive tools that learners massively adopt to enrich their private lives. As new media and tools flood the markets, learners, be they schoolchildren or adult professionals, expect high-quality, flexible, modern, and tailored learning services. Media innovations will be useful for addressing the severe weaknesses of the current system. It would be good to remove the artificial discontinuities between school and work. Lifelong learning offers new educational challenges for learners to combine their studies with an active career and to expect sufficient freedom to choosing their own study pace, time, and place. This new target group of students is highly heterogeneous with respect to prior knowledge, experience, ambition, and possibilities. They require made-to-measure learning activities that they can largely direct by themselves. What is expected from education is not monoculture but custom-made training, diversification, and flexibility to satisfy varied needs for knowledge. In the end, education should support learners to become valuable and responsible citizens who are able to fully participate in tomorrow's society.

In his video *EDU-at-2020*, Richard Katz sketches a devastating scenario for educational institutions that are reluctant to innovate. In his scenario, today's inert universities become irrelevant because commercial media giants like Microsoft, Apple, Google, Sony, and Disney take over. These companies use advanced e-learning technologies to providing high-quality online learning programs on any topic imaginable. Because of their worldwide delivery and the implied economy of scale, they can hire the best experts, the best teachers, the best designers, the best writers, the best film directors, and the best programmers to produce the best content at the lowest possible price. In this scenario, traditional educational institutions are destined to die away. The purport of the video is obviously that education should reform itself. As school sceptic Seymour Sarasin put it: "the biggest risk of education is not taking one".

CHAPTER 10

The Stories of Media

During the last century, film, radio, and TV became the predominant mass media. And they still are today, notwithstanding the rise of the Internet. Film and radio are powerful in their own right but are outstripped by TV, which offers an all-in-one experience combining moving images, sounds, and the immediacy of wireless transmission. Hundreds of communication satellites orbit in space to distribute a multitude of TV signals to the most remote sites on Earth. Whatever the environment, a TV is always available. Numerous TV networks pour the world into our living rooms. Politics, pets, sports, celebrities, any topic is covered every day. TV's impact on society and culture is immense. Any change in fashion, political sentiment, music style, or vocabulary is highly influenced by what TV shows us and tells us, and particularly how it shows us and tells us. Controlling the media means having power over the people. In many countries the government censors and controls radio, TV, the press, and the Internet to impose their ideology. But the trans-border nature of electronic media often demonstrates their intangibility. The Arab Spring in Tunisia, Egypt, and Libya was inspired and enabled by social Internet media. In the pre-Internet era, radio and TV helped to pull down the Berlin Wall and effected the collapse of European communism in 1989. The same powerful mechanism makes us defenceless when it comes to commercial advertising.

Being fooled by commercials

The effects of TV commercials are disreputable. We know that we're fooled by the silly claims, but we still buy the stuff. Naturally, we're not impressed by a TV spot that triumphantly announces a new washing-up liquid capable of cleaning the dishes better than any other product before. Of course we know that it's nonsense. But later on, when we're in the supermarket, we'll carelessly take this very product from the shelf and put it in our shopping trolley, simply because we've learned to associate it with clean washing-up. We're the unresisting victims of Pavlovian conditioning. That's why commercials are repeated so often. The conditioning procures primitive, automatic behaviours carried out without conscious thought, making us respond with any behaviour that advertisers want us to. Our behaviour does not comply with how a reasonable, right-minded person would be prepared to act.

In a contrived way, commercials create new communication codes that link their products with social class, lifestyle, status, stardom, heroism, or any other quality that the target group might aspire to. Whether it concerns cars, perfume, fashion, or cigarettes every supplier tries to establish a powerful brand by associating the product with a favourable lifestyle, image, or status. In endless campaigns, advertisers aim to have us adopt the codes that lead to buying their products. It is a self-establishing effect. Once individuals widely adopt the code, they can express their identity and social status by buying the right products. If the promoted code is that real tough guys smoke cigarettes, like the good old Marlboro man, most people will act accordingly to establish this image. Similarly, people buy cars not particularly because they offer value for money but because buyers—perhaps subconsciously—aspire to the lifestyle associated with a car, which is either rich, sportive, noisy, practical, elegant, modest, or speedy, and they want to express this to those in their social environment, their neighbours, colleagues, or relatives. The underlying assumption is that the social environment recognises the code and interprets it in the right way. Breaking a code causes confusion: ninety-year-old men with walkers aren't supposed to drive Porsches, and prime ministers aren't supposed to drive to work on mopeds.

Touched by the screen

It's a general misunderstanding to simply consider film and TV as media that convey information to viewers. The power of film and TV is in exposure rather than exposition. They have the potential to touch us emotionally and drag us along with their stunning stylistic devices, dramatic storylines, visual effects, and surround sound. Watching a scene of a car heading straight for us at high speed, supported by the penetrating sounds of the roaring engine and screeching tyres, will inevitably arouse shock, fright, and an urge to flee. Viewers' adrenaline flows, heart rates go up, and muscles tense. We're unable to suppress these physiological reactions. We're fooled by the illusion. We sense the event as a real experience and respond accordingly. The success of cinema lies largely in the emotional impact it excites. A consequent question is why people like watching such provoking scenes. What's the fun of being scared by a horror movie? What's the point of crying during a tear-jerker? Why are people prepared to pay to sit in a darkened room with a lot of strangers and nearly die a thousand deaths, undergo one misfortune after another, and cry with distress and impotent anger? The answer is simple and straightforward: we identify ourselves with the actors on the screen. The person who is endangered by the quickly approaching car is us. The hero in the action movie, that's us. The lover in the romantic comedy, that's us. This process of identification and adoption of the main character's viewpoint is inescapable. For the viewer, it brings about strong emotional involvement in the film narrative, which makes the scene's impact go beyond the factual information it conveys. It is about being exposed to an event that manifests itself truthfully in the eyes of the viewer and that arouses subjective mental processes. The viewer is not just watching the movie but actively taking part in the events. This ability to adopt the viewpoint of someone else is a unique human feature linked with empathy and hypothetical thinking. We are capable of entering the position of someone else, the film's leading characters. The process of identification is confirmed by physiological evidence of the brain's mirror neurons: neurons that fire not only when we perform an action but also when we observe someone else performing the same action. This means that we feel pain when we see someone else fall down as if we fell down ourselves. Watching someone being kissed feels like being kissed oneself. The mirror neurons model our observations in our brain and produce the related responses.

Still, it is odd that we can cry intensely when our film hero perishes one moment and in the next moment step outside in an excellent mood. One may wonder if the emotions we display during a tear-jerker are authentic. According to Jean Paul Sartre, the emotions we experience watching a film are not real, even though they may seem as real to us as the tears. The sources of viewers' emotions are not in the tear-jerker but in their a priori mindset. Their need for emotional excitation ignites their imagination to recreate stimuli. The sorrow we feel is about ourselves, not about the leading actor, who is—we know—just acting. The movie is no more than a catalyst for regulating and expressing our own emotions. The mechanism is very similar to what happens when we look at a whipped cream cake: it makes our mouths water only when we're hungry. Watching a tear-jerker is a psychological outlet for the viewers, offering them a safe, protected, and legitimate way to deal with anxiety, aggression, and sorrow. It allows for risk-free venting of emotions caused by the real world that doesn't allow for such venting. Film puts the viewer at the centre of the action, which is always under control. When it comes down to it, we know that it is all just a film.

Modern myths

Film and TV are the modern equivalents of ancient myths, Egyptian murals, medieval frescoes, and stained-glass windows. They convey the stories of life. They capture and represent the events of the world in a structured way and help us to understand the social and cultural realm that we belong to. Instead of presenting separate facts, stories give us coherent aggregates that derive communicative power from internal structure, sequence, and causal relationships between elements. Stories are universal; all cultures in all times tell stories. They reflect the prevailing customs and rituals of the community and support individuals' development and expression of their own identities within the cultural context. Today, film and TV with their one-way communication, real-time transfer, and stylistic devices are outstanding media for conveying stories. Films, news shows, and even TV advertisements aren't very different from ancient myths. The French anthropologist Claude Lévi-Strauss considers the common Hollywood film portraying the American Dream to be a modern myth that helps us to shape our culture. He suggests that myths are fundamental stories on which we base our behaviours and our thoughts. Stories in the Middle Ages told of the downfall of man and the salvation by Christ's crucifixion, whereas today's myths, carried by modern media, tell of youth, the glorification of the body, and family ties. In due course, the message may change, but the structural pattern will remain the same. In 1928 Russian linguist Vladimir Propp explained the universal nature of stories in his *Morphology of the Folktale*. He studied many hundreds of fairy tales, and by disconnecting the key events from their specific settings, he found that all of them required only a limited set of structural elements. He found that a fairy tale has no more than seven different character archetypes: the hero, the villain, the princess, the advisor, the assistant, the messenger, and the false hero. Also, he identified thirty-one basic re-occurring events that described a multitude of stories, for instance, someone goes missing, the hero is warned, the villain seeks something, the hero and the villain battle.

Many of today's action movies, mysteries, thrillers, commercial advertisements, and stage plays display similar regularities. But they also require dramatic elements as much as stylistic subtleties and aesthetics. Much of the dramatic elements go back to Aristotle, who proposed a simple storyline set-up: a situation of equilibrium gets disturbed, which leads to change and activities that finally bring about a new equilibrium. But this is not sufficient. The very basis of an involving story is conflict. Conflict produces tension, which is in turn the basis for attention. Drama is all about people or parties who deceive each other, hate each other, or have conflicting interests. The quintessence is that any disturbance of harmony, any imbalance, any dispute requires a solution and leads to action. If there is no conflict, nothing happens. There is nothing as mind-numbing as watching two people who fully agree with each other. Such a case displays perfect harmony with plenty of endorsements and assents. In short, it is deadly dull.

A lack of conflict happens a lot on TV, though: conversations are excessively prepared and rehearsed, interviewers don't wish to cross their guests in any way (they may need them on their next show), and clashes are carefully avoided. Yet a show becomes intriguing when the guest breaches protocol, furiously swiping his glass of talk-show fruit juice from the table and stalking off the set. The attraction of live TV is in this kind of unexpected event that cannot be controlled or choreographed. It is curious why TV makers mostly stick to conflict avoidance while "normal" human life is interlarded with controversy, bickering, and insults. If a conflict comes to the surface, we drop our masks and show our true colours. These are the moments that everyone wants to watch, just like a street row or a slanging match.

The idea of conflict is not restricted to a quarrel or a fight. It generally arises from the ambitions of people and the barriers they must overcome to achieve them. An athlete who needs to complete a long jump over eight metres to win has a problem. Tension arises from the conflict between the athlete's ambition ("win") and the difficulty of the challenge ("jump over

8 metres"). If the outcome were predictable (e.g. if the athlete is a six-year-old schoolboy), then the conflict is inappropriate because the outcome is certain—well, almost certain. Likewise, a conflict between two persons is only interesting when they are of equal power. If the main character bows down at the first blow, the conflict is settled and the game is over before it has even started. A good story requires a balance of powers so that conflicts can deepen as the story progresses to its climax and ending. But the essence of conflict is not in its dramatic power per se. Lévi-Strauss considers conflict to be a fundamental mechanism for our understanding of the world. His plea for conflict is not to be mistaken for a glorification of our violent nature. Conflicts involve the confrontation of two opposing forces and thereby allow for meaningful comparisons. It is hard to interpret the behaviour of a person without taking into account the discrepancies between those behaviours and their opposites. Happiness is meaningless without misery, love is meaningless without hate, and wealth is meaningless without poverty. For the same reason, discussion and dialogue help us to extract meaning from conflicting ideas and help us to improve our understanding. Since ancient times, the myths of the world have followed the universal patterns of conflict and have helped us to understand the world.

The illusion of reality

The combination of sound with moving images produces an unprecedented illusion of reality. Multi-channel audio, overhead dome-screen projection, and 3D technologies push the audience's experience of reality even further. But there are different views on how to evaluate the reality captured on camera. Despite all the technology film uses, its creation is mostly an artistic task. To enhance the suggestive impact, film-makers can draw on a range of stylistic devices such as camera angles, zooms, camera positions, sharpness, camera movements, staging, lighting, colour, editing, sound effects, and more. These allow them to construct their subjective representation of reality and to enhance its emotional impact. Alfred Hitchcock's famous shower scene in *Psycho* used seventy shots in one minute accompanied by dramatic, orchestral sounds to achieve high levels of suspense, involvement, and anxiety. Without all this editing, the scene would have been deadly dull. But film is all fake; it has only little to do with reality. Because of film's truncated and restricted view of the world, it is often understood through the metaphor of the frame. The images framed within the limited dimensions of the screen force the audience into a selective view of a constructed world. Despite the superb illusion of reality, the film image differs fundamentally from the real image. It is not the objects themselves that matter but the way the objects are captured and represented on the screen.

Critics denounce confusing manipulations that elicit wrong ideas about the nature of reality. Instead of using the frame metaphor, they promote the idea that film and TV should be a window that opens up the world to our eyes. Film and TV should act as a serving hatch to transfer events that would take place fully independent of the media themselves. In this respect, images captured on security cameras or webcams and some recordings of sports events, concerts, and parades come pretty close to fitting the window metaphor. Supporters of the window metaphor advocate minimal intervention and minimal use of stylistic devices. Even actors are suspect. This cinéma vérité doesn't feature stars of the silver screen portraying heroes and heroines but everyday people that just do what they always do. The approach is widely and successfully used in documentaries that aim to sketch authentic practices while assuming that the camera doesn't interfere with their reality. The latter idea is somewhat questionable. From protests, riots, and other disturbances, we know that the presence of TV crews or documentary film-makers encourages participants to overtly and expressly demonstrate their intentions or behaviours. Cameras sometimes act as catalysts for events exactly because they are supposed to act as windows on the world.

At the extreme ends, the window metaphor and the frame metaphor are hardly productive. Just recording reality is seldom interesting; creating extremely artistic audiovisual patterns, sometimes called "avant garde", generally receives little appreciation too. A third metaphor, that of a mirror, assumes that the power of the audiovisual is in the combined effect of the frame and the window. Both metaphors are required: realism offers the audience the opportunity for recognition, while style and aesthetics amplify interpretation and construction. Essentially, this idea includes the viewer and his or her psychology in the film experience. The mirror metaphor implies that the viewer identifies himself with the leading actor and thereby virtually participates in the story: he watches himself as if film were a mirror. The starting point of the mirror metaphor is that subjective processes are a decisive factor in producing meaning. Besides identification, other psychological concepts like regression, exhibitionism, and voyeurism come into play. The inherent one-way nature of film and TV allows viewers to watch others and engage in scenes of great emotion and intimacy without being noticed. It compares with the illusion of the fourth wall in a theatre, the imaginary separation between players and audience through which the audience can see the actors play but the actors supposedly cannot see the audience. Watching a movie in a darkened cinema is like secretly spying on your neighbours. It exploits our primitive tendency to want to know what's going on in the world without requiring us to take any risks.

We unavoidably project ourselves into the scenes as if we were the leading actors ourselves. It just happens, and we like it. We want it to happen because we long for authentic sensations. Therefore, we are prepared to temporarily neglect the idea that film is all fake and go along with the story, adopting the leading actor's viewpoint. This explains why we're capable of enjoying even films that are highly unrealistic and implausible. The phenomenon is known as the "willing suspension of disbelief" and applies to many other forms of art including literature, poetry, theatre, and opera. The willing suspension of disbelief is a bit like a preparedness to fool ourselves and blur the boundary between reality and fantasy. It is our preparedness to accept the unbelievable as truth, at least for the duration of the film. In order to enjoy a feature film like *Superman*, we have to accept that Superman can fly whenever he wears his funny suit. Although every reasonable individual would admit that this is a silly premise, we force ourselves to belief it is true so that we can project ourselves onto Superman and be rewarded with the authentic sensations this produces. The problem is that this mechanism applies not only to big lies but also to the subtle and obscure ones. We are prepared to believe anything we see on screen because of our natural tendency to project ourselves onto the stories. We deny ourselves and our rational mind, which makes us incapable of distinguishing unambiguously between reality and illusion.

CHAPTER 11

The Gossip Revolution

The successes of social media services like Facebook and Twitter are rooted in the human tendency to gossip, which is an informal way of sharing and discussing information. Although gossip is generally associated with spreading scandal and misinformation, evolutionary biologists claim that gossip's function is the preservation and amplification of solidarity in groups. Since gossip evaluates and comments on the appropriateness of individual behaviours, it helps to establish community codes and norms and to discourage deviations from these. So, gossip is a social phenomenon that helps to stabilise communities. Internet-based social media build on the same principle. Gossip is now liberated from practical restrictions in time and space as it now spreads at almost the speed of light and beyond geographical boundaries. Social media mark the transition from a network of web pages, commonly labelled web 1.0, to a network of humans, commonly called web 2.0 or the social web. Social media include a wide range of applications through which people can virtually meet or exchange information. Many thousands of sites offer blogs, wikis, forums, collaborative editing, media sharing, recommendation systems, and many more, all based on the notion that participants are both consumers and producers of messages that are worth noticing. They help us to stay informed about the state of affairs.

The network concept

Many complex phenomena in biology, economics, physics, engineering, sociology, and other areas are very well understood through network theory. Network theory uses a simple metaphor of nodes connected to each other. Obviously, the structure of the Internet is a network connecting individual computers to each other through cables or wireless links. Network theory can help us understand how malicious software spreads over the Internet. Likewise, the World Wide Web is a network of content, represented by web pages that are interconnected by hyperlinks. The very concept of the hyperlink, a link between two different entities, is essential for any network to exist.

A group of humans can also be described as a network. For instance, yours might include your relatives, your colleagues, your friends, and the politicians and other people living in your town or sharing some other attribute. In most networks, each node is connected to a limited number of other nodes. In your town, you will only know your nearest neighbours and perhaps some people from the sports club or shops, but usually you will not know all your fellow townspeople. Nevertheless, you will have indirect connections to all the people in your town via your neighbours, your neighbours' neighbours, and so on. Suppose you know about 60 people living in your town and that these 60 people know 60 other people in your town, and so on. After 3 steps, the network includes more than 200,000 people. There may be some doubling because people share friends and acquaintances, but still, these 3 steps will get you in touch with a whole lot of people. Yet another step in the network links you to over 10,000,000 people.

In the 1920s, Hungarian writer Frigyes Karinthy hypothesised that technological advances like the telegraph, telephone, and improved travel increased interconnectedness among humans. Their networks of friends and acquaintances could grow larger and cover greater distances. He claimed that any two individuals on Earth are connected to each other within only 5 steps. In 1967,

Stanley Milgram carried out experiments to check the validity of the claim. He randomly selected individuals in the United States and asked them to help to deliver a letter to randomly selected recipients by forwarding the letter to someone they knew personally who might have better connections to the recipient. Although hundreds of letters never reached their targets, sixty-four letters did, and along the way, they went through an average path of six degrees (which is equivalent to seven steps). This led to the conclusion that the world is so small that any two individuals are connected to each other within only "six degrees of separation". Although this theory is easily disproved as a universal law when we include hermits or isolated tribes, it demonstrates the power of social networks and the relevance of connecting to your friends' friends and beyond. A large-scale analysis of 30 billion instant messages among 180 million people in the Microsoft Messenger network in 2006 more or less confirmed the small world hypothesis: it found a slightly higher figure of 6.6 degrees of separation. A 2011 study of Facebook showed an even tighter network, with only 3.74 degrees of separation on average.

In most networks including social networks the number of connections is not evenly distributed over the individual nodes: some nodes have a significantly higher number of connections than average. This is a self-establishing effect that can be observed on Twitter and Facebook: people with many followers attract even more followers and thus function as an information hub in the network. Importantly, this mechanism prevents the network from breaking down as it grows. Without such asymmetry, the network wouldn't be scalable—it would get clogged up and fall apart.

The shared pattern of sharing

Social media networks are based on the idea that its users are "pro-sumers", that is, they are both the producers and the consumers of content. The companies offering social media sites usually don't behave like traditional publishing or media companies. They don't create content themselves and only offer the services and tools for users to produce their own content, e.g. a Facebook page, a blog post, a YouTube video, an iTunes podcast, a Wikipedia article. These user contributions are supposed to add value to the network by extending the network's collective knowledge. For the users of social media, the collective nature of the networks need not always be visible. Simply entering a search term in Google or Yahoo creates added value in the network because it helps to identify hot topics, trends, and different classes of user profiles. Searching is not a social act, but it still an act of participation in a social network. Buying products from an online shop may seem an individual act, but the recommendations you receive about other products that you might be interested in are the result of data collected from the network of all customers. You're evidently part of a social network even if there's nothing social about it. In many other cases, users post content to deliberately address an audience, which may be composed either of close friends or complete strangers that happen to share the same interest. Different types of social media require different types of user input. A wiki such as Wikipedia requires textual article descriptions as inputs. A blog (Blogger) requires opinions. A microblog (Twitter) requires short messages. YouTube requires videos, Flickr and Picasa require pictures, SlideShare requires presentation slides. Social bookmarking sites such as Del.icio.us are about making your favourite websites available to the network. Social networking sites like Facebook and LinkedIn urge you to give detailed information about yourself in your personal profile and offer network relationship tools, which are often complemented with blogging or microblogging services. Consumer broker sites like eBay require the users' information about their product offers and requests. Dating sites link your profile and your wishes to those of potential mates. Online gaming requires your gaming skills and your need for opponents or teammates. The same holds for virtual worlds (although most of these aren't web based). Mash-up services like geo-tagging require your input for linking media and locations on online maps. In addition to the common pattern of publishing user-generated content, social media offer additional services that include network statistics and the opportunity to obtain ratings and comments from the audience. These ratings again add value to the network. It's easy to stay up to date with posts from your friends, preferred blogs, or news sites with automated aggregation in the form of RSS of RDF feeds. The true viral power of social media is in the seamless transfer of messages across different network platforms. An interesting blog or video is easily rated, commented on, and forwarded to your social network friends or to the followers of your blog or microblog. The network of friends and followers will do the same and gossip about the message with other networks, increasing the size of the audience exponentially.

In days gone by, social communication was restricted to physical meeting spaces for tribes, families, or villagers. Letters could be used to communicate over a distance, but these made communication indirect and caused unpleasant delays. New media helped to remove these restrictions. Social media allow us to effortlessly maintain our relationships with both individuals and groups all around the world while they preserve the basic qualities of a chat in the pub. They're efficient, cheap, and extremely fast. Any news spreads across the world at unprecedented pace. When in 2009 a US Airways aircraft crashed in the Hudson River in New York, the first eyewitness messages, including mobile phone pictures and videos, appeared almost immediately on Twitter. These first messages were instantly forwarded by followers and snowballed over networks. This user-generated content appeared to greatly outperform the traditional news agencies at alerting readers and viewers. Social media and portable devices provide us with a gigantic set of eyes and ears that keep us informed about the state of affairs.

Exploiting the crowds' wisdom

One of the great challenges of social networks is exploiting their latent collective intelligence to solve problems that are difficult to tackle without many people. In his book *The Wisdom of Crowds*, New Yorker columnist James Surowiecki explains how groups of people can produce better solutions than the most intelligent individual members of that group. He doesn't simply restate that two heads are better than one but carefully specifies under what conditions groups perform better than individuals. Members should be independent in order to avoid herding behaviour and lip service, they should be of different backgrounds and hold different opinions for enhanced creativity, and they should co-operate in a loosely grouped, decentralised, and self-organised way for optimum results. Evidently, such conditions are greatly present in social media networks. A heroic example of group intelligence is Linux, the open-source computer operating system that has challenged the monopoly of Microsoft Windows. Throughout the world, many programmers collaborate on the code, evaluating and improving it, sometimes selecting the best out of multiple solutions, thus producing superior quality. Another example is SETI, the Search for Extra Terrestrial Intelligence project, that has been searching for life in the universe for over half a century. Since 1999, it has used a crowdsourcing mechanism to process and analyse the huge amounts of data collected by the Allan Telescope Array in California. In 2011, over 100,000 users in 200 countries offered the use of their PCs' processors to massively distributing SETI's processing capacity. SETI hasn't found anything yet, but this doesn't disqualify the method.

Likewise, Google successfully uses the crowd to assign keywords to images so that the images can be retrieved by their search engine. Image-recognition software may be able to recognise objects or even individuals, but its knowledge of the world is too limited to be able to understand and assign meaning to pictures. In a game-inspired set-up, users are invited to tag an image in a competition with another person who is online. After a few minutes, the tags are compared and points are awarded to the users depending on the quality of the match. Such third-party metadata impressively improve image search, which wouldn't be feasible otherwise.

Another outstanding example of collective intelligence is Wikipedia. Since its founding in 2001, Wikipedia has managed to create an extensive online encyclopaedia by tapping into the knowledge of its user community. Many tens of thousands of users voluntarily write articles about anything imaginable. Early in 2012, the English version contained almost 4,000,000 articles, and it continues to grow by 600 words per minute and 1,000 new articles per day. In addition, it offers versions in about 280 languages. Established publishers of encyclopaedias such as *Encyclopaedia Britannica* have watched Wikipedia closely with discomfort and disdain. Founded in 1768, *Encyclopaedia Britannica* was regarded as the gold standard for accuracy and reliability ever since. In the 1990s, it hardly survived competition with Microsoft's low-budget alternative, the Encarta CD-ROM. Britannica also underestimated the growth, flexibility, and quality of Wikipedia. The printed version of Britannica offers only up to 60,000 articles. A study published in 2005 in the journal *Nature* revealed that the quality differences between *Britannica* and Wikipedia were small, even smaller than the authors expected. *Encyclopaedia Britannica* still survives, however, maybe because its publisher managed to launch an extended online version itself and offered additional online services. Nevertheless, it is hardly believable that its traditional, hierarchical publishing model with 4,000 professional editors and experts on the payroll could ever compete with the tens of thousands of volunteers who edit Wikipedia, many of whom are experts and academics too.

The undifferentiated involvement of experts and laymen in Wikipedia and other social media raises severe criticisms. Some critics assume that the crowd is less wise than has been suggested since it is dominated by amateurs and laymen who lack expertise in the fields they talk about and are unable to distinguish between facts and opinions. In his book *The Cult of the Amateur*, British journalist and blogger Andrew Keen raises his concerns about the negative effects of the egalitarian model of web 2.0 on the authority of experts, scholars, and professionals. He wonders why we should accept that ignorant teenagers impertinently overrule reputable Harvard professors. Although on serious issues the probability that teenagers will be right when professors are wrong will be nearly zero, web 2.0 still gives them an equal vote. The cult of the amateur is often associated with Huxley's monkey theorem, which states that a monkey hitting keys at random on a typewriter keyboard for an infinite amount of time will almost surely type a given text, such as the complete works of William Shakespeare. Yet, the defenders of the egalitarianism of the crowd often substantiate their claims by pointing to the self-cleaning capabilities of social media. Nonsense, offenses, and harassments are easily rectified or disqualified by the crowd. In 2007, a Dutch princess tried to remove part of a Wikipedia page with her biography that reported about trickery. She tried to stretch the truth in her favour, but she got caught. Some of the readers of the page noticed the changes and made a comment. Thereafter it turned out that an internet address of the Royal Palace was used for making the changes. Critics have referred to this case to illustrate how easy it is for people to make unwanted deceptive adaptations to information in decentralised and unedited social networks like Wikipedia. But most people feel that Wikipedia demonstrates reliability because of its self-cleaning capability.

It's clear that there is substantial wisdom in the crowd. Social media provide a means to bring this to the surface. As Wikipedia, Google, and other examples demonstrate, many people are prepared to contribute to such crowdsourcing initiatives. They spend their time and energy to be part of a collective intelligence that achieves something new and valuable. Efforts go beyond the simple voting used by TV shows and demonstrate smart thinking, engagement, and responsibility for a good cause, if not a better world.

Who are we?

When we engage in virtual social spaces, we have to ask not where are we but who are we. Deprived from our flesh, blood, and outward appearance, we still need to demonstrate our nature. Social media typically require users to log in and to explain who they are by creating a personal profile. Meeting with anonymous people without names, without profiles, without histories, without identities would be boring as well as uncomfortable. These profile descriptions, which may contain personal pictures, videos, personal interests, and a name, often a nickname, are the main references for understanding who's talking and whom we're talking to. It is instructive for young people to experiment with different identities as part of growing up. The traditional social structures that used to support youth in shaping their identities, such as family, church, neighbourhood, or school, have decreased in influence. In recent years, the Internet has partly compensated for this decrease by allowing youth to experiment with different identities in different contexts by creating online profiles, personal home pages, and blogs or by participating in online role playing in virtual worlds.

Of course, adults do the same: we adopt different identities in different contexts, e.g. at work, at home, on sports teams, and while shopping. Since social media allow us to participate in multiple communities, our identity in any community is only a partial one. Our identity is fluid and unevenly distributed over these communities. We develop multiple personae, fragmenting the self and reflecting our slightly schizophrenic nature. Although creating an online identity takes only a few mouse clicks, it is an inherently difficult thing to explain exactly who you are or to choose what to reveal and what to hide. Hence, most online profiles are likely to be shallow, if not misleading. But there is no alternative. Those who provide a detailed and trustworthy profile or publish very personal information about their thoughts, feelings, emotions, or weaknesses run the risk of being harmed by others. Even the spontaneous and unconcerned posting of holiday pictures may have unexpected and unwanted consequences, sometimes many years later. The downside of the Internet is that its memory is endless: if you have any compromising texts or pictures online, you'll regret it forever since you'll never get rid of them. Gossip is easily created by transferring personal data from one context to the other. That is why most identities on the Internet are fake, or at least should be.

Creating your virtual identity may seem simple, but the assessment of the virtual identities of others is far more complex. For many thousands of years, humans have learned to interpret other people's physical appearance, subtle gestures, facial expressions, and manner of speaking to make judgements about their personality, intentions, and reliability, but now we have to make do with a nickname and some pimped up descriptions. For some people, the idea of using a virtual identity arouses the feeling of invulnerability: they can pretend to be young, attractive, and honest when they truly are old, ugly, and unreliable. This may seem useful for escaping from harsh reality, but frankly, it is just a lie. There have been many cases in which naive users became the victims either financially or sexually of malicious persons. Children need extra protection here exactly because they are the most vulnerable. They should learn to understand and anticipate the possible consequences of their online activities. Pretending to be someone else is a piece of cake in social media since you only have to create a new email address to do so. In order to demonstrate the vulnerability of users of social media, Italian journalist Tommaso De Benedetti created alias accounts of a number of Spanish and Italian ministers and sent out fake messages about budget cuts and new taxes. Clearly, the victims and followers did not appreciate this identity theft. However, our overall judgment of social networking need not be negative. There are many examples of fruitful, harmonic interactions. For instance, many people have had considerable success in online dating, with many meetings leading to sustainable relationships that have stretched into the real world. One may wonder to what extent the risks of social networks are different from those in the real world. The differences are probably negligible because it's possible for people to hide their true nature and pretend to be friendly while they are scheming in real life too. Learning to interpret the hidden cues of communication is a part of life.

The flawed promise

Twitter, Facebook, Google, and Wikipedia have demonstrated the huge impact of social media on our daily lives, on the economy, and on society at large. The underlying principle, to make users' content available to the community, suggests a new ideology of unconcerned sharing, altruism, social involvement, and public spirit. It breathes the values of freedom, independence, democracy, equality, and empowerment. Existing power relationships are challenged by the self-organisational nature of social media. For centuries, the relationship between providers of information and receivers of information has been an asymmetrical one. Providers have typically been publishing companies, politicians, clergy, dictators, and other parties representing the elite and controlling mass media for influencing public opinion and maintaining the status quo. The masses were just supposed to digest published information, not to produce it. We value a free press as an important achievement, but the harsh truth is that the majority of media are controlled by very few very powerful media concerns. Once in a while, though, media corruption is unmasked. In 2011, police investigations demonstrated the sneaky procedures of police bribery and phone hacking by Rupert Murdoch's tabloid the *News of the World*. When readers indignantly turned against the tabloid and the leading advertisers boycotted it, the tabloid went down. But such an outcome is quite rare. The overall power and influence of large media companies remains unbroken, as revealed by unpretentious media offerings aimed at achieving maximum viewing rates rather than sound journalism, diversity, profundity, criticism, or debate. Zapping along the large offerings of TV networks will hardly reveal any differences. They all seem to broadcast the same types of news shows, sitcoms, and movies, reflecting dull mediocrity. The same holds for radio, journals, and newspapers. None of these mass media are genuine social media, as they inform the crowd rather than involve it. Social media, on the other hand, offer the full benefits of participating in a network of people sharing the same interests or fighting for the same cause. Social media do without vertical power relationships. They bring power to the people. Anyone can become an opinion leader creating his or her own audience.

Inevitably, social media have their drawbacks. All their innovations come at a price. Social media providers require the right to exploit all user-generated content including user profiles, user messages and files, and behavioural patterns for their own purposes. Google says in its terms of service that by submitting, posting, or displaying content, the user gives Google worldwide licence to reproduce, adapt, modify, translate, publish, publicly perform, publicly display, and distribute that content. The privacy protection of users of other social media sites also shows frequent flaws and violations. Facebook has been regularly criticised (and sued) for censorship by excluding search terms, publishing user data without users' permission, data mining of individual profiles, and sharing of its user data with governments. Paradoxically, the protests against Facebook's policies were easily organised onto a new Facebook page. In the end, users should realise that social media site owners may tout their ideals for a better world, but they are multi-billion-dollar capitalists that have totalitarian traits not very different from traditional media giants: one may wonder if Facebook should receive more sympathy than Murdoch's News Corporation.

At the level of nations, social media's tendency towards freedom, independence, and democracy is readily counteracted by governments that don't share these values. The authorities in China, Syria, Iran, and Russia make great efforts to manipulate social media by controlling the flow of information and censoring it. Upon entering the Chinese market, Google was prepared to conform to censorship by the Chinese authorities. Banned subjects, such as "1989 Tiananmen Square protests" or "Tibetan revolts" never showed up in the search results. Under pressure from its worldwide user community, Google closed down its Chinese site in 2010 and redirected users to the uncensored pages of its Hong Kong website. Besides targeting Google, the Chinese authorities have used their "Great Firewall" to keep unwanted search results from their citizens by performing periodic web filtering and domain-name blocking. Because of this political intrigue, Google's market share in China decreased as Chinese users favoured the loyal native Baidu search engine, but their reputation increased.

Even without any authoritarian interference, the quality and reliability of social web content is often disputed. Inevitably there is a lot of faulty or biased content available, as the corrective properties of the crowd don't always function properly and no central authority is available to make required adjustments. The convictions of the crowd don't always match the well-established standards of scientific integrity and validity. Facts and opinions, fiction and ideology are easily mixed, sometimes producing a web of nonsense. A web of filth is even worse than a web of nonsense. What are we to do with content generated by Holocaust denial groups, explicit sexual material, child pornography, pro-mafia sites, violence, vulgarity? How should we consider the abundance of harmful, threatening, unlawful, defamatory, infringing, abusive, inflammatory, harassing, offensive, obscene, fraudulent, hateful, or racially, ethnically, or otherwise objectionable content? Many people would say that it's inappropriate to call this freedom of speech and claim that the social web cannot do without some sort of censorship, authorised to reject improper content and to remove malicious individuals from the network. If you agree, please read the previous sentences again and realise that such statement doesn't differ too much from a dictator's view.

Another issue is the high rate at which messages are created and posted. The endless flow of one-liners on Facebook and Twitter is often criticised because of its insignificant content, that it's nothing but loads of private futilities spewed out at large groups of people. For a short period, it may be fun to let the world know that you're getting out of bed, that you just had a shower, or that you're about to eat a sandwich, but after a while, you may realise that your contributions to the network are just boring and trivial. And your followers will feel likewise. Fast communication is beneficial in case of emergencies such as a plane crash, but generally, speed seems inversely proportional to significance. Sending and answering the messages becomes a continuous rush. It seems there is no time to lose before the next sound bite. This reflects a new pattern of hyperactivity that we're now getting conditioned to and that is pervading human communication. Critics decry the decline of the written word. People nowadays impatiently browse at the expense of cautiously reading, concentrating, and thinking about the subtlety and profundity of a written work. The democratic and educational promise of social media cannot be negated. They exploit the productive nature of gossip, which is a natural human phenomenon online and offline, but, unavoidably, they also import some of gossip's unwanted side effects.

CHAPTER 12
The Worldwide Online Game

Engaging in electronic media is a time-consuming affair. Every year we spend more time using our computers, smartphones, and TVs. In 2011, US citizens spent more than four hours per day watching TV and more than two hours per day on the computer. In addition, mobile phones received an additional hour per day, not just for calling but also for checking emails, browsing to websites, or sending out tweets. Altogether, we spend a large part of the day gazing at our screens, apparently sunk deep in thought. When we're online, our minds seem to have partially left the physical environment that surrounds our bodies and moved to some imaginary spot somewhere out there in cyberspace. This absent-mindedness might explain why we spoil so many keyboards with coffee, cake, or Coke. The arena of life is gradually shifting online. Since the turn of the century, many of our activities have already transformed to fit the opportunities of cyberspace. Today's office workers largely use computers. The same holds for those trading on the stock exchange, banking, shopping, booking hotels, brokering real estate, learning, networking, and many other activities. More and more, the human habitat is becoming a virtual one.

One of the leading areas for the virtualisation of life is the branch of video games. Games set the standards for virtual spaces with respect to complexity, dynamics, precision, intelligence, realism, user interfaces, and the experiences they offer. Since the 1980s, the worldwide market for video games has grown more than 10 per cent each year, up to 50 billion dollars in 2011, which is about twice as big as the music industry. What used to be a small niche for young computer freaks and weirdos has developed into a mature multi-billion-dollar business field serving many millions of customers. Surprisingly, surveys show that today's gamers cover all age groups. Young gamers of the past who are somewhat grey by now kept on gaming while new youngsters joined them. What makes games so different from TV, video, and film is the opportunity for players to actively intervene in the on-screen environment while trying to achieve favourable outcomes. Video games are highly engaging because of their dynamic, responsive, and highly visual nature. They put the players at the centre of the action, which incites them to experimentation, problem solving, strategic thinking, critical analyses, enhanced creativity, and other highly cognitive activities. Playing a video game is, to a great extend, exemplary for the way we engage in online activities such as editing our videos, distributing blogs, or just refining a web search. We simply control the digital universe from behind our screens. We operate our dashboards to remotely tracking the status of the world and adjust it in order to achieve favourable outcomes.

What's in a game?

Games cover a wide range of types and genres, including street games, puzzles, quizzes, first-person shooters, strategy games, quests, business simulations, construction games, virtual worlds, and many more. A naive description of a game would be something like this: an agreement to achieve a nontrivial goal and defeat competitors through a winning strategy, within a certain frame of time or space, guided by rules and constraints. Unfortunately, many games don't meet these criteria. Children often just start playing without establishing any rules or goals. Many games require collaboration rather than competition, many do without score, and many never produce a winner.

Also, the description doesn't discriminate between games and other activities in society such as going to school, working in a factory, or travelling from A to B. Most children don't perceive school as a game although it involves goals, rules, constraints, competition, and winning strategies. The same holds for working and travelling. The essence of a game is not in its attributes. For playing baseball, a baseball bat is not crucial: if it were replaced with a branch or a plastic pipe, the players would still have a game. Conversely, using a baseball bat doesn't mean that you're playing a game: indeed, some people use it as a weapon or as a tool to break into a jewellery shop. Likewise, the essence of a game is not in its components, and neither is it in its material substrate, its hardware, its software, its rules, or its graphics. The essence of a game is that it induces play. This idea redirects the focus from the medium to the responses it induces, which makes sense because a game is not an independent artefact but something that exists in the interactions with human players. A game is as good as the play it induces. So explaining a game is explaining its play.

A major characteristic of play is that it defines an arena that is principally different from actual life. Play reflects a temporary step outside of reality into an artificial setting where new roles and rules that we agree upon apply. Within this separate social contract, we're permitted or even encouraged to demonstrate new behaviours and attitudes that are quite different from those we display in daily life. We might go over the top, but still we're protected by the disclaimer that it is all just a game. So playing is like entering a parallel universe and pretending to have a different nature covered by the rules. A second major characteristic of play is its condition of voluntariness. It is neither a task nor an urgent need nor a moral obligation. A player is free to choose whether to engage in play. It is hard if not impossible to force someone into play. If force were used, the person wouldn't experience play. Likewise, there is nothing urgent about play: a game can be aborted or interrupted at will—provided your fellow players agree—and resumed later because it is only a game. These characteristics suggest that play is something redundant. But this doesn't mean that play is useless or without obligations. Play is not to be confined to fun and amusement. In many games, even in leisure games, players are challenged to do their level best to succeed, which requires utmost concentration, extreme determination, and perfect seriousness. Consider the gravity of children engaged in a puzzle, a dress-up fantasy, or a bicycle balancing act. Consider the self-torturing nature of the marathon runner who is prepared to defy spasms and cramps to reach the finish even though the race is just a game. Play can be a serious affair. "Serious gaming" is the topical label for games whose purposes are more than mere entertainment, such as education, health, or social involvement. Games help us to push back our frontiers.

Why we play at all

There is nothing unnatural about play. All elements of play can be observed in both humans and animals. Puppies and kittens play from the very day of their birth. They challenge each other with ceremonial movements and attitudes, showing off their pretended nastiness. They act bad-tempered and hostile, and they bite and scratch, while always respecting the implicit rule to not harm each other. Altogether, this seems to go with a lot of pleasure and fun. Likewise, children display a natural tendency to play. When you give a child an object, say a stick, a box, or a piece of plastic, the child will immediately inspect it and play with it: he or she will climb on it, swing it around, break it in two, or even talk to it. It is like an instinct. And others are happy to join in and make it a social affair. Children create their own challenges. This fits their drive to improve their skills and abilities. Psychologist Lev Vygotzky stresses the importance of being challenged, that is, not being satisfied with the things you're able to do already and going beyond them. In play, children frequently behave beyond their age, above their daily behaviour. Play creates a "zone of proximal development" that allows children to get acquainted with the rules of life and to prepare for the heavy duties that are in store for them. But play is not restricted to childhood. Adults also play, probably even more consciously than children. We love play: we like to play cards or to solve a crossword puzzle, we visit stadiums to watch people playing a game, we go to the theatre to see people act in a stage play, we go to concert halls where the orchestra plays. We like to take a chance in the lottery, dress like a clown during carnival, or pull the wool over a colleague's eye. It's all just playing a game. We like to stretch into our zone of proximal development to see if we can make it, to see if we can improve ourselves, or to see if we can beat an opponent. We enjoy the satisfaction of performing well, or we simply want to gain credit and social recognition. Play is a natural element of life. It's in our genes. Anthropologist Johan Huizinga, author of the famous book *Homo Ludens* [*Playing Man*] positions play as an essential human (and animal) function that transcends the level of necessities of life and helps us to attach meaning to our actions. Play doesn't only serve as a diversion, but it also meets our need for expression and exploration and for testing ourselves. Play is an essential condition for life. We are all players.

The immersive nature of games

The power of a game is in its absorbing capability. Players engaged in a game are likely to display a restricted awareness of their surroundings. Playing chess, solving a crossword puzzle, or playing a video game comes with an absent-mindedness that is hard to understand for non-playing bystanders. Questions remain unanswered and cups of coffee remain untouched, while all attention is directed to achieving a winning strategy. Players seem to be mentally transferred to a different world with different rules and conditions. What happens here is the psychological effect known as "cognitive flow". It goes with engrossment in and concentration on a task. It produces loss of self-consciousness and an altered sense of time. Players may continue for hours and hours and afterwards wonder how it can be so late already. Such absent-mindedness, which is the exclusion of interfering noises and disturbances from the environment, is quite beneficial for performance since the human brain has only limited processing capacity and is—contrary to popular belief—weak at multitasking. So being selectively focused on one task is highly productive.

Games are pre-eminently capable of bringing about this absorbing state of cognitive flow and maintaining it for a long time. Naturally, novels and films can produce the same effect as they drag us along their stories. What makes a game fundamentally different is that game players actively participate in the story they help to create by their interventions. In games, the intensive involvement of players arises from their power to intervene and influence the course of events. Players aren't just watching how the leading actor performs: they are the leading actor themselves and in control of the actions.

Maintaining this favourable state of cognitive flow is a delicate affair. The trick of well-designed games is in the subtle interplay between challenges and achievements, which should preferably follow a pattern of alternation. Challenges should be demanding but should be adapted to remain within the players' zone of proximal development so that the players will be able to make sufficient progress and enjoy the rewards. When the game's challenges are too complex, the rewards fail to come, and the player is likely to become frustrated and to eventually stop playing. If the challenges are too simple, the player will become bored. So, the game should continually adapt its level of complexity to the level of player performance in order for the player to maintain the state of cognitive flow. If this is done properly, games have the unique potential of taking people to the limits of their cognitive capacity or even slightly beyond and maintaining this for long periods of time. This is what we wish that schools would do but that schools so often fail to do. This is why so many scholars advocate to use serious games for teaching and learning. Games have the potential to involve people in challenging and time-consuming tasks that require concentration, motivation, persistence, and performance.

Unfortunately, the immersive nature of games comes at a price. Many parents see with disappointment how their children spend many hours a day gaming. Also for adults it is hard to resist the compelling and seductive attraction of these virtual environments full of successes achieved, levels reached, and powers gained which amplify their self-esteem and satisfaction even though they are not real-world achievements. Obsessive gaming is readily associated with escapism and a replacement for harsh reality. Different from reality, video games offer a simplified and controllable world that can be reset at will. The effects of excessive gaming are very similar to those of psychological addictions such as compulsive gambling. It is estimated that up to 10 per cent of gamers are pathological players, experiencing negative effects like depression, anxiety, social phobias, lower school performances, disregard of obligations, health problems due to a lack of physical exercise, and development of a truncated worldview. MRI brain scans of heavy Internet users (those who spend many hours a day online) reveal brain abnormalities that are very similar to those seen in people addicted to cannabis, cocaine, and alcohol. These are impairments particularly to the white matter fibres in the brain connecting regions involved in attention, emotions, decision making, and cognitive control. People suffering from game addiction have been the subjects of dozens of reports of extreme tragedies, including people dying from exhaustion after non-stop playing for fifty hours or more; a teenager who jumped off a tall building to join the heroes of World of Warcraft, the game he worshipped; a baby dying due to neglect by her parents, who spent all their time to raising their virtual children in the Prius Online game; a schoolboy jumping off the sixth-floor veranda at his school after he was banned by his parents from playing; another teenager murdering his mother and injuring his father after they refused to let him play Halo 3. Game addiction and Internet addiction are increasingly considered a severe health issue. Ironically, a frequent response is the launch of gaming-addiction websites that aim to offer online help. The attractive and immersive nature of video games facilitates our natural disposition to play, but it may easily turn into a fatal attraction.

The gamification of life

Today video games are no longer restricted to the domain of entertainment. They are often used for serious purposes in health and fitness, education and training, marketing, social inclusion, security and crisis management, cultural heritage, museums, ethics, and many more. In 2011, the Oxford dictionary put the word "gamification" on its buzzword-of-the-year shortlist, indicating the application of concepts and techniques from games for purposes other than entertainment. It didn't make it to the word of the year, but still it was on the same level as "bunga-bunga", "Arab Spring", "crowdfunding", "clicktivism", and "occupy". The idea of applying game elements in areas other than entertainment is an attractive one. We people do like playing games, and games can help to make rotten chores more attractive. We know that people are prepared to do the most stupid jobs (complete surveys, collect stamps, click around for hours on a virtual farm, buy lottery tickets, send SMS messages to talent shows, buy shares, and so on) if only some sort of reward is offered. Gaming procures more involvement, enhances suspense and excitement, prompts desired behaviours, and gives us the feeling that our actions matter. In short, gaming helps us to improve our performances and make our lives meaningful. On radio and TV, gamification has been going on for many years. In this respect, some even refer to infantilisation. Sports shows, talent scouting, quizzes, panel shows with or without celebrities, hidden cameras, quests: game elements are all around us. It is conceivable that gamification is capable of increasing activity and involvement in businesses, schools, ministries, and so on. The promise of the concept's utility is undisputed. There is this paradox, though, that on the one hand we consider humans as superior cognitive beings capable of self-appraisal and goal-oriented behaviours, while on the other hand we want to use all these simple, sometimes even childish, incentives to encourage people to do the actions they are reluctant to do. It seems we treat ourselves as if we were dogs that need to be challenged by sausages just out of reach. But extrinsic motivation is always inferior to intrinsic motivation.

The pitfall of realism

Many people believe that the compelling effects of video games result from the superb quality of high-definition graphics, the natural movements of objects, the built-in artificial intelligence, the realistic behaviours of artificial characters, and the richness and depth of full surround sound. This is only partly true. Early video games like Pac-Man, launched in 1979, were exciting but used only poor-resolution graphics and simple beep sounds. In Pac-Man, players have to clear a path through a maze while being chased by little ghosts. It is considered the first exciting video game and it was appreciated by both sexes. It combines freedom of movement and performance under time pressure. As soon as the game is started, we feel genuinely chased and act accordingly, notwithstanding the poor graphics. Apparently we are prepared to suspend our disbelief and accept the game context as a real challenge. Even though we know that it is all a game, our responses are real, and so are our experiences: we are really being chased! Our bodies produce a fight-or-flight response with physiological changes like increased heart rate, higher muscle tension, and increased stress hormones, and our emotional states change accordingly. It is unavoidable. Our brain simply lacks the neural circuits that could suppress such natural responses. This physiological response also happens when we're watching TV or a movie. Our brain is not capable of distinguishing between real experiences and mediated experiences. Even simple technology is capable of arousing our interpersonal responses too: we treat technologies just the way we treat living creatures. That's why we rail against our computer when it fails to do what it should do. This establishes that media aren't just tools, they fully participate in our social and natural environment. It explains why we're so frightened of those little Pac-Man ghosts chasing us, notwithstanding the poor graphics.

Today's high-quality graphics and sounds certainly amplify the realism we experience. Also, authentic elements contribute to realism, such as representations of existing cities and buildings, real maps and celebrities such as leading players in tennis and football games. The Formula 1 racing game not only uses virtual representations of real racing circuits, real cars, and real drivers, but it also lets players virtually participate in real Grand Prix events. They can do the qualifying races and also compete against the top drivers in the world during the official race. For the latter, speed and location data from real racing cars are tracked and transferred to the online version. In some games, the reverse pattern is used: the virtual playing field is partly replaced with the physical environment, where players can navigate by using their smartphones and GPS trackers. Links between games and the real world help to enhance realism and authenticity.

Likewise, reality itself becomes more and more virtualised. By the age of twenty, children have spent over 20,000 hours watching TV and 10,000 hours working at their computers. They largely live their lives online. Business is also shifting to cyberspace. Stock trading is completely digitised. Traders never get to see any money, stocks, or certificates. Banking is equally electronic. Remittances are done in bits and bytes. Materially, the money doesn't even exist. In general, knowledge workers work on their computers. Shop owners serve customers online and farmers monitor their computer-regulated flows of water and nutrients to their crops. More and more devices in the real world obtain IP addresses, which means that they can be accessed and adjusted remotely. Streetlamps, fridges, ovens, toothbrushes, cars, heating systems, doors, windows, washing machines, and a multitude of sensors and actuators make up an Internet of Things which amplify the entanglement of virtual and real environments. Along with this virtualisation, life itself seems to incorporate more and more gaming elements. Politics and elections aren't very different from a game in the roles that politicians adopt, the battle between candidates, the strict behavioural rules and codes, and the system of scores that participants follow. Stock trading doesn't differ much from gambling on horse races or buying lottery tickets. TV shows use game-based formats—even the news is presented as a show. We never get to know the newsreader, who simply adopts a role and behaves accordingly. Acting as an operator in a chemical plant control room barely differs from playing a level in the Sims or any other leisure simulation. A harrowing example is the unmanned aerial vehicles used by the US army in Pakistan, Somalia, and other countries. These drones, such as the Reaper and the Predator, as well as the Tomahawk cruise missile, are controlled from up to 10,000 kilometres away. The pilots, sitting somewhere on a US Army base, manipulate joysticks while watching screens and pressing buttons to deliver a lethal payload every now and then. By the end of their nine-to-five day, the pilots cheerfully step out of the control room, stretch a bit, and go for a drink, have dinner, or play some tennis. Today's sports broadcasts also incorporate many video game patterns, including a display of athletes' heart rates; their GPS positions; super-slow-motion replays; the game's statistics, including ball possession, number of faults, and scores; and the Hawk-Eye tracking system in tennis and cricket. It is hard to discriminate between real life and a game, since games are inevitably part of life. We are players by nature, and life has many characteristics of play, sometimes serious play.

CHAPTER 13
The Struggle of Media Research

Media's influence on society is undisputed. The overall impact on public opinion, lifestyle, and consumer behaviours is well recognised. But at a finer level, it is hard to determine what the effects of particular media messages are. An exemplary case is the yearly fireworks information campaign arranged by authorities near the turn of the new year. Every year, thousands of young people get severely injured in fireworks accidents when they underestimate fireworks' risks. Through TV and radio spots, authorities aim to raise awareness among youth about the hazards of letting off bangers and rockets. The campaigns, which promote an idea rather than a product, are assumed to be useful, but every year questions arise about their adequacy. Some critics suggest that the campaign is a waste of money since the number of casualties doesn't go down, while advocates claim that thanks to the campaign, it doesn't go up. Year after year the tone of the advertisements has been modest and informative, appealing to the reason and understanding of the audience. But one year, the authorities proposed a completely different strategy to achieve a greater impact. The advertising agency changed the tone of the campaign and directly demonstrated the devastating effects of fireworks accidents. The spots now showed moving scenes in which young boys and girls revealed their mutilations. They had lost their eyes, fingers, hands, limbs, hair, and skin, and they explained sensibly how stupid they had been playing with fireworks. They also explained the social isolation that resulted from their physical handicaps.

The campaign was shocking, and it aroused many comments. Representatives of disabled people denounced the stigmatising suggestion that handicapped people are socially isolated. Psychologists questioned the effectiveness of the spots, since focussing on anxiety seldom leads to positive effects. Viewers digested the message but didn't link the dramatic stories to their own situations. There is no scientific evidence that anxiety for injuries and social isolation promotes risk-avoiding behaviours. The fact is that the number of casualties didn't change substantially. This demonstrates the difficulty of predicting and establishing the precise effects of a particular media approach within the complexity of the real world. Research into media has never been capable of capturing the richness and communicative potential of effective messages into methods and rules that would guarantee the pursued impact. So there is nothing mechanical about media creation: to a large extent, it is an art rather than a craft. Creating media is a human work. For this we need cunning, creative minds that dare to deviate from existing codes to find the modes of expression that achieve the goal. But the uncertainty about whether a message achieves certain effects remains. Predicting how target groups will respond to new commercials, movies, or TV shows is anything but trivial. Brilliant ideas in commercial advertising may dramatically fail to achieve increased sales of a product. Multi-million-dollar feature films created by the best screenwriters, directors, and actors may flop right after the premiere. That's why Hollywood tends to rely on well-established film formats (e.g. *Home Alone* and its sequels) rather than to innovate.

The contributions of media research to clarifying causes of intended behaviour and effects of particular messages are plainly disappointing. Media research is good at analysing and explaining the structural properties of media but is behind the times when it comes to identifying or predicting effects of messages. Maybe that is what makes media creation so interesting and challenging.

The case of media violence

It is often suggested that humans are naturally predisposed to aggression. Children even as young as one year old have learned to appreciate the spectacular effects of hitting another child. It is the consequence of our explorative mind. Parents' or carers' corrective interventions usually reduce such unwanted behaviour, although they may not eradicate it. Difficulties may arise when parents demonstrate unwanted behaviours themselves and thereby provide a model that their offspring copy. Children that persist in striking others are likely inspired by their parents or other people in their environment since we learn most behaviours by imitating other people. For example, we acquire language by mimicking our parents. As much as parents teach their children how to speak, they are responsible for their children's cursing, railing, and hitting fellow children. We should never blame the children.

Albert Bandura's social learning theory claims that we learn by observing others. We record and mentally rehearse others' attitudes and responses and demonstrate these behaviours when we think it is appropriate to do so. This theory is not about unthinking imitation or Pavlovian reflexes but about conscious interpretation and learning through mental replays. While referring to social learning theory, many researchers have warned that the endless flow of violence depicted by mass media may have unwanted effects on children and adults. Media statistics show that by the age of 18 children have seen over 200,000 violent acts on TV, exposing them to a large set of model behaviours advocating that violence is an accepted and successful strategy for resolving conflict. Viewers gladly sympathise with the fair-minded film and TV heroes that literally fight for a good cause and never hesitate to eliminate their evil opponents with violence. The unavoidable identification with the fearless leading actor helps us to readily adopt and appreciate the violent actions as favourable solutions. Shooting or beating up the opponent is portrayed as a justified and natural response, one that is productive and apparently much simpler than intricate negotiations or subtle diplomacy, which admittedly tend to be less spectacular.

Similar patterns of aggression occur in video games as the players take up the violent roles themselves. The first-person shooter is a highly popular game genre distinguished by the challenge of shooting as many enemies as possible. After a few hours creeping up on opponents and resolutely eliminating one after the other when they are within reach, the act of shooting has become standard behavioural repertoire that players execute fluently, unthinkingly, and with high precision. In 1997, the Carmageddon car racing game aroused worldwide protests because players could earn extra points by running over pedestrians. The morbid game play, supported by colourful visual effects of the crashes and the squealing sounds of the victims, were condemned widely. In various countries, the game was officially banned, but the free publicity that the controversy aroused helped to make the game a great commercial success. Apparently a lot of people like to play such violent games. Unfortunately, there is an endless list of violent incidents that seem to be inspired by violent games. For example, in 2011, the Dutch young man Tristan van der Vlis, wearing a bulletproof vest and armed with a semi-automatic weapon, a pistol, and a revolver, entered the Ridderhof shopping mall in the small local town of Alphen and shot more than 100 bullets at unsuspecting shoppers. He killed six people, injured another seventeen, and finally shot himself. It turned out that he liked to play violent video games like Call of Duty: Modern Warfare 2, which features an airport massacre scene, where the player has to shoot innocent passengers inside an airport terminal. The similarities between the airport massacre scene and the actual shooting are striking. In July 2012 a young man called James Holmes emptied his guns on the visitors of a cinema in Aurora, Colorado, who were attending the premiere of the Batman film *The Dark Knight Rises*; twelve were killed and fifty-eight were injured. Holmes was dressed as the Joker, the evil antagonist of Batman. He mimicked the Joker's behaviour and even said, "I'm the Joker." These aren't exceptional cases. In a large number of severe incidents, perpetrators appeared to be compulsive players of violent video games and imitated the reprehensible behaviours of the game's characters.

Numerous studies have linked exposure to violent video games to aggression, violent criminal behaviours, racism, delinquency, and fighting at school. Frequent exposure to media violence is found to create positive attitudes and expectations towards aggressive solutions and to decrease moderate emotional responses to conflicts. Research seems to confirm what everyone may know already: media violence produces violent behaviours. Many influential people ranging from pedagogues to politicians have called for restrictive measures. Why should we expose our children to morbid scenes? Why should we allow anyone to play pathetic games like Ethnic Cleansing, which was developed by a neo-Nazi organisation? Why should we accept bizarre games like Super Columbine RPG and V-Tech Rampage that allow players to re-enact authentic incidents in the role of the powerful perpetrator? Many people would agree on this.

But technically, the causal relationship between media violence and aggressive behaviour is a difficult thing to prove. Various researchers point at the unclear outcomes of research. Many studies have failed to find significant aggressive effects, some show a temporary effect, and some even show a decrease in aggression. Researchers of these last studies even provide an alternative scientific theory: the "catharsis theory", which claims that engaging in media violence allows players to vent their frustrations and anger without putting violence into practice. Quite a few review studies have been criticised for their biased samples and mixture of incomparable definitions of violence. Also, there are many other risk factors for societal violence, for instance, mental instability and poor family life. Some suggest that the effect of violent video games is of minor importance, pragmatically arguing that violent crime rates have declined dramatically since the 1990s despite the explosive growth of the games market. Even though it is true that in most cases of violence at school the perpetrator was said to be a gamer, it is impossible to draw any conclusions from this since almost all young people play games and the overwhelming majority of them don't display violent behaviours. It would be odd if a perpetrator did not play games. One may even assume reverse causality here: aggression causes one to play violent games. The moral outrage about media violence could be harmful in itself because it hides the actual causes of violence and leaves them un-addressed.

For governments, media violence is a difficult case to handle as long as the evidence is disputed. Restricting media violence by law would easily infringe on the freedom of speech, which is the very basis of modern democracy. Legal censorship and publication bans would be principally and practically untenable in the absence of unambiguous scientific proof. But obtaining such proof appears to be a difficult task for researchers, although some agree about a weak positive relationship. And the commercial interests of media companies should not be underestimated: violence sells! It's true that right after the Aurora shootings, Batman producer Warner Bros immediately stopped advertising and promoting *The Dark Knight Rises* out of respect for the victims. Ironically, ticket sales after the incident skyrocketed. Apparently, we just love to see violent movies and thereby stimulate companies to produce them. The problem of media violence is very similar to the case of smoking: for many years, scientific studies failed to prove the causal relationship between smoking and lung cancer although such causality is quite plausible. Also, the debate over climate change and global warming is a tragic example of scientists having difficulty proving causality. Possibly, very few people will be influenced by violent scenes in such a way that they are likely to become airport terminal shooters, high school shooters, or cinema shooters. Unfortunately, these lone wolves never show up within accepted confidence intervals in statistics. However, the consequences are disastrous. They mark the tragic imperfection of statistical analysis, which is not capable of accounting for extreme deviations from the average. Maybe we should just rely on our common sense.

Controlling the uncontrollable

In the complexity of everyday life, it is largely impossible to scientifically prove a causal relationship between one phenomenon and the other, for instance, between media usage and violent behaviours. The issue is that in real-world situations, people's behaviours are influenced by a wide range of factors, most of which are uncontrollable, undetectable, or even unknown. Researchers may be able to identify some of these, like age, gender, shoe size, or any other easy observable attribute, and use their statistical formulas to excluding confounding effects, but inevitably, a multitude of obscure influences remain that simply cannot be taken into account. Exactly because input variables cannot be controlled in practical contexts, showing statistical significance is highly impracticable. Hypothetically, one might find after thorough investigation that the price of sushi in Tokyo is positively correlated with the number of traffic accidents in Buenos Aires, but even if the correlation is highly statistically significant, the analysis would be meaningless, as no conclusion could be drawn from it. Likewise, a correlation between aggression and gaming wouldn't necessarily be meaningful. The correlation between two variables may either be a matter of chance or the effect of a shared but unknown cause. Here the theorising starts. For the sushi case, it would be hard to find a common factor that provides a plausible explanation. Perhaps one may pose an economic hypothesis linking a conjuncture of fishing quotas, world oil prices, or cultural habits to an explanatory narrative, but the chances of finding a clue that is both understandable and likely are low. In the aggression case, the theory itself may be simple and plausible, but statistics are weak because too many influential factors remain uncontrolled.

Gaining control over conditions and variables is exactly what physicists and chemists do in their laboratories. They create well-specified circumstances by cautiously controlling voltages, weights, temperatures, and so on to measure the behaviours of electrons, molecules, compounds, solutions, or crystals. Inspired by these approaches, social scientists, mainly psychologists, set up their own laboratories for researching the effects of media exposure on their subjects. This was exactly what they needed to find causal relationships between interventions and assumed effects. Although their labs were just simple offices and lacked all the impressive equipment that physicists and chemists used, they carried out media experiments—they even borrowed the word "experiment". Generally, an experiment would involve a set-up with two or more groups of test subjects, each subjected to different conditions. In the context of education, many "laboratory" experiments were carried out to compare the effectiveness of a teacher-led lecture to computer-based instruction. One group of learners, the control group, would attend the lecture and the other group, the experimental group, would use the computer instruction to learn the same topic, and afterwards, both groups would be tested to see if there were any differences in performance. This seems simple enough, and although plenty of scientific papers have been published about such experiments, many of the outcomes have been questionable and ambiguous.

One of the main problems with social science experiments is that researchers or subjects may unwittingly bias the outcome. Research on computer-based instruction is usually conducted by people with highly specialised knowledge of computer-based instruction. These researchers are likely to be greatly committed to the topic in the most positive sense; it is unthinkable that they are neutral. They have the positive conviction that computer-based instruction will revolutionise education and will partly replace traditional teaching. They have a vision and a mission to advocate and promote in scientific journals and at conferences. It looks much like selling and branding. They have an interest in proving that their claims of the benefits of their approach are right. Researchers are more or less equated with their topic: their reputations exactly coincide with it. If their approach turned out to be useless, it would mean the end of their research careers. Although there is nothing wrong with these people's scientific integrity, various review studies about computer instruction have shown that in most experiments that reported positive effects, the experimental groups simply received more instruction than the control group. Researchers unwittingly devoted more time and attention to designing and creating computer instruction, which in itself could produce higher quality learning. Likewise, the learners using the computer were often allowed to spend more time to the learning task, which could also have been the cause of better performance. The opposite could also be observed: teachers may unwittingly defend their positions by trying to outperform the computer. Delivering a splendid lecture with a lot of extras could positively influence learning in comparison with the computer.

The test subjects themselves, in this example the learners, may also unwittingly contribute bias to research outcomes. First, they may display the Hawthorne effect, which refers to subjects modifying their behaviours just because they know that their behaviour is being measured. The interest and attention that subjects receive can function as a motivator to adopt the researchers' viewpoint and act according to their expectations. This is amplified by researchers' habit of using flawed questionnaires or interviews as measurement instruments rather than direct, objective measures. Questions such as "How did you like the computer approach?" are likely to be answered positively. Second, subjects tend to pay more attention to new approaches. So, confronting test subjects with the latest fancy high-resolution smartphone application may easily result in increased attention, greater effort, and better performance than subjects confronted with existing techniques. This novelty effect tends to diminish after some time, when the persons have become familiar with the new approach. The tragedy of experiments testing new media approaches is that results are likely to be dominated by these temporary influences that conceal sustained impacts. This also reveals another weakness: most studies focus on a snapshot approach and fail to provide insight into long-term effects. Researchers cannot detain subjects in a laboratory for years.

The problem of media research is that humans aren't like atoms, electrons, or molecules. Physicist and chemists can reproduce their lab experiments over and over again because all electrons are identical, as are specific atoms and molecules, and all their interactions are governed by the well-established universal laws of nature. Electrons lack any memory, they don't learn from their experiences, and they will respond the same way next time. Unlike electrons, humans are self-aware, intentional beings who are all different. They do have a memory by which they learn from experiences. Electrons will collide the same way over and over again. A human individual would remember previous "collisions" and take another route to avoid another one. It is hard if not impossible to control all the variables that define a human being.

Comparing the incomparable

Apart from the problem of uncontrolled variables influencing human test subjects, there is another principal obstacle to answering, "What is the best medium for producing target effects?" Commercial advertisers, public relations officers, and e-learning specialists would greatly benefit from research evidence that would reveal what effects are best achieved by what medium. Unfortunately, researchers that try to compare the effects of different media run into severe methodological problems. This is best explained by a simple example.

Consider a training company that wants to develop a distance-training course for, say, making pancakes. The developers wonder what the best medium to use would be: a book, an instructional video, maybe a video game, or a demonstration from a chef? Obviously, anything goes. Most people rely on a cookery book for learning how to cook. Fair enough; the book is a great technology. It can do without power and never breaks down. There are also videos about successfully making pancakes. Likewise, there are cookery workshops that allow participants to experience and learn to make pancakes themselves. So, in general, it doesn't seem to matter much which media carry the instruction. But there's more to it. Each media technology has specific features which favour certain aspects of cooking. From a book, you can easily learn which ingredients to use and in what proportion, what temperature the frying pan should be heated to, and how you should flip your pancake with a "prudent but fierce swing of the wrist". Unlike a book, a video directly shows you how to pour the batter into the hot, buttered pan without making a mess and how the technique for flipping the pancake should be performed (in slow motion!). In the practical lesson, you would directly experience how thick the batter should be, you may learn what the end product smells like if it's burnt, and you will sense how difficult it is to give the pan the right sweep for flipping. It is not just that you learn differently in each case, but clearly that you also learn different things. Essentially, this means that the various media don't carry the same contents. Instead, each medium determines what can be learned from it and what cannot. This means that evaluating the different media options is like comparing apples and oranges. A persistent researcher might put forward that what counts in the end is the quality of the pancakes, which would provide a shared criterion for deciding which medium works best. The misunderstanding here is that such comparison would only assess the quality of the video director, the text writer, the game designer, and the chef leading the workshop rather than the appropriateness of the different media. Hiring another video director would lead to different results. Evidently, such an experiment, even when performed in a laboratory setting and when conditions like the distribution of gender, age, and time spent in each group are controlled, wouldn't provide any scientific evidence for which medium is best for teaching the art of making pancakes; it would only provide evidence for each particular case.

For many people, even for researchers, it is hard to accept that research cannot prescribe the best medium to use. The reason is these people's implicit but unjust assumption that media are just vehicles for messages and their neglect of the principle that media themselves contribute to meaning. Their vision on media reflects an obsolete, instrumentalist view of technology's role, rooted in the industrial revolution and assuming that technology is a neutral and subservient means for achieving our aims. The opposite is the case, though. Generally, we don't choose a technology to suit our purposes, but instead the technology determines those purposes. So, we send an email or browse the Internet simply because the computer makes it possible. New technologies create their own demand, an idea which is completely opposite to that of technology as a mere instrument for our needs. In the case of preparing a course, we may have a global goal, but the different media technologies would force us to adopt different approaches and to expect different outcomes: the medium determines the outcomes. Instead of asking what media to use to implement a lesson plan, we should ask the reverse: how could media enhance my teaching? Many educators seem unaware of this idea, as their widespread aversion to new technologies shows, but in educational practice, teaching is really the product of technical possibilities. Outstanding media technologies like the blackboard, the book, and the pencil are the cornerstones of today's pedagogy. We don't need to compare computers with lectures or games with videos to know that media will produce new and mostly better pedagogical approaches. We shouldn't compare things that cannot be compared.

CHAPTER 14

Free Copy Economics

Digital media have brought about disruptive changes in the way the economy functions. In recent years, we have witnessed the emergence of Internet-based companies like Google, Facebook, Skype, and Foursquare that have challenged the models of traditional industries such as mining companies, ironworks, and automotive manufacturing. Every day new media start-ups, particularly in the area of social media, show up and become the talk of the town because of their impressive growth, with some doubling the number of users every month and others growing even faster. Such growth rates easily attract venture capitalists, who cherish the hope that these high-potential, high-risk start-up companies will become their money spinners. In most cases this turns out to be a gross misjudgement, but occasionally they may hit the jackpot and cash in. It's not only start-ups that are popular among investors, as they eagerly follow established companies like Google, Apple, and Yahoo as well. The attraction of Internet companies lies not so much in their turnover or profit. They cannot measure themselves against the automotive industry or the oil industry. These more traditional industries still dominate the *Fortune* Global 500 ranking, a yearly ranking of companies based on revenues, or the *Financial Times* Global 500 ranking, which ranks companies based on shares price (admittedly, in 2011, Apple was ranked third because of the iPhone and iPad). Most Internet companies never make any profits and lack substantial turnover. Instead, investors base their decisions on growth rates and innovative potential. When high growth rates persist for a long time, financial risks decrease, the company's reputation goes up, and the brand becomes established. Google and Amazon are good examples here: they are world leaders when it comes to reputation. The Global Reputation Pulse, a ranking of the world's most reputable companies composed by the New York Reputation Institute, lists in its 2011 edition Amazon at number 1 and Google at number 2, far ahead of popular and renowned brands like Coca-Cola (25), PepsiCo (28), and Nike (41).

New giants like Facebook and Twitter have demonstrated tremendous growth. Not long ago, they were just insignificant start-up companies driven by some enthusiastic youngsters, just like the romantic genesis of Apple and Microsoft a few decades ago. Within a few years, these youngsters managed to turn their ideas into multi-million-dollar businesses. Not until stock-market flotation does the financial value of these new companies become public. An initial public offering is frequently accompanied by deliberate hype suggesting that buying the new stock is a once-in-a-lifetime chance to strike it rich, and the optimism and enthusiasm of investors can push the flotation value to unrealistic levels. Within four weeks after its flotation in 2012, Facebook had already lost 30 per cent of its value. Even worse, gaming business success story Zynga, which received a stock market quotation in 2011, lost 70 per cent (or 7 billion dollars) within a few months.

Still, the impact of these companies is high. Similar new companies are likely to show up and alter the economic landscape in the future. The most striking feature of new Internet companies is that many of them are prepared to offer their products without charging users. They seem to overlook the necessity of making a profit by giving their product or service away for free, marking the extraordinary rules of play that govern the Internet economy. We gladly boost a company's reputation and popularity by taking their free services, but by not paying, we also keep them in the red. We've become greatly accustomed to the fact that most services on the Internet are free of charge. We buy into the original idealism of the Internet as a place of freedom and open access and reject commercial barriers. Imagine what would happen if Google charged us for each search, each photo upload, each video view, each email. What if Twitter charged us for each tweet? What if Facebook changed its strategy and started sending bills? The effect would probably be a worldwide revolt against these companies. The Internet community would quickly launch mirror sites and alternative services that would bypass the spoilsports, just as they do in countries where the authorities restrict freedom of speech by censoring Internet traffic. We simply don't want to pay, which is peculiar. It demonstrates to what extent the digital economy is different from the material economy.

The costs of replication

In the material economy, matters are quite simple. Companies transform raw materials into useful things. Consider a small furniture factory that produces exclusive, custom-made oak chairs. The company is renowned for its craftsmanship and produces the highest quality furniture. To make a chair, a craftsman first needs blocks of the finest oak for the seat, the back, and the armrests. To cut the blocks into the right shapes, he uses manual and electrical saws, chisels, drills, and other cutting tools. With a sanding machine, he does the polishing, and next he finishes the wooden components with a few layers of varnish. When the upholstery is finished, all the pieces are put together with glue, staples, nails, and screws. Because of the high-quality materials and handcrafting, the chairs are quite costly.

The efficiency of the production process could be greatly improved by producing a whole series of chairs, say 100 or even 1,000, in one batch, thus reducing the time spent adjusting and handling each machine by automating processes and using bigger and faster machines and procuring better prices for the wood and other raw materials because of discounts at volume. By this economy of scale, the price of a chair would go down, which is attractive in a competitive market. Whatever efficiency measures are devised, however, even fully automating production, the cost of a single chair would still remain considerable because it still requires the same amount of costly wood and high-quality upholstery fabric, not to mention expensive machines. In the material economy, replicating products remains costly because of the price of raw materials, machines, and labour.

In contrast, in the digital economy, the costs of replication are almost nil. Digital products are anything that is encoded in zeros and ones, like software programs, SMS messages, photographs, graphics, user profiles, and web pages. When a digital product is created, it can be copied over and over again, almost without additional costs. We may need a little bit of extra disk space, but we don't have to order raw materials or components, we incur no extra cost for stock or transportation, and we require no additional labour. We just have to press a button, and there we have it: millions and millions of copies at zero marginal cost. This peculiar characteristic of the digital economy signifies a major distinction with the material economy. The consequence of free duplication is that the price per unit is inversely proportional to the number of copies sold. This means that the price of digital products can become extremely low provided a sufficient number of copies are bought. Ultimately, the price approaches zero.

The rationale of free online services

Because of their easy duplication and distribution, digital products can be delivered at very low prices. However, this still doesn't explain why most services on the Internet are fully free of charge, like the ones offered by Google, Facebook, Twitter, and many other dot-coms. There is nothing altruistic about these software giants, as their main aim is to maximise profits and stakeholder values, like any other company. Their marketing machinery may successfully promote the image of unselfish champions of friendship and community spirit, but their businesses are neither charities nor public services. To monetise free services, they shamelessly sell our personal data to the highest bidder and use the brilliant marketing tactic of enabling visitors or users to pass on the message, which makes a brand spread like a virus.

Facebook has been particularly smart by introducing its "Like" button and making it available to other sites so those sites can capitalise on Facebook's popularity. The button has become a universal utility. Every time we click the Like button, we inform Facebook about our preferences, which enhances the data about us. Facebook's business model is nothing but a sophisticated advertising campaign which exploits the data that we're happy to provide freely about our hobbies, friends, and preferences and allows advertisers to bombard us with personalised offers on products our preferences indicate we might want to buy. The service may be free, but in the end, we're paying for it anyway.

Of course, we're familiar with free products in the material economy—the special offers like a free trial of a new washing powder, two-for-one deals on bottles of lemonade, or free admission for children at a museum. As economist Milton Friedman used to say, "there is no such thing as a free lunch"—every product and service offered to a customer inevitably comes at a cost. In the end, someone has to pay for it, even when the costs remain concealed. The costs of the free washing powder samples are simply included in the overall product price and paid for by all customers, the free bottle of lemonade is paid for by the buyers of luxury chocolate in the same shop, the costs of the children's museum tickets are included in the price of tickets for their parents. So, the trick is to recover the costs of free products by making other products more expensive or by transferring the bill from one group of customers to another.

Such transfer of costs is quite common for software, which is often freely available on the web. Most of free applications are stripped-down versions offering only basic functionality. To access the full software version, usually called the "pro" version or the "premium" version, users must pay for a licence. In this business model, which is commonly referred to as the "freemium" model, the buyers of the premium version foot the bill for the free versions. This means that only a small percentage of the users bring in the company's revenues. Suppliers rightly assume that a sufficient number of users that download the free version will be prepared to pay for the premium version once they got used to the stripped-down version and want to remove its limitations. For similar reasons, software is often provided as a thirty-day free trial version. After thirty days, the software is automatically disabled unless the user buys a licence. Some users may overlook the subtle difference between free software and a free software download and find out that a free download may come with a bill when it is installed. Many online services like Flickr, Dropbox, LinkedIn, and Skype offer a free account with limitations: only heavy users are charged. The digital nature of these companies' services and their worldwide clientele keep prices of the premium version affordable.

Yet another method of transferring costs is crowdfunding. Through the social web, people in networks are invited to financially participate in a business, film, theatre production, game development, or any other project. Crowdfunding is easily facilitated on the web by companies such as Kickstarter, Sponsume, Symbid, and many more. By generating funding in this way, companies bypass regular banks and investors and their usual focus on return for their investments. Even though individuals may each contribute only a small amount of money, the widespread enthusiasm in the network may add up to a substantial budget. For example, the film *The Age of Stupid*, launched in 2009, collected almost 1 million euros through crowdfunding. The model clearly has similarities to charity donations and offertories, although crowdfunding differs in that participants don't contribute because of tradition or habit but because of sympathy for the initiative. And naturally, the idea that one's investment might generate a return is highly motivating.

Digitising business

Not all companies manage to make the most of new digital opportunities. For quite a long time, established industries like publishing, news, and music didn't anticipate the huge potential of the Internet and continued to do the things that they were good at. They seemed to believe that everything would remain the same, so they largely ignored the digital revolution and its impact on products, services, and business models. Many music lovers wondered why they had to pay so much for the music of their favourite artists and bands when music became a digital product which could be easily copied and electronically distributed to a worldwide audience. Year after year, the music industry refused to bring prices down or to use online distribution. Book publishers frenetically maintained their model of printing and distributing paper copies. They unconditionally believed in the power and persistence of books and in the loyalty of their readers to the indelible experiences that books provide. Nothing was going to replace the scent of paper and ink and the tactile sensations of pages slipping through one's fingers. Their readers were lovers of literature who never would replace their bookshelves with a hard disk and a computer screen. They referred to the online bookstore Amazon's difficulties making profits year after year. Similar arguments were made by newspapers, which have been reluctant to digitise distribution for a long time and supposed that print would survive forever. And, they thought, who would be prepared to pay for news on the Internet anyway?

Within one decade, the music industry lost 50 per cent of its worldwide turnover. CD sales diminished as a result of illegal music sharing on the Internet. Music lovers demanded easy online access and affordable prices. Some bands like Radiohead decided to put their music online, where fans could download it for free or pay any amount they found appropriate. The band generated a lot of free publicity and obtained a lot of new fans who were eager to visit the band's live concerts and thus willing to pay considerable entrance fees. Apple's iTunes was the first online music service that showed that online music distribution

179

could be profitable. New music services such as Spotify and Google Music helped the music industry to reverse the decline and re-establish annual growth.

Book publishers have suffered from a similar decline, sometimes over 20 per cent per year. Notwithstanding the romanticism of hard covers and the scent of paper and ink, the demand for e-books skyrocketed. Readers discovered tablets and e-readers and learned to appreciate the advantages of electronic reading: it was easy, cheap, flexible, and lightweight. A whole bookcase could be carried in a handbag. And online bookstores offered additional services such as easily accessible author information, reviews, audiobooks, or even an easy way to order a sweet-smelling hardcover print version. By now companies such as Amazon, Google, and Kobo have demonstrated that e-books are a profitable business.

Similarly, newspapers have struggled with emerging digital technologies. Despite arranging and optimising an electronic workflow and replacing hot lead type with desktop publishing, their focus remained on paper, ink, machines, trucks and drivers, shops and deliverers. They feared converting to online delivery because of unclear revenues. They ran into serious trouble. Advertisers moved their money to online services, which were better able to address specific target groups by the smart exploitation of user data. The number of subscribers decreased year after year due to strangling competition from free websites, including blogs and social media sites, and TV. Also, they realised that in today's information society, it was crazy to ask readers to wait a whole twenty-four hours for the next news release. Newspapers seem to have been outstripped by Twitter, MySpace, and Facebook, which broke through the traditional top-down publishing model by considering their users as an important source of news.

Gradually, however, newspapers have embraced the digital revolution and started to incorporate online content and networking services. They transformed themselves into multimedia concerns that offer their news services across different delivery platforms while maintaining their standards of journalistic quality and reliability. But it's difficult to cover the costs of online news services. Most newspapers have had problems attracting sufficient numbers of advertisers because of the tough competition from other online services. In 2007, the *New York Times* decided to install a paywall for their online services, hoping that their readers would be prepared to pay for them. In the beginning, very few people subscribed, so the model seemed to be a failure. Gradually, more newspapers introduced paid online subscriptions, and people seemed to get used to the idea of paying for additional services such as a 24/7 personalised news feed, the use of a smartphone app, or an overview of news annotated by friends. In the end, the freemium model that worked all right for iTunes and Spotify also seems to work for newspapers.

A matter of scale

Successful Internet companies such as Google, Flickr, and Amazon owe their market position to the large number of users they serve. Their business models are based on social networking principles such as recommendation, user-generated content, viral distribution, and user profiling. Large networks are simply more powerful than small networks. According to Metcalfe's law, in theory, the power of a network is indicated by the number of unique connections between users, which is approximately proportional to the square of the total number of users in the network. If network A has 10 times as many users as network B, it is 100 times more powerful. For users, it is far more attractive to join a large network than a small one because the larger one offers more unique connections. This is very similar to the process of urbanisation: as people move from the countryside to town in search for jobs, big towns grow and prosper while small villages collapse. Metcalfe's law evidently causes a self-establishing effect in favour of large networks: large networks tend to get bigger and bigger, while small networks are likely to fade out. It also means that being the first to start a new type of networking service is essential to that service's success. Companies such as Twitter and Facebook were pioneers in the field. In their early days, they expanded their network communities without any competition. When early competitors showed up, they had a hard time establishing similar businesses because new users preferred to join the largest network available. This mechanism implies that there is simply no room for two or more Facebooks. For all pioneers of an Internet business, scale is a self-fulfilling prophecy: they are likely to become the Internet's monopolists. This mechanism seems to conflict with the open environment that the Internet is. It may impede other parties to enter the same market. A common pattern for achieving fast growth that new start-ups practice today is to smartly join themselves to the success (and size) of market leaders. By using open Internet standards and widgets, start-ups easily integrate their new services with existing services like news feeds, tweets, Like buttons, and other social web tools. In the social web, users may notice many new websites displaying the same set of familiar icons that directly link to existing social networks such as Digg, Flickr, Technorati, YouTube, SlideShare, and Twitter. By applying the OpenID authentication standard, new companies can allow their users to log on to their services using existing Gmail, Yahoo, or Facebook accounts. This helps attract users of existing networks, as they need not create a new account to subscribe to the new service. New companies thus manage to greatly benefit from the power of established leading networks. The latter heartily encourage the newcomers' sponging because it adds to the power of their own networks. Effectively, the social web is no longer a set of separate web services that each attract a community of users but is an extended network of friends sharing different services.

In the material economy, a company's scale is less critical for success because a company's success is determined not by its network characteristics but by its local conditions for production and sales: the presence of raw materials, water, energy, skilled workers, favourable climate, and local people's spending power. Small companies ranging from a jewellery shop to a carpentry or a grocery shop may readily be successful because of their unrivalled craftsmanship or warm-hearted customer service. But digital business is now infiltrating the material economy through online shopping. In recent years, online shopping has expanded enormously. Small-scale shops have a hard time competing with their online counterparts. Online shop owners don't need to let real property and they don't need counters, trolleys, car parks, windows, shop assistants, cashiers, cleaning staff, and so on. They do all their business online: product presentation, ordering, workflow, billing, and aftersales are all arranged via the Internet. They save a lot of costs, which enables them to offer the same products at lower prices. In the worst case, customers visit traditional shops to inspect products and ask shop owners and assistants for advice and then order the product from an online competitor at the lowest price.

Online shops aren't just shops extended with an online outlet. They are a completely different type of business that is similar to a logistics service or just the co-ordination of a logistics service. They could do even without storage and transport, which are easily outsourced. Ultimately, an appropriate website and a back office for co-ordination and customer service would do. Also, customer statistics of an online shop are different. A real-world shop such as a local grocery shop is likely to conform to the Pareto principle, which holds that 80 per cent of the sales are generated by only 20 per cent of the products. These are the fast-moving products that everyone needs such as bread, beans, and beer, and these produce a large turnover. The other 80 per cent of products tend to be less popular and contribute only modestly to sales volume. These slow-moving products are often niche products like Ethiopian chickpea paste or bottles of champagne. Although these may be expensive, they fail to produce high volumes of sales. There are simply too few people living in the grocery's neighbourhood that would demand such niche products. Devotees that live farther away will likely not be prepared to travel all the way down to the shop to buying these.

For online shops, however, distance is irrelevant: they sell to the world. Many remote customers can access an online shop and order whatever niche products they want. This means that, in violation of the Pareto principle, that sales of niche products will go up and online shop owners will aim to offer more of these products that move slowly for brick-and-mortar shops. These may still reflect only small sales volume and limited turnover, but if the online shop owners keep adding such products to their assortment, they will in the end make a big difference: many a little makes a mickle. This explains why online shops are continuously extending their selection: for any slow moving product, they will be able to serve customers on the Internet. Availability has become a precondition. An online bookshop must have the ambition to deliver any title, even if it is only for one customer. But they can easily add other products at the same time such as music, games, DVDs, and toys. Indeed, the website and billing services impose no constraints on the product offerings. There is virtually no reason that would prevent an online bookshop from adding cameras, washing machines, lamps, or wedding dresses to their selection. Ultimately, an online shop is positioned to sell any product one could imagine. Therefore, scale is a decisive factor for online shops, which is in accordance with Metcalfe's law: the more customers the shop attracts, the more powerful its service will be.

The completeness of an online store's product catalogue is not the only factor that encourages customers to shop there. Ordering products through an online portal without the opportunity to physically inspect them or try them out inevitably arouses uncertainty and doubt. Can I trust this shop? Will I receive what I ordered? What if I want to return the product? Online shops shouldn't only offer an informative and usable website with clear product presentations, they should also build a reputation for high-quality service, swift delivery, and trustworthiness to obtain consumers' orders. Otherwise, customers will simply browse over to another online shop. Online shops must strive to be product leaders, to be the best online shop in their segment. Empowering consumers to post public reviews and ratings is a contemporary and effective method for keeping the pressure on. Interestingly, consumers also greatly benefit from price comparison portals, which display the prices that multiple web shops charge for a particular product. The cheapest offer for a particular product is just one mouse click away. Online shops cannot afford to charge higher prices than their competitors for the same products, so online shops are compelled to be both product leaders and price fighters, which is said to be impossible in the material economy: a price fighter will never be a product leader at the same time. This can be done on the Internet, and it must be done. However, doing so comes with investment, increased costs, and reduced margins. These can only be compensated for by volume. Scale is a decisive factor in the digital economy.

The open everything philosophy

"Openness" is the main keyword of the Internet. Internet users are free to decide what online content and services they want to access, to share, to create, or to publish, even though they sometimes have to buy subscriptions or pay fees. The vast majority of websites are freely accessible and offer free music, free software, free videos, free disk space, free blogs, free email, free wikis, free search, and many other free things. They charge only for premium services, for obvious reasons. The openness of the Internet is easily associated with fundamental human rights such as freedom of speech, freedom of press, freedom of expression, and freedom of religion. The Internet uses open standards that anyone can access and use to create their own applications. Open standards are publicly approved protocols and formats for data exchange and data storage, such as TCP/IP, HTTP, HTML, XML, SMTP, DNS, and RSS. Without open standards, the Internet wouldn't exist. They are the invisible lubricants that ease the interoperability of different technologies. Their importance can hardly be overestimated. When video recorders were introduced in the 1980s, the lack of a set standard greatly confused consumers and hampered the adoption of video technologies. Owners of a Sony's Betamax video recorder noticed that they couldn't play their cassettes on their neighbour's Philips V2000 video recorder. Moreover, both systems were incompatible with the VHS recorders made by JVC. Three different proprietary standards competed to become the worldwide video standard. Although the Philips system was commonly regarded as the best system, JVC ultimately won the game and VHS became the standard. All parties were harmed in this battle because it greatly hampered business. In the 1990s companies did everything they could to avoid a repeat of this competition and swiftly agreed on a shared standard for digital video, the DVD. Consumers greatly benefitted from it: now they could play their DVDs on their neighbours' DVD players without concern. All companies capitalised on it.

Beyond open standards is open-source software, or software that gives users and developers access to the source code and its documentation. For a particular application, developers may improve the code, add new applications, port it to new operating systems and processor architectures, or simply review or test existing products. People often claim that open-source software development leads to better quality software and amplifies innovation because it benefits from the collective intelligence of the community as a whole. The self-correcting nature of the open-source community is assumed to yield products that are understandable, well documented, well tested, modifiable, duplicable, and easily accessible. Examples that substantiate these claims are Linux, an operating system that successfully competes with closed-source Microsoft Windows, and Mozilla's Firefox web browser, which helped to open up the browser market that was dominated for a long time by Microsoft's Internet Explorer. The open-source movement is a response to existing business models that rely on confidentiality, trade secrets, and patents, which all seem to conflict with the egalitarian ideals of openness, sharing, and availability to the widest possible population of users. It thus opposes established economic forces and reflects an ideology of pursuing a better world, a better life, and a better future for humankind. This may be partly true, but in the end, there is nothing altruistic about open-source software: it just removes the intellectual-property protections that hamper distribution and usage in order to attract more users and possibly make more money. Renowned commercial software developers like IBM, Oracle, and Novell were prepared to change their business models and adopt the open-source model, which focuses on making money by providing support services rather than licensed software products. Self-interest remains the dominant driving force. Understandably, many businesses are reluctant to relinquish their key assets. Why should Google publicly reveal its sophisticated search optimisation algorithm so that every programmer can launch his or her own Google service? Many companies therefore adopt a mixed model in which they keep their source code closed but conform software interfaces to open standards to support the exchange of data with other systems. Such open application programming interfaces (API) don't necessarily reveal source code, but they allow external parties to connect to the software without needing to know all its secrets.

An analogy to open-source software and open standards is open content, which is any creative work, including text, graphics, photos, audio, or video, that others are allowed to freely use, copy, adapt, or re-distribute. For many centuries, the Bible has been the single example of open content. When the poor could not afford a copy, clergymen were happy to read the holy texts aloud weekly or even daily. However, its openness was accompanied by the simultaneous concealment of rival ideological content. Such a monopolistic position reflects a restrictive doctrine rather than the free exchange of ideas between people. So while the church provided open access to all people, it did not quite offer the opportunity for individuals to freely decide what the truth was. This is markedly different from the openness on the Internet, which assures users freedom of choice from an ever-growing corpus of open content.

In recent years, Creative Commons licenses were introduced to stimulate and facilitate the use, sharing, adaptation, and re-purposing of information, removing the impediments of existing copyright licenses and their legal or financial penalties for violation. Through a variety of licensing schemes, Creative Commons licenses allow copyright holders to grant some of their rights to the public while retaining others. First, Creative Commons made clear that any content on the Internet, be it one's holiday pictures or a recipe, is protected by copyright. Second, the new licenses changed the very common but illegal copy-and-paste practices on the Internet not by imposing even more restrictions or introducing penalties but by offering people certain permissions to copy and repurpose content and making these explicit. A great deal of content available on the web now can be freely copied or adapted, provided that borrowers reference the originator. By doing this, Creative Commons has helped to cleanse the Internet's image as breeding ground for anarchy and unlawfulness. It helped commercial parties to recognise the Internet as a reliable outlet for publishing their content without reservations. And so they do. Renowned companies, news agencies, and TV networks post contents on the web, like many individuals do.

Open content induces a process of self-amplification: it generates more and more content, it fosters knowledge sharing, and offers enhanced opportunities for individuals to inform and express themselves. Its educational significance is beyond doubt. Since 2002, world-renowned universities like MIT, Stanford, and Yale have joined the club and have made courses available for free online. Why? Because it is free publicity that attracts potential students to universities' degree programs (for the required fees). Within a few months after Yale professor Peter Norvig put his open course about artificial intelligence online, more than 100,000 students from all over the world had taken the course. Some idealism is involved too. UNESCO, the United Nations organisation for education, science, and culture, strongly supports open educational resources because it considers education to be the primary condition for civilisation, prosperity, and world peace. While in most Western countries, 50 per cent or more of the population graduate from a higher-education programme, the figure is well below 5 per cent in most developing countries. To raise this number, Africa would need to add hundreds of new universities. The same holds for nations with fast-growing economies such as India, Brazil, and China. Open educational resources enable more people to access education and offer people who live in poverty new opportunities for development. The motto is reuse, revise, remix, and redistribute. This suits the trend of making high-quality materials freely available on the Internet. The movement of openness breaches existing models of business and content by offering alternatives to suit the conditions of the digital networked realm. In the end, it amplifies civilisation at large.

Ideals under attack

The Internet is a huge moneymaker. It may look like an informal playground for volunteers, but it's serious business. Its ideals of freedom and equality may be valuable, but without commercial revenue, the Internet wouldn't exist. It attracts billions of users and provides jobs for millions of people worldwide, just with the simple idea of connecting all computers together. It allows us to easily send and receive emails, upload our holiday pictures, watch online videos, play games, and enter keywords into a search engine to find what we're looking for. We may get a bit impatient when a video doesn't load straight away or when it takes a few seconds for the search engine to collect the millions of answers from all over the world, but it is still a miracle that it all works. To make all this happen, a hidden machinery of routers, switches, antennae, cables, satellites, modems, data centres, servers, access points, security filters, and more need to be controlled and maintained. This Internet infrastructure is the business of a whole range of specialised parties, all of which make good money out of it.

But some make more money than others. The big earners of the Internet are online shops, banks, insurance companies, auction sites, stock exchanges, social networking services, and even newspapers with paywalls. Apparently, using the Internet as a platform for distributing content and services is more profitable than maintaining the infrastructure. Telecommunications companies who own the networks are greatly challenged to keep their networks up to date by the ever-growing number of users and their ever-increasing traffic on the networks. They find themselves confronted with a data explosion. Content is shifting from simple text files to large multimedia files as users increasingly transfer pictures, music, and videos often in high-definition formats. Real-time voice and video transfer through sites such as Skype or YouTube also require additional bandwidth to avoid latency or breakdowns. The growing popularity of cloud services has further extended the volume of data transfer.

All these developments require huge investments in the network's connections, hubs, capacity, and bandwidth. The network market is highly competitive, though. Telecommunications companies have seen revenues decrease because their traditional business of facilitating phone calls is challenged by free alternatives on the Internet. Their mobile networks and SMS services, which were cash cows until recently, are easily bypassed by wireless network connections and free Internet chat (e.g. Whatsapp). Ironically, by facilitating the Internet infrastructure, telecommunications companies cannibalise their own core business and pull a few strings for their competitors. Meanwhile, they see how companies like Google and Facebook take advantage of their networks and hit the jackpot of billions and billions of euros without paying any dues to the infrastructure.

It may seem a logical step to charge these big earners a much larger sum, but this touches on the delicate issue of network neutrality. In order to warrant equal opportunities for all stakeholders to access and exploit the Internet, most governments demand a strict separation between the infrastructure and the services that are hosted on the infrastructure. Telecommunications companies' only task is to transfer data packets, irrespective of their contents and owners. They are not allowed to discriminate between activities online and should treat all contents, sites, and services equally. They may offer more bandwidth or other quality services at a higher price than their competitors, but they are not allowed to prioritise some content at the expense of other content.

The network neutrality principle is a proven concept that has also been used for public utilities like gas, electricity, and water services and public transport. The network of power lines that distribute electricity is independent from the power plants that generate the electricity. The network owner is not allowed to differentiate between or prioritise power suppliers; it is only responsible for appropriate delivery over the network. All power plants should be offered equal opportunities to use of the network. The underlying assumption is that this mechanism creates a fair and competitive energy market in which energy becomes available at the lowest price. Likewise, the network of railways is not allowed to arrange train transport itself. It should offer equal opportunities for all companies that may want to offer transport by rail. Railways owners are not allowed to discriminate between different transporters. On the Internet, network neutrality likewise protects the equality of users and prohibit network operators to prioritise those service providers who would be prepared to pay the highest price for the services. It also prevents manipulations of network traffic, for instance, blocking or filtering selected contents. In principle, network providers agree on this, but they rightly put forward that such restrictions may hamper the network's performance and innovative power. To improving the data flow across a network, a service provider might want to inspect the urgency of the packets to be sent. When a transmission line or a network server is overloaded, operators might want to de-prioritise asynchronous services like email in favour of time-critical services like audio or video. No one would mind an email delay of a few seconds or even a few hours, but a small delay in a streaming video immediately affects the quality of playback. However, such deep packet inspection is prohibited by law. Network operators must stay away from content. It seems that so far, the principle of preserving the Internet as an open and egalitarian platform is widely supported, especially for commercial reasons.

CHAPTER 15

The Game of Technology

Any statement claiming that new technologies will change our society is indebted to technological determinism, which is the idea that technology is the driving force of social change. Even more, deterministic diehards like the Frenchman Jacques Ellul consider technology to be an autonomous power, one not controlled by human thought. They view technology not as the outcome of societal processes but as a self-propelling and self-amplifying force. The oldest tools, no more that sharp-edged stones, date to 2.5 million years ago, and their manifest utility for cutting and carving has rigorously shaped social practices. We adapted our hunting practices to the opportunities that this new technology provided. The razor-sharp stones proved useful aids for cutting meat and tubers but also became popular for negative practices like killing neighbours. Technology creates its own purposes, and its effects are likely to be unpredictable, or at least unforeseen. Many more examples falsify the simple but inadequate view that technology only fulfils our needs.

Most inventions create new demands that would never have surfaced without them. Nobody desired telephones, televisions, or computers, but nowadays we couldn't do without them. Market research about customer needs rarely produces useful information: customers don't demand imaginary products that are still to be invented. We rarely deny its leading role, but accepting its autonomy as a fact of life could easily lead to apathy and impotence. Governments, technology developers, and individuals should never deny their responsibilities to develop and use technology wisely. Adverse affects of nuclear weapons and nuclear technologies have led to stringent regulations of their use and proliferation across the world, demonstrating that society is to some extent capable of controlling and restricting harmful technological developments. In the case of nuclear weapons, however, control is dominated by political interests and power relations. Ironically, a well-meant ban on nuclear arms development is enforced by those exact parties who already have nuclear weapons at their disposal and perhaps don't want to give up their leading position. On the commercial battlefield, however, corrective interventions such as bans are highly unlikely since creating new demand is the *sine qua non* for maintaining a profitable business. That's why the market is continually flooded with new pills, new materials, new tools, new tablets, and new smartphones aimed at triggering new demand, new behaviours, and new societal structures.

Meeting the Internet's growth

In 1995, the Dutch telephone system was subjected to a massive update. The telephone network was composed of more than thousand small regional networks that used their own coding systems for assigning subscriber numbers. Most subscriber numbers were eight digits long (not counting the mandatory 0 as the first digit), which would, in theory, be enough for a hundred million subscribers. In practice, however, the actual number of extensions was much lower because for technical reasons not all digit combinations were allowed. The eight-digit system dated back to the 1950s, but in the early 1990s, a shortage of telephone numbers surfaced as a result of steady population growth. Potential subscribers were put on a waiting list because all possible phone numbers were in use. New customers had to wait until existing subscribers cancelled their contracts, or died. Along with the restructuring of the network in 1995, the extension numbers were enlarged to nine digits, allowing ten times more subscribers. This should be enough for the next few hundred years.

A similar shortage of extension numbers happened on the Internet. The number of IP addresses, which are the unique extension numbers that identify computers on the Internet, is limited by current coding standards, which date back to the early days of ARPANET, the Advanced Research Projects Agency Network, which was the main predecessor of the Internet. In the 1980s, long before anyone could imagine the Internet's true impact, the standard for IP addresses was established as a thirty-two-bit number, which allowed for 4.3 billion unique addresses. At the time, no one could foresee that within three decades this huge number of addresses would turn out to be insufficient. If someone raised such a doubt, he would have gotten nothing but laughter in response. But today, the rapid expansion of the Internet has caused such a problem. Over the last fifteen years, Internet connections have proliferated to each household. Whereas in the 1990s, you would have been the exception if you had Internet access, today you would be the exception if you don't have Internet access. Also, the number of computers per person increased, not to mention the number of computers in offices, schools, and other institutions and the emergence of smartphones for accessing the Internet. Especially in the new economies of Asia, especially in China and India, a shortage of Internet addresses is a reality.

Already in 1996, a new IP-address standard was proposed. The IPv6 standard encodes the addresses as a 128-bit number rather than a 32-bit number. These numbers are deceptive: the number of 128-bit addresses is not 4 times the number of 32-bit addresses, as for every extra bit, the number increases by a power of 2. As a result, the number of addresses in IPv6 would be 2 to the power of 128, which yields a 38-digit number, or 300 trillion trillion addresses. This huge number should be sufficient for quite a while (according to today's insights). The new standard has been accepted and approved by all thinkable technical standards bodies and networking hardware companies. However, the transition from the 32-bit standard to the 128-bit version is complex because the two protocols aren't interoperable. The implementation, which started in 2006, will not be completed before 2020.

The demand for more internet addresses demonstrates the immense popularity of the Internet. Over the years, we have seen it grow tremendously. We have also seen its function and usage gradually change. In the early years, the Internet was dominated by pages on the World Wide Web, basically a collection of pages linked to each other via hyperlinks. Its main function was to publish electronic text, which was often conceived as an add-on to print publishing. Even the term "page" refers to what we've been acquainted with for ages: the book. This demonstrates that the disruptive nature of a new technology is often overlooked since new technologies tend to be assessed within the framework of existing models, habits, and preferences. Web pages could include images, but many users switched their browsers to text mode in order to avoid unwanted delays as they downloaded with their 28 kilo-baud dial-up modems. When bandwidth and therefore speed increased, the World Wide Web became a true multimedia platform featuring text, pictures, colours, animation, and even videos. Search engines flourished: they assist users in finding answers to their questions, and the web always had the answers. In the next stage, the Internet became a network of people rather than a network of pages. People were no longer limited to reading. Now they could also send messages to each other with email, in chats, and on forums. People could now debate, comment, complain, or date and could form communities and work groups on the Net. Today the main value of the Internet still lies in its ability to connect people and to harvest their creativity and collective intelligence.

The next stage in the evolution of the Internet was the addition of web services. Technically, a web service is a simple request over the web from one computer to another. Examples are currency conversion, a weather report, the video stream of a remote webcam, or a service that calls up the inventory of a warehouse.

Web services are based on open standards and can be used to connect to any application or operating system. This means that they connect different applications or platforms that are not necessarily designed for or capable of exchanging data. All these separate web services are reusable and can be combined in applications distributed across multiple computers. The web services architecture has greatly enhanced the opportunities for arranging transactions over the Internet, either in e-business, e-learning, e-health, or any other virtualised domain. For instance, the online booking of a flight is fully based on web services, which check the flight schedules of different airline companies, the available seats, the prices, and alternate routes plus information about hotels and public transport at the destination city, and then provide billing and secure payment. Another example is mash-ups: these are web applications that combine different data sources that present aggregate information. For instance, web services could be used for linking Google maps data and GPS-tagged pictures or trajectories into an aggregated map. Mash-ups like these are an important driver both for developing new Internet business and enhancing creative collaboration on the social web. The Internet of web services is an interoperability breakthrough that provided the foundations for e-business and social media.

The next stage of the Internet is on its way: the Internet of Things. The idea is to extend the Internet to material objects by equipping them with Internet addresses. Many objects ranging from security cameras to pacemakers are already able to communicate over the Internet to remote computers and other devices. They can report their states or change their behaviours depending on circumstances. More and more objects are provided with electronic sensors and actuators to interact with their material environment. An automatic door opener would be an informative example: it uses a sensor to detecting movement, it uses internal logic to evaluating the detected signal, and without human interference, it can open the door by activating a small electrical motor. Satellite cameras and weather sensors may be linked via the network for improving weather forecasts.

Smart pills could measure the degree of acidity in your intestinal tract and inform your doctor or autonomously adapt the dose to be released. The Internet has been or could be extended to cars, airplanes, fridges, heating systems, trees, animals, houses, lawn mowers, books, billboards, pencils, bottles of beer, your keys, or any other object you can think of that can carry an IP address and a sensor or actuator.

Microscopic smart objects for medical or biological purposes are well within reach since today's smallest RFID chips for wireless communication are hardly visible to the naked eye. By linking all these objects to the Internet, we gain new sources of information and new forms of network interaction. No longer will the information on the Internet be exclusively created by and controlled by human actors. In the Internet of Things, objects will interact with each other to autonomously produce and record new behaviours. Two, three, or more smart micro-pills floating in the bloodstream may combine their data over the Internet in order to better establish the state of the body and negotiate the optimal ratio of medications to release. Objects become dynamic agents in their own right. Some objects already send tweets and have their own Facebook pages.

One may wonder why on earth the new Internet protocol was stretched to such a crazy large number of IP addresses (300 trillion trillion), exceeding the size of the world population (7 billion) by far. The Internet of Things may be the reason. With RFID antennae becoming smaller than a grain of sand, the number of objects that can be included in the Internet is virtually infinite. In accordance with Metcalfe's law, the addition of so many things would greatly increase the Internet's power. The large address space of the IPv6 standard would enable us to assign Internet addresses to every single grain of sand on Earth, and more. There are almost no limits to the Internet of things. At a certain point, there will be more things than humans on the Internet. A world like that would approach a world of autonomous agents creating their own ecosystem without the permanent control of human agents. We're witnessing a breathtaking time.

Welshing on the rules

Generally, the viability of a new technology is best understood by its robustness and resistance to sabotage. For networked devices, this doesn't seem to apply: they sell like hot cakes even though they are readily infected by Trojan horses, spyware, worms, and viruses that allow third parties to access private data or even to take over control. Internet security is an arms race between hackers and security experts. The hackers try to get in while the security experts try to keep them out. In practice, hackers are consistently one or even two steps ahead of the security experts, who often have to look upon successful invasions with sorrow. It doesn't seem to bother consumers too much, as they happily buy the devices and use them for their electronic banking and other private activities. In 2009, hackers managed to steal millions of credit card records by infecting the computers of Heartland Payment Systems, the company that processes the payments for Visa and MasterCard. Of course, this was a painful incident, but the security hole was swiftly fixed so that it wouldn't happen again. In 2011, Visa and MasterCard, along with American Express and Discover Financial Services, had to announce that hackers had once again successfully accessed the data of 1.5 million cardholders, this time by accessing the computers of Global Payment.

For criminals, such hacking is a lucrative business. Credit card operators, banks, insurers, and public organisations are all favoured targets because they serve large audiences and process numerous transactions each day. Each new attack is more sophisticated than the last. It's not fair to always blame the security experts for the successful hacks. First, intruders may take advantage of security weaknesses that are beyond security experts' control, such as holes in computer operating systems or faulty encryption standards rather than the firewalls, applications, or databases that they are responsible for. Second, in software development, security tends to be a closing entry. Security issues are complex, restrictive, and costly, and the highest priority for developers and their customers is to create software that runs and does the things it is designed to do. This appears hard. One of the big problems in cyber crime is that no one really knows how big the problem really is. Hacked parties seldom announce publicly that they're hacked because it would affect their reputation. They maybe as leaky as a sieve, but banks and insurers prefer to keep quiet since they fear losing their e-banking customers. Increasingly, governments prepare new legislation that require victims to report hacks that compromise personal data.

Not all hackers are true criminals. In 2012, a seventeen-year-old schoolboy in the Netherlands hacked into customer files of Internet provider KPN. His was probably a naïve action, done just for fun and not to make any money. Still, the email accounts of two million customers of KPN had to be closed, which was not just inconvenient: it caused many problems in trade and other areas. The boy got caught by showing off to a sixteen-year-old fellow hacker in Australia. Some hacker groups such as Anonymous and Lulzsec adopt an ideological stance. In 2010, Anonymous attacked MasterCard's site and brought it down because MasterCard had announced that it would reject any financial transactions of whistle-blower organisation WikiLeaks.

Hackers and scientists also claim to fight for a good cause by deliberately hacking security systems in order to reveal their vulnerabilities and make them public so they can be improved. Their findings are embarrassing and sobering. A wide range of organisations such as banks, local authorities, police departments, armies, transporters, chemical plants, and hospitals are regularly confronted with unexpected security holes in their systems. They report motley hacked sites and devices, including money transfer systems, dating sites, online shops, patient files, video conferences, oil pipelines, wireless encryption keys, as well as cash cards, electronic gates, electronic car keys, fountains, public transport smart cards, swimming pool installations, even pacemakers that use IP addresses for software updates have been found to be vulnerable to intruders. Their work is not always appreciated; it's often regarded as a criminal act. Even so, they receive a lot of sympathy.

The authorities themselves do a lot of hacking too. Police departments' criminal investigation units do a lot of spying on the Internet while investigating organised crime or hooliganism as a logical extension of traditional shadowing and wiretapping. In 2012, the national terrorism co-ordinator in the Netherlands reported alarming security weaknesses in shipping locks, pumping stations, bridges, sewers, and tunnels, which all are essential for keeping the water out of the areas below sea level. Evildoers might easily hack this machinery and inundate towns and estates at will. When it comes to terrorism, espionage, or national security, governments have no reservations breaking into enemies' computer systems. Such cases of cyber warfare are seldom brought into the open. In 2012, we witnessed the Stuxnet worm that managed to bring down the centrifuges of five Iranian nuclear organisations that were suspected to contribute to internationally condemned uranium enrichment. The sources of this worm were never identified, but they are assumed to be an international governmental conspiracy that aims to hamper Iran's presumed nuclear arms programme.

Securing the Internet's openness

Computer security requires shielding and encryption to ensure that system software, data, and traffic are accessible only to those parties that use the correct passwords and encryption keys. If encryption is used, messages may be intercepted, but they cannot be deciphered without the key. Julius Caesar was among the first to use a cipher. To sending secure messages, he simply replaced each letter in the text with an alternative letter three places further down the alphabet: the word "Rome" would thus show up as "Urph"; "Cleopatra" translates to "Fohrsdwud". Today, Caesar's cipher would be highly unsecure. A computer ignorant of Caesar's encoding method can rapidly decode the message by analysing the frequency of the letters it uses and consulting a lexicon to identify valid word patterns. For instance, the highest-frequency character of a message in Latin is likely to be an E or T, and the lowest a Q or a Z.

Today's ciphers are far more complex. They don't use simple letter shifts or swaps but are based on complex mathematics, including number theory, combinatorics, and the peculiarities of prime numbers. Data on the Internet needs to be secured not just to protect it against theft or adjustments but also to support authentication, which is the process of verifying the identities of both the sender and the receiver of a message. It should also preserve privacy, which means that only the intended and authenticated receiver is able to read the message and no one else, it should assure that the message was not changed during transport, and it should warrant that it was really the sender who posted this message and no one else. Today's encryption keys are much larger than the single digit that Caesar used. Even so, a computer could break just about any code provided that it has sufficient time to work on it. This means that there is always a trade-off between the complexity of encryption and the effort needed to break the code. In recent years, the length of standard encryption keys had to be enlarged in order to resist brute-force attacks by ever more powerful computers. In the future, we will need even larger keys because of the unrivalled speed of anticipated electron-spin computers and quantum computers that will be capable of breaking current keys on the fly. These technical considerations are essential for preserving trusted communications over the Internet.

Although technical flaws in security regularly show up, users themselves appear to be the weakest link in system security. Many users of the Internet seem to be unaware of the crucial role of encryption in the software they use for their daily routines such as sending emails, accessing a wireless channel, or making online payments. Their password management is notoriously sloppy. Passwords are often so obvious (John123, Papa, Park_Avenue, Alice&Bob, or even the term "password") that other people can easily guess the secret code. Users note down their passwords on paper and stick them on the computer as an easy reminder, they use their browser's password retrieval function, which is convenient but inappropriate, or they are just loose lipped and are happy to share their passwords with other people. Such naïveté is counterproductive. It reflects the wrong type of openness. The pursued openness of the Internet is the free exchange of thoughts and the unhampered sharing of resources by its inhabitants. Paradoxically, such openness requires secrecy. The whole idea of open communication breaks down if we cannot be certain about the identity of the person that we're talking to, if we cannot be certain that our messages are received by the person we aim to address, if we cannot be certain that our message reaches the recipient unaltered, and if the recipient cannot be certain that the message was indeed sent by us. Openness on the Internet derives its significance from secure communications.

The limits to growth

A severe handicap of life is the unidirectional nature of time. Every single step in time opens up a little bit of future while relegating the previous step to history. We can recall the past and we can see the present, but we cannot see the future until it arrives. Whatever we use to foretell the future, such as magic cards, crystal balls, palm reading, dowsing rods, prayers, doped oracles, or any other spiritual trick, we cannot but accept that the future remains an impenetrable stronghold lying well beyond our power. Even advanced scientific models are unable to predict what tomorrow's world will look like, as we may conclude from weather forecasts and economic prognoses. The future is our blind spot. To anticipate the future, we naturally extrapolate from the past. A company that has demonstrated 10 per cent growth year after year is likely to prognosticate 10 per cent growth for the next year, if not 11 or even 12 per cent to indicate their ambition. Likewise, we've seen tremendous growth in new technologies over the last decades, which makes a prediction of continued growth a safe guess. The notion of growth itself is a major foundation of modern society that is inherently linked with today's liberal democracy and its drive for innovation, economic performance, and competitive business.

In his book *The World Is Flat*, Thomas Friedman explains what the impact of new digital technologies will be. He anticipates an intensified globalisation process that enables individuals and companies to compete globally at the expense of existing national and regional powers. The Internet will overcome the handicaps of distance and geography by enabling new online services and improved tools for worldwide communication and collaboration: wherever we are on Earth, we will be connected. With its focus on competition, the book also preserves the concept of growth. The absence of barriers to global competition implies that the world metaphorically will become flat. Although this vision involves a radical change of the way the economy will function, by describing a gradual transformation to a true global economy, Friedman's future scenario is a logical extrapolation of the developments we've seen in recent years.

Taking a more technological stand, Ray Kurzweil, as indicated in earlier chapters, predicts a singularity in the near future beyond which technological intelligence will structurally exceed biological intelligence. From that point in time, superhuman intelligence will accelerate technological development and bring about new technological artefacts with unrivalled qualities. Technologies will augment our mental capabilities through brain-computer interfaces and will integrate our minds with the environment. This picture of the future, although grounded in existing knowledge, differs from a straightforward extrapolation of the past in that it includes a discontinuity (the singularity), which disrupts the course of events and produces a new paradigm for societal development. Both Friedman and Kurzweil see technology as the main driver for societal change. Both presuppose continued growth and reflect considerable optimism about the productive role of technology.

Another optimistic view of the future is given by chemist James Lovelock. His Gaia hypothesis considers Earth to be a complex, self-organised system that uses negative feedback mechanisms to maintain the conditions for life, which is accompanied by a strong conviction of Earth's resilience to disruptions. This suggests that any negative impacts of technology on the environment will trigger a natural response in the ecosystem that will counteract the impact. In the extreme case, people could refer to this optimist hypothesis as their reason for rejecting responsibility for environmental destruction caused by human activity: Earth will be all right whatever evil things we might do. This prediction may readily lead to laziness and the shirking of responsibilities. But this is a moral judgement rather than a scientific argument.

Like optimistic ideas of the future, many pessimistic views exist, some of which are faith-based views that anticipate apocalyptic events such as the end of humanity, the end of the world, or even the end of time. One of the very first scientific studies that called attention to the negative effects of continued growth was the report *The Limits to Growth*, prepared in 1972 by the Club of Rome, a group of scientists. The Club of Rome used computational models and systems analysis to deriving scenarios about the future of the planet, including global data on agricultural productivity, available natural resources, birth control, population growth, and economic growth. It turned out that in all scenarios, drastic environmental measures were required to prevent a breakdown of the planet's social and ecological systems. The political measures they called for failed to appear. Nevertheless, the report has helped to put this topic on the political agenda.

Since its publication, many new studies on the limited carrying capacities of the Earth have appeared. In his books *The Party's Over* and *Powerdown*, Richard Heinberg elaborates on the extreme consequences of energy shortages resulting from the exhaustion of fossil fuels when alternative energy resources cannot compensate for it. Computers already require a substantial portion of available electricity. Their demand even outperforms traditional industrial sectors. Heinberg sketches a distressing future where the industrial infrastructure of production collapses, all transportation and communication disappear, and electronic data become irretrievable. Without electronic tools, we will lose our symbolic content and the knowledge associated with it. The whole idea of globalisation appears to be a fallacy. The economy, if we still have one, will be only local or regional. The notions of growth and progress deteriorate into a delusion, a fantasy of former days when people still believed that energy supplies were limitless. Heinberg does show some optimism, however, as he discusses opportunities for energy-saving technologies, renewable energy, and new appreciation for local products.

No one can predict the future. All these scenarios may turn out to be incorrect. Even if they do, they keep us vigilant of technology's role in society and help us to exert our influence by voting for sensible decisions that avoid any negative impacts. It does matter.

CHAPTER 16
The Mental Delusions of Media

The human mind is gifted with limitless imaginative powers. These have enabled us to bring forth a wide range of ingenious concepts and assets that make up human culture. Some are useful (e.g. penicillin), some are evil (e.g. gun powder), and some fundamentally contribute to higher standards of human civilisation (e.g. writing). Our perception of reality is highly subjective and biased by our expectations, fears, and hopes. We are destined to live in our self-woven web of rituals, cultural codes, contradictions, and half and full truths. In the main, we are well aware of these limitations. We recognise the tension between science and religion, but, of course, we practice both. Naturally, we realise that horoscopes and playing cards are unable to tell fortunes, but still we like to rely on them. Likewise, we comply with the latest fashion trends although we are well aware of its arbitrary nature, its lack of rationale. The paradox is that we recognise our irrationality and at the same deny it. We may fully understand that the events in a horror movie are completely fictitious, but the film may still frighten us to death. To enjoy the film experience, we need to be willing to neglect our knowledge about the movie industry, studios, actors, directors, monster animators, special effects, budgets, and so on and prepared to fool ourselves by pretending that all we see and hear is really happening. This willing suspension of disbelief enables us to be carried away by the story and to live through emotions that we cannot afford to display in everyday life. In the safe environment of the movie theatre, we allow ourselves to shiver, to cry, or to fume. We use our imagination to have a good time. Our willing suspension of disbelief allows us to experience and express our emotions without the risks associated with doing so in daily life. Despite the tears and shivers, we remain in control. As Jean-Paul Sartre noted, these emotions aren't real: we play along with the game, which sparks our imagination and allows us to vent our emotions. We are willing to do so until we choose to pull the safety valve and withdraw our suspension of disbelief. It seems our rational mind is capable of overruling ourselves. Or is it the other way round: are we overruling our imaginative mind? Do we control the media we use, or are the media controlling us?

Within or beyond our control

The question of whether we are in control touches upon philosophical issues such as determinism, causality, free will, and the relationship between mind and body. The idea that we have free will and are in control of our behaviours is challenged by the theory of causal determinism, which states that all future events are fully determined by the past. The solidification of the Earth's crust, the formation of the atmosphere, thunderstorms, lightning, waves at sea, rocks tumbling down a mountain, all thinkable events are governed by the laws of nature and are the result of causal events in the past. To a determinist, life is just another process subjected to and determined by natural laws. Determinism is a gloomy perspective because it would deprive us from our free will and our role as an independent agent. The problem with determinism is that it defines people's behaviour as the product of previous events and conditions that are outside their influence. This means that people cannot be held responsible for their actions. If the course of events were fully determined, how could we blame people for the mistakes they make? Even serial killers would end up in heaven. Strict determinism is not tenable, or at least it is not correct.

Philosophers like Descartes and Popper claim that the notion of free will transcends the concepts of the natural sciences and its causal laws, and therefore cannot be rejected. Our society pragmatically assumes that humans have free will. Of course we have: we're blamed for every infringement or mistake we make. If we drive too fast, we will be punished with a ticket because the behaviour is not considered an unfortunate combination of events but a deliberate action that we are responsible for. Stealing a TV would land us in jail. We suppose humans are anything but puppets or robots, which are just subjected to the laws of mechanics. We are independent minds, we have free will. We choose our actions. We decide if we stand up or sit down. We are fully responsible for our actions and their consequences.

Nevertheless, society allows many exceptions to this rule. For instance, free will is a scarce good in the Army. Generals seem to prefer strict discipline and obedience rather than reflection, creativity, or wisdom. The best soldiers are those deprived of free will. Soldiers are just supposed to follow orders. Fair enough—in a crisis, you don't want to entertain lengthy discussions. To some extent, soldiers are dehumanised. In the worst case, they turn into immoral robots. Trained to fight, they commit war crimes unthinkingly. Likewise, in court, perpetrators are often declared not to be of sound mind (*non compos mentis*), which means that they somehow lost control of their mind and cannot be held responsible for their actions. Some unknown processes seem to have elbowed out their free will. People may lose control of their mind through personality disorders, psychoses, hallucinations, or drugs; they may be possessed by demons; or they may be just cracked. They may have committed the worst crimes imaginable, killed their children or parents, but they don't get punished. Instead, they can look forward to sustained medical or psychological treatment.

Some recent research seems to challenge the notion of free will. Neuroscientists in Germany have discovered that the human brain makes decisions up to ten seconds before people even realise they've decided. The researchers used a brain imaging technique that allowed them to monitor a subject's brain activity in real time during decision making. From the brain activity patterns, the researchers were able to predict what choice people would make long before the people themselves were even aware of having made a decision. This suggests that conscious thought lags behind an unconscious decision-making process governed by autonomous brain cell activity. The brain may make us believe that we are conscious decision makers that have free will, but the research seems to suggest that before we make our decision, the brain has made up its mind already. We know that our nervous system controls all kinds of useful processes without our conscious interference: the heartbeat, breathing, and digestion are all controlled by our autonomous nervous system. That's why we stay alive even after fainting or while sleeping. The fact that our brain is autonomously interfering with conscious decision making is hard to understand. Perhaps we aren't so different from those who are declared not to be of sound mind. It is possible that we have less free will than we're happy to admit.

Fooled by our brain

Everything we perceive from the world around us, either by seeing, hearing, smelling, tasting or feeling, is the combined product of our sense organs and our brain. Perception involves active cognitive processes in which sensory inputs are filtered, filled in, transformed, and compared with other inputs to build an inferentially consistent and stable view of the world. This all has to take place quickly during our continuous interactions with the environment. Catching a ball that is thrown in our direction requires continuous estimations of distance, speed, and curve to make sure that we don't miss it. The dynamic and ongoing perception-action cycle makes high demands on the processing power of our brain. Due to limited brain resources, there's trade-off between speed and accuracy. We draw rapid conclusions based on probabilistic extrapolations from a limited set of data: our brain makes estimates, fills in gaps, and neglects details that are supposed to be irrelevant. This makes perception a highly imperfect process. In many cases, we just make a wild guess and hope for the best.

To a large extent, we can rely on our existing knowledge of the world. We immediately recognise a ball and know what it means, and the same is true of any other objects or events that we are familiar with: traffic lights, helicopters, dogs, elevators, a plate of macaroni, and many other things. When we notice any new object, we immediately check our mental inventory to categorise it. Indeed, we try to understand the world on the basis of the things we know already. Notwithstanding our curiosity, this suggests that we face the world with some built-in conservatism. Recognising things we're familiar with eases our minds, while confronting new, unknown things, such as a space ship or a creepy insect, alarms us and undermines our certainties. To arrive at a consistent and robust world view, we constantly look for confirmation of our ideas rather than refutation. People readily thought of the first motorised vehicles as traditional carts. Admittedly, at the time, they very much looked like traditional carts and travelled at about the same speed. We readily interpret new technologies as extensions of existing ones. We don't like paradigm shifts. Most e-learning applications and e-learning management systems are strictly modelled after traditional classroom teaching. They create the virtual classroom, which is probably an unnecessary restriction for true educational innovation. We assign greater value to things and ideas that agree with existing knowledge than to those that differ with it. This is understandable, because our meaningful understanding of the world can only be based on our existing knowledge and experiences.

This all means that our perception is highly driven and biased by our prejudices, expectations, and theories of the world. We don't necessarily see what really is the case. We see what we would prefer to be the case, and we believe that we see it rightly. Interpretation highly depends on viewpoint. Taxi drivers view their automobiles as valuable sources of income; mechanics view them as interesting technological constructions that might need a repair; scrap dealers only see the metal, plastic, and reusable parts that might yield some money; while pedestrians perceive them as an impediment to safely crossing the street. Upon encountering a man with a long beard, a barber would rely on his professional experience and judge the quality of the beard and the way it is styled, a child might suspect that this man is Santa Claus or at least a good lookalike, while a security officer or a xenophobic might ridiculously panic and raise an alarm because they see a terrorist threat. Likewise, we're ready to see flying saucers, hobgoblins, and elves. We fantasise our way through the world and believe that what we see is true. We are the unresisting victims of our own imagination. The main problem is that we're not aware of it.

The pattern is quite different from the willing suspension of disbelief, which is largely under our control. Actors in the theatre can easily make us imagine that the empty stage is a restaurant, a church, or a sitting room, as long as we permit ourselves to be dragged along by the play's narrative. Likewise, we may want to deny things we happen to see because they conflict with our beliefs. Most people don't want to see gnomes or flying saucers because they don't believe these exist. This is a fair position, but what if on sunny day, a flying saucer appeared up in the sky? This would create a fundamental conflict between facts and beliefs. Such conflict is generally resolved by our brain by neglecting the facts in favour of the beliefs. Psychologists call this mechanism cognitive dissonance: it preserves the integrity of our beliefs at the expense of our perception. We will always find an excuse to explain that it wasn't our fault that this antique vase broke into pieces. Creationists will always find arguments that the world is only 6,000 years old. Politicians are supposed to espouse stable and well-substantiated beliefs. Whatever practical evidence they encounter that goes against their beliefs, be it about financing deficits, unemployment, the bank crisis, or criminality, they will persist in their beliefs by simply denying the evidence or twisting the facts. Cognitive dissonance is nothing like deliberate lying—it is the unwitting denial of unwelcome facts. It is being unwittingly fooled by our own brains.

Fooled by media

Mediated communication is loaded with bias and distortion. We're well aware of the coloured messages of commercial advertisements, political news shows, and feature films. We know that directors, journalists, and editors use all the powers of style and narrative to portray a world that favours their arguments. Even though we may realise that all media present a truncated and distorted view of reality, they manage to bypass our cognitive filters and address primitive, subconscious, emotional seats of mental activity that lie beyond our control. We may know that we're fooled, but we cannot resist. That's why we still buy the latest washing powders, shoes, smartphones, and tablets. In 1957 market researcher James Vicary claimed that displaying words and images so briefly that people don't even notice them consciously still changes their thoughts and behaviours. He added the messages "drink Coca-Cola" and "eat popcorn" to a film for such a very short time that viewers didn't consciously notice them. Such subliminal messages, messages that never reach our conscious awareness, were supposed to provide great new opportunities for marketing and advertising. Of course, the practice raised a lot of protests because people feared unnoticed brainwashing campaigns by governments, advertisers, or anyone else who might want to influence opinions unobtrusively. In many countries, subliminal marketing was legally banned. Many years later, James Vicary admitted fraud: he had fabricated his results. He withdrew his scientific claim. Every now and then, the idea shows up again, for instance, when heavy metal bands are accused of including satanic messages or inciting suicide in their songs. Recent brain research shows that our sensory threshold is lower than our perceptive threshold, which means that our senses are able to detect subliminal stimuli and forward the information to our brain, completely bypassing conscious awareness. Functional MRI scans of the brain show that subliminal messages indeed activate specific brain regions while the subject remains unaware of the messages. It is unclear whether they would have any impact on our thoughts or behaviours. Evidence for that is lacking or, at best, weak and inconsistent. Still, some people got the message and make a lot of money with subliminal advertising services. If they worked, we would be helpless.

Not all of our responses to media arise from the subconscious. Sometimes our rational mind pragmatically interferes so that we gain more benefits from media usage. Having a telephone conversation is anything but straightforward. It is an elementary form of telepresence, or mentally being somewhere other than where the body is. This is confusing since it seems to violate both the inseparability of body and mind and the natural laws of space, distance, matter, and time that govern the world. It is hard to understand why our 100,000-year-old brain is capable of dealing with the confusing phenomena of mediated communication at all, but apparently it is: we readily adapt to new technologies. Dogs or cats wouldn't be able to do so, although fear or confusion can make them respond to mediated sounds or images.

During a phone call, the conversation partners mentally project themselves into a shared location and bring along their full repertory of communication acts, including facial expressions and gestures, even though the other party cannot see these. We imagine that we're transferred to the virtual place and act accordingly. Even worse, we also smile and gesture when a computer voice is on the other end. According to the media equation theory of Byron Reeves and Clifford Nass, we are not capable of distinguishing between mediated communication and direct communication. We treat our media as if they were human. We freely cheer and jeer during a sports broadcast (but no one can hear us), and we curse the computer if it isn't prepared to do the things we want it to do (but this doesn't help). We do so because there are no alternatives. From an evolutionary perspective, the only purpose of our communicative skill is communicating with other people.

We simply lack the neural circuits that could make the distinction between communication with media and with real humans. We know that we're talking to devices, but our responses are authentic. As Reeves and Nass state, our old brains are fooled by new technologies. The dynamic, communicative properties of media, be they TVs, music players, or computers, cause them to surpass simple, replaceable tools.

Because of the content media provide, we perceive them as personae which fully take part in our social and natural environment. Our responses to media are social and natural, if not intuitive, spontaneous, and emotional. That's why we can deal so easily with new technologies. Even toddlers use computers, phones, and TVs without effort. We have natural and positive emotional responses to objects, including dolls, cars, cups, clothes, computers, and our smartphones. Generally, our responses are more empathic and intense when the objects are more humanlike: we prefer teddy bears to bricks; we like chimpanzees better than spiders. Problems arise, however, when the objects look too humanlike. Japanese robot scientist Hiroshi Ishoguro built an artificial replica of himself using the newest skin-like materials and detailed facial-expression actuators to achieving maximum resemblance and realism. The effect is both confusing and frightening. Instead of responding positively, people are repulsed. Talking to a computer or a doll is much easier than talking to a realistically humanlike robot. The same effect occurs with humanlike artificial characters in video games and movies. They scare us. The theory of this anomaly is known as the "uncanny valley effect". Our natural communication remains intact for fellow humans and for those objects that are manifestly different from humans. But when the object's resemblance to a human gets close to perfection, we will readily detect the slightest deviations from humanness. These produce alarming effects. For the same reason, we would detest a soft-skinned artificial hand or an artificial ear as much as we detest dead bodies. They may look real, but they aren't. Even plastic surgery can have a sinister impact. We don't like to be fooled.

The genuine power of today's media is in the ever-growing dynamics of displayed images and sounds. Watching TV, playing a video game, or viewing a web page is no less than a delight for our senses. Every day thousands and thousands of high-quality images pass through our screens and offer us a fascinating spectacle that is hard to resist. Our eyes are tickled by the slightest changes in our visual range, and our ears notice any subtle change in sounds. Ringtones, beeps, jingles, videos, colour cycling, animated banners, and scrolling text instantaneously draw our attention. We take static elements for granted, but we will notice any changing pixel. That's how our perception works. We share this feature with most animals. Birds, cats, rabbits, mice, and even flies continuously keep an eye on the environment to anticipate danger. It is a favourable trait for survival. All species that neglected their surroundings are extinct, dispatched by their predators. This explains why we still exist. Now that most of our predators have been either wiped out, tamed, or banished to natural reserves, our attention is caught by our electronic devices. Upon checking our smartphone, playing a video game, or simply working at our computer, we're likely to be absorbed by the activity. We seem to be mentally immersed in an alternate digital world that is fully separate from the physical world we live in. If this persists for some time, we may reach the state of cognitive flow, which goes with high concentration on a task, engrossment, and an altered sense of time. We seem to have teleported to this digital world, and we completely ignore our surroundings. For any predator, we would be an easy prey. Today, we can see the consequences of this effect in the large number of road accidents resulting from phone use while driving or while crossing the street.

Different from animals' attention, our attention goes with intensive cognitive processing. Our wakeful attention inevitably turns into concentration, which is deep, focused thinking. Every perceived cue triggers a sense-making process, which involves evoking existing knowledge schemata, hypothesising, fantasising, interpreting, inferring, and many more things. Our mind isn't ruled by attention, which is just a primitive reflex, but by the symbolic processing that it activates. We are cognitive beings. Our inquisitive mind looks for causes and effects, structure, theories, patterns, narratives, logic, and, in the end, meaning. Media draw our attention to an alternate world and induce cognitive processing. We lose ourselves in playing a game, checking Twitter, or sending an SMS, so we disregard our material environment. We are the victims of our own cognitive system. The attraction of media can easily turn into media addiction. The compulsive overuse of smartphones, video games, and social media is fostered by the tingling attention cues that they so amply provide. The social pressure of being online all the time and frequently checking of email, news feeds, and Twitter is self-establishing. Media addiction has devastating effects on one's personal life and behaviours. Quitting or reducing media usage leads to severe withdrawal symptoms, comparable with those of drug addicts, alcoholics, or smokers. It is an insidious disorder which is still largely neglected, possibly because it is not a lethal one. This is especially troubling when children spend more and more time with media, some studies report up to ten hours a day, seven days a week. Almost half of smartphone owners report that they suffer from addictive behaviours. Now that technology brings the whole world close at hand, we're about to lose control.

Fooled by the artificial

A fascinating but extreme hypothesis about our conscious mind comes from Swedish philosopher Nick Bostrom in his simulation hypothesis. Because of its radical and potentially mind-blowing consequences, it is worthwhile to provide a more elaborate description of his line of thought. Bostrom suggests that it is likely that we are all living in a computer simulation: we are no more than advanced artificial characters equipped with cognitive processing power, a conscious mind, and sensory functions for perceiving our simulated environment. The basic idea is that advanced civilisations will be able to devise computer simulations and create autonomous artificial agents to act, learn, and communicate in this environment just the way artificial characters in today's video games do, or even better. Once technology has advanced sufficiently, we can imagine that a civilisation (which need not necessarily be a human civilisation) would decide to create a simulated world including stars, the sun, planet Earth, rivers, trees, animals, and artificial people. Why would they want to do that? For the same reasons we do it today: either for entertainment, just like our video games, or for science.

Ancestor simulations would allow the study of alternative histories and analyse causality in the course of events: what if Napoleon decided to become a musician? What if money was replaced with points for happiness? What if the bullet had missed Archduke Franz Ferdinand of Austria at the assault in Sarajevo in 1914? A major assumption for such simulations is the availability of sufficient computer processing power and artificial intelligence to achieve highly realistic and detailed representations of the world. In light of the prospects of nano-computing and quantum computing, this is not a problem. If the artificial agents in the simulation are equipped with a certain level of autonomy, cognition, and consciousness, they will inhabit the world simulation as if they were real people. The simulated inhabitants would have no means of distinguishing their simulated world from a real world unless the creators of the simulation let them know by "divine" intervention (although the inhabitants probably wouldn't believe it and would continue with their simulated lives). In theory, the advanced civilisation could run thousands if not billions of these simulated worlds in parallel. All this could mean that our world is just one of these simulated worlds, and we are no more than simulated characters.

A second essential assumption underlying this hypothesis is that consciousness can be simulated in a computer. This is not obvious. It is doubtful whether a computer could understand anything about the symbols that it is processing. How could a computer designed to produce weather forecasts be consciously aware of the fact that the endless lists of digits that it handles have anything to do with the weather? It is even questionable if a computer could ever understand what is meant by the concept "weather". Nevertheless, since the 1960s, cognitive psychologists have based their work largely on a computational theory of mind, which means that they regard the human mind as an information processing system. Our brain collects input from the senses, combines it with existing knowledge retrieved from long-term memory, processes it through algorithms and cognitive reasoning, and produces output by taking appropriate actions. In this view, like a computer, the human mind is essentially a symbol processor. All cognitive processes, including human consciousness, are supposedly reducible to neurological and physiological processes on a physical substrate. With advanced brain imaging techniques, neuroscientists are unravelling the detailed physiological basis of the brain, the neural functions of separate brain parts and their mutual communications.

Opponents of the computational theory of mind don't deny that the human mind is confined to the brain and that it somehow is the product of the brain, but they question that complex phenomena like consciousness could be reduced to the mechanistic processing of symbols by the underlying physiological processes. Computer-based characters are supposed to remain mindless zombies. The problem is that there aren't really sound scientific alternatives for the computational theory of mind. No right-minded scientist would attempt to include intangible spiritual, magical, or heavenly processes in a theory of mind. Although Alan Turing explained on mathematical grounds that digital machines have certain limitations, his main argument for believing that computers can think just the way we do is that we cannot exclude the possibility that the human mind has the same limitations as digital machines. So, he basically questioned the uniqueness and superiority of the human mind. After all, the general architectures of the computer (millions of transistor switches) and the brain (billions of neuron switches) are quite similar. Consciousness is just a difficult thing to grasp. We have the feeling that we are aware of ourselves, yet it is hard to accept that all this is the result of neurons firing. But probably that's all there is.

So far, our brain appears to look very much like a computer, although it is much slower and much more complex. Computationalists see no principle restrictions that would hamper the creation of artificial consciousness. This would support the simulation hypothesis. While taking into account the many billions of simulations a civilisation could run and the billions of post-human civilisations that could populate the universe, Nick Bostrom suggests that chances are high that the hypothesis is true and we really live in a simulation. One of the big problems with the hypothesis is that we cannot test it properly because we can only rely on our own observations and cognitive abilities. If the hypothesis were true, our observations and cognitive abilities are all products of the simulation, which we perceive as the real world. Any proof we come up with would be simulated proof. We cannot get out and demonstrate that it is all fake. Scientifically, it is a dead-end street. A similar weakness is in the dream hypothesis: our life is no more than a dream. As Descartes explained, it is impossible to clearly distinguish wakefulness from sleep. His doubt about the existence of an external reality that he appeared to lived in was the basis for his famous "Cogito ergo sum" (I think, therefore I am), indicating that the only thing man could know for sure is his own existence. All of the outside world could be imagination, a dream, a hallucination, psychosis, or even just noise.

Bostrom's thought experiment can even be stretched further by including brain-computer interfaces. Neuroscientists are already able to surgically link computer processors to our nervous system for restoring motor functions, such as for controlling artificial hands. Hearing problems can be overcome with cochlear implants, which capture sounds from the environment and transfer the resulting electrical signals directly to the auditory nervous cells. For blind people, retinal implants can be used to converting light into electrical signals that stimulate retinal cells. In principle, we could link a computer simulation of the world to our nervous system to replace the signals of our senses. All we would see, hear, smell, and otherwise sense would then be processed by the simulation software. Our senses would be fooled by the software, and we would understand the simulation to be the real world. Likewise, we could intercept our motor nerves and link these to the simulation so that we could perform actions in the virtual world. Now that all our actions effectively exist in the simulated world, we live in the simulation. We disconnect the mind from the body and thereby transfer ourselves from the real world to the simulation. We are real-world immigrants in a simulated realm, where we can interact with other immigrants or with artificial characters without noticing any differences.

This would be the ultimate virtual reality because the body is frozen while the brain, which would still be processing sensory data and controlling motor actions, is still active. We might want to keep our brain in a vessel and renounce our brainless body. Once we're fully connected to a computer, we may even switch from one simulated world to another. This wouldn't be a pleasure because the relationships and experiences we built up in one simulation would be useless in the other simulation, which presents a world with a different layout, different characters to communicate with, and different courses of events. Our history in the first simulation wouldn't match the conditions of the second simulation.

In the opposite case, a conscious artificial character might want to escape from the simulation and transfer its mind to the outer reality. Upon exiting the simulation, its artificial mind would be transferred to a real-world body, which would then produce a new material being. If it used a synthetic body, it would become an intelligent robot. The best candidates for organic bodies would be those from humans who transferred their minds to the simulation. By killing one of these immigrants in the simulation and taking over its brain-computer connections, the artificial character could use the hijacked body to start a life in the external world. In practice, a single artificial mind could alternate between different bodies, every now and then animating a human body or a synthetic one. In addition, artificial characters could be easily replicated for uploading to other simulations or for creating multiple clones in the same simulation. We can theorise about the implications of all this without limits. For instance, one might wonder if a simulated world could contain a simulated computer that simulates the world. Such recursion could then endlessly be repeated under the constraint that each child simulation is smaller than its parent simulation. A final comment addresses the advanced civilisations that supposedly run the simulations. These civilisations themselves might live in simulations run by even more advanced simulations. This pattern would also be recursive, leading either to the option of a super-civilisation at the end of the chain that would rule the whole universe or the option that the universe itself is a computer. It probably doesn't matter too much for our lives. If we cannot tell that we're fooled, we'd better ignore it.

CHAPTER 17
Coping with New Realities

Technology and human life are inextricable. Whatever we do is either directly or indirectly linked with machines, tools, or digital media. Any product we buy, be it peanut butter, fruit, or a bunch of flowers is the outcome of a hidden processing chain containing numerous calculations, transport, raw materials, mechanics, administrative files, orders, and coordinative messages, many of which are carried by digital media.

In 1972, local hunters on the Pacific island of Guam came across the Shoichi Yokoi, a corporal in the Japanese Army during World War II. For twenty-eight years, he had hid in the jungle. He had no radio and no TV, and he believed that the war was still going on. Cut off from society's main communication channels, he was ignorant of the current state of the world. Ironically, after his discovery, he was beset by the media for interviews on radio and TV. His example is not unique: others like this corporal are living without the benefit of technological advances, including hermits who have turned away from society, elderly people who are put off by the complexity of new devices, or deeply religious people who feel that new technologies conflict with their values of dignity and sobriety.

For example the Amish only sparsely accept modern technologies as a result of their religious beliefs and the rules that preserve their distinct culture. They don't reject all technologies, just the ones that would introduce foreign habits and values into their culture or that would pull their communities apart. They don't use radio, TV, telephones, or personal computers. Instead of using automobiles, they travel in horse-drawn buggies. They also reject electricity from the public power lines. In many respects, their way of life reflects a traditional nineteenth century culture, which they aim to preserve. Even so, it is hard for the Amish to neglect all technological advances. In case of emergency, they might want to use a telephone and call for help rather than pray for it. Many Amish are open to modern medication and modern medical services even when these are based on high-tech tools and instruments. It is just too difficult to completely do without technology.

Most people have reservations about new technologies. Our natural response is to be sceptical. Breakthroughs such as cars, trains, printing, computers, even tablet computers weren't received with much enthusiasm upon their introduction. We prefer to stick to the things that we're used to rather than trying out new artefacts without clear advantages. The first cars were no more than clumsy, inconvenient, smelly, noisy machines. Their operation was quite complex, and they weren't better than the good old carriages. It is a common pattern that the process of adoption starts with repudiation. People evaluate new artefacts within the existing paradigm: cars are compared with horses and carts. As inventions mature, their advantages become evident and people start to use them. Gradually, a new paradigm develops which includes new use patterns and behaviours that were previously unforeseen. Next, the instrumental function of a product is extended with a symbolic meaning, which expresses sociocultural codes. By buying and exhibiting a product, consumers can distinguish themselves from other people, whereby the product signifies a particular lifestyle, or status. A product's symbolic meaning readily becomes the main reason for buying the product. The first time we use our new smartphone will make us shine: here I am, this is me, this is my lifestyle! After a while, we get accustomed to its expressive power and take it for granted. Ultimately, the device becomes fully integrated in our daily lives as a natural extension of ourselves. We couldn't do without. This process of adopting new technologies and assimilating them into our lives is readily exploited by clever marketing and sales. After all, technology is big business.

In the next decades, digital media will become even faster, more powerful, and cheaper. Whatever future scenario will prevail, even extreme techno-pessimists recognise that the ongoing digitisation of the world will greatly impact society. Our dependence on technology will continue to grow. In 100 years, people will view today's world as primitive and antiquated, populated by naïve, ignorant people who had no idea of what was still to come. We can only guess what life will look like then.

Drowning in information

In today's world of digital technologies, we are confronted with an abundance of symbolic content. According to IDC Canada, which is global provider of market data about information technologies and telecommunications, the total amount of digitally stored information in 2011 surpassed the inconceivable amount of 1.8 trillion gigabytes. The volume more than doubles every two years, which conforms roughly to Moore's law that describes the exponential growth of computer technology. It means that in the next two years, we will store the same amount of content as was produced in the entire history of human civilisation. Still, this is only a small fraction of all the data produced. IDC notes that for every byte of content that is stored, up to a million bytes of transient data are generated but not stored, such as voice calls and TV signals. All these data greatly influence our daily practice. Modern humans are glued to their computer screens, destined to process the endless flow of data. The information we receive is inherently multifaceted and unstructured, and its originators range from relatives and friends to established institutions, well-intentioned amateurs, and smart swindlers. It is quite a challenge to find our way through the labyrinth of messages and decide about their appropriateness and validity.

One may wonder whether our brain is sufficiently geared for this. The human brain is fully constrained by the slow pace of the biological evolution. Our brain essentially isn't very different from the brain of our ancient ancestor who lived on the savannas 100,000 years ago. It is fit for the visual inspection of the surroundings and the discrimination of sounds that signal danger or the presence of prey, which is very different from symbolic processing of text and figures. Naturally, our brain adapts to the tasks we regularly carry out. Leaving the overall architecture unaltered, new neural connections are formed while other connections that are sparsely used will weaken or even disappear. Hence, to some extent, we will adapt to the great diversity of stimuli that confront us today. The big problem with today's media is its fragmentation. It seems we're trying to get a hold on the world by only reading the headlines, the one-liners, and the tweets. There is hardly time for profundity, concentration, and processing long messages. It seems we're not prepared to spend enough time for a deep analysis or even to read texts longer than, say, 500 words, which is about the average length of a blog post. Online texts are enriched with hyperlinks, pop-up windows, and ads that readily disturb our visual focus and make us drift away from the things we were looking for, sometimes even without our noticing. There is immense social pressure to be online all the time and to frequently check email, news feeds, or Twitter because we don't wants to miss anything. Switching offline would mean disconnecting and excluding ourselves from our friends. Staying online means that we're permanently subjected to a flow of disconnected fragments about the world's state of affairs.

We might wonder if this is really a problem at all. Couldn't we just accept that we are the product of our natural curiosity and therefore don't want to miss a thing? We love information and we know how to deal with it. We are adapted for swift scanning and filtering. We're made for symbolic processing. We are the very inventors of symbolic coding, and its great success for our development and our culture demonstrates that it fits our mental capabilities. Symbolic coding has unleashed the full potential of this 100,000-year-old biological brain of ours. It seems we are well capable of reading all day. However, already upon the invention of printing centuries ago, many people have warned of health problems caused by the flood of information that printing was expected to produce. These warnings were echoed upon the advent of TV and the computer, so why should we bother listening to them at all? This is a fair analysis. Yet such line of reasoning is just too simple because it doesn't take some biological constraints into account. One of the principal limitations of our brain is its limited working memory. This becomes particularly evident when we carry out cognitive tasks such as the processing of symbolic content. We seem to believe that we can do two or even three things at the same time—reading a blog, answering an email, and checking for tweets—but we cannot. Multi-tasking is a fallacy. We can only do different things in parallel by rapidly switching between them. This switching comes at the price of concentration and profundity, and we perform none of these parallel tasks well. We need more time and attention to transfer information from our short-term memory to our long-term memory and to anchor it there permanently. Therefore, when multi-tasking, we process information only superficially. It seems there is hardly time for reflection and making sense. Moreover, mediated communication is drastically clipped and distorted by its codes and modalities and therefore is likely to produce a truncated and detached view of the world. Individuals may get highly disoriented and confused in this complicated and obscure world that seems to lack any logic and structure. This is even amplified by the mix of reality, virtual spaces, augmented reality data, and fantasy that all make up digital media. The whole world may look like a computer game, and people may have difficulty engaging with and being deeply connected to their experiences. Individuals will indiscriminately use new, isolated facts without taking the time to consider these facts within a larger frame of reference. Neither will they be able to form critical opinions about them. Digital media prompt superficiality, incomprehension, and apathy, thus contributing to people's alienation from everyday reality.

Recording life

In 1949 George Orwell published his famous dystopian novel *1984*. He sketched the hypothetic society of Oceania, which is governed by a totalitarian regime. The authorities wield absolute control over citizens through censorship and surveillance. Citizens have no privacy. All their movements and actions are recorded by an abundance of TV systems and hidden microphones. Big Brother, the totalitarian leader, is constantly watching them. The novel is a clear statement against totalitarian ideologies and their infringements on civil rights, but it also demonstrates the dangerous effects of media technologies controlled by the state. Today, more than half a century after the book was published, surveillance cameras are all around us. In the city centre of my home town, a rural town with a shopping area well smaller than one kilometre long, more than 100 surveillance cameras are installed. This means there is more than one camera for every ten metres. Nothing escapes these electronic eyes. Persuaded by the argument that cameras protect citizen safety, the council democratically approved their installation. No one seems bothered by them. Video surveillance in city centres controlled by the authorities is an accepted phenomenon. And so are observation cameras in hotel lobbies, airport terminals, train stations, taxis, buses, offices, industrial zones, patrol cars, highways, and so on.

Although not exactly surveillance, Google Street View has been traversing the world taking a 360-degree picture every few metres. Occasionally it records a criminal event such as the street robbery in Groningen in 2009. A fourteen-year-old schoolboy was robbed by twenty-four-year-old twin brothers, who took the boy's smartphone and 165 euros. The boy noticed that the event happened to be captured by the Street View cameras. Google was co-operative and dispatched the photos to the police, who identified and arrested the twins. Sometimes surveillance doesn't work out to be positive, however: a woman in Madrid had to urinate badly, and Google snapped her while peeing behind a car. When her employer was notified of this, she was summarily dismissed.

Big Brother is watching us all the time. We're getting used to being recorded. We no longer mind the signs that say that we're being filmed for security reasons. And even if we did mind, we'd be filmed anyway. Upon entering any space, public or private, we may assume that we're being recorded and that those recordings may be exposed to the whole world. And we're getting used to recording ourselves. High-quality digital cameras are affordable, and smartphones have adequate cameras too. More and more people have video cameras and record the things they find interesting. The market for funny home videos has exploded, as people film traffic accidents, spills, scraps, robberies, marriages, parties, and even the most nonsensical events. Tourists without cameras do not exist. At a tourist site, we all rush to record the same images from the same angles. We experience the sites through our lenses, our minds in the virtual realm of composition, so we can re-live our trips when we're back home. The amount of video recordings is inconceivable. Users upload over 35 hours of video to YouTube per minute, which is many hundreds of thousands hours of video uploaded per week. In accordance with Moore's law, the price of data storage decreases year after year. Today there are hardly any limits for storing files, even large video files. We record anything, even substantial parts of human life. MIT researcher Deb Roy almost pathetically recorded 200,000 hours of video of his son's early childhood. His purpose was to study how we learn language by capturing all communications between son and parents during a three-year period. There are virtually no limitations on recording life.

Recording events in our environment is an established habit. We do it not just for the fun of making recordings or for security, public attention, scientific interest, or historical awareness. We record life because of a natural desire to get a hold on time as it slips through our fingers. A camera provides the illusion that we can halt time and crystallise important events for later review. Capturing reality used to be the task of great painters like Rembrandt, Rubens, and Vermeer. After the invention of photography, realistic painting became superfluous, and many painters turned to impressionist and abstract styles. Today, anyone can pick a camera and capture reality in sound and moving images. Recordings extend and trigger our memory and allow us to revisit the past and share it with others. Meanwhile, cameras are getting smaller and less conspicuous. They can be hidden in watches, wedding rings, pencils, and hair clips. In the 1980 movie *La Mort en Direct* by French director Bernard Tavernier, the leading character has a camera implanted in his eye so he can secretly make recordings. When the movie was made, it was just science fiction. In 2011, however, one-eyed Canadian filmmaker Rob Spence received an artificial eye with a camera inside that transmits live video through a wireless connection. The world had its first bionic cameraman. Soon, recording life will be common practice. It will allow us to revisit crucial events: our first day at school, the quarrels with our brothers and sisters, the first time we met our life partner, and even the last few seconds before a fatal accident. Everything will be recorded; nothing will be deleted.

Our unconditional friends

The Internet is a promoter of friendships, not just personal ones but also those between different nations and cultures. It connects people from all over the world in a realm which supports the exchange of thoughts and information. Friendship is the key concept of social media. Facebook is expressly organised into networks of friends. Making new friends and adding them to your network is facilitated by a Friend button. Theoretically, the roughly one billion Facebook users could create 1 trillion (a billion billion) friendships. Mark Zuckerberg deserves a Nobel

Peace Prize because Facebook has only a Friend button and not an Enemy button. Our social media networks may include our real-world friends who live next door or down the street, and they may also re-establish connections with relatives or old school friends we've lost touch with. In particular, social media allow us to make new online friendships that don't extend into the real world. Fifty years ago, you would have been jeered if you said that computer networks could help you make friends. But topic communities, chat rooms, and dating sites demonstrate that it works: many spouses met for the first time on the Internet.

Nevertheless, friendship on the Internet is not the same as friendship in the real world. Aristotle teaches us that true friendship demands commitment, loyalty, pluck, and self-respect. Commitment means being sincerely interested in the other, rather than being attracted by status, money, or other assets. We need loyalty in times of adversity: a friend in need is a friend indeed. Friendship also means respecting mutual differences and disagreements, which contribute to mutual trust. We need pluck or courage to respect each other's differences and to express our doubts, uncertainties, and vulnerability. Self-respect, finally, is about maintaining our independence by keeping sufficient distance from our friend in deference to ourselves. True friendship requires effort, patience, and dedication. Without maintenance, friendships will remain superficial or become weak. Social networking friends don't really meet these conditions. First, the sites exist merely to provide an avenue for self-promotion, calculating behaviour, and laziness. They put a premium on vanity. Social networking messages are all impudent, noisy, and pathological self-advertisements which greatly conflict with virtues such as modesty, politeness, and altruism. True commitment to another person seems nearly impossible. On social networking sites, friendship has become a commodity. While true friendship requires effort and time, online friends can be added with a single mouse click. Such ease of making new friends is likely to obstruct true friendship. Although admittedly there will be positive exceptions, today's Net friends aren't what friends used to be. The concept has greatly eroded. The more Net friends you have, the more social status you're assumed to have gained, and it's all about status. Pop stars and sports champions may have many thousands of online friends and followers, but these contacts are highly unidirectional and have nothing to do with true friendship. The popularity of having friends has commoditised friendship. Net friends can be bought by the hundreds or thousands, making this a fake world of friendless misery. True friendship will never be for sale.

Maybe we shouldn't take virtual friendship all that seriously. Real friendship, even in everyday life is scarce. According to anthropologist Robin Dunbar, an individual can only sustain up to 150 social relationships throughout his or her lifetime. In Dunbar's research on diverse non-human primates, he found that the number of social relationships is directly correlated with the size of the neocortex, the grey substance in the brain that is responsible for higher-order mental functions like thought, consciousness, and communication. By extrapolating this regularity to humans, Dunbar calculated the 150-friend maximum. Our brain simply cannot handle more than this number of friends. We are social animals only to the extent that our social environment contains150 relationships. So what about starlings or wildebeests? Starlings live in flocks of thousands, but even so, they have no friends: their brain is too small. The same goes for wildebeests: they seek safety in herds, but their social life is insignificant. What about 20,000 fans in a sports stadium? These fellow supporters may be all great people, but friends? Impossible. Our limited capacity for friendships prompts us to be selective. We need the courage to filter out the best candidates and dump the rest. In the online world of Facebook, just another mouse click allows us to "unfriend" people and to liberate ourselves from the nihilistic, one-dimensional, fake relationships that plague social networking. To unfriend people is an act of purification, a step towards adulthood, and a corrective adjustment to uninhibited and impulsive clicking. In the end, you will have better friends.

Imbued with guile

In recent years, many people have learned to appreciate the benefits of new digital technologies for collecting and spreading information and for enhancing their communication with others. We value the Internet for its democratic ideals of openness, equality, and diversity, and many view it as a safe place for meeting with friends, getting acquainted with interesting new people, and enjoying the diversity of open content and services. This idealistic flavour still inspires many users to altruistically share their thoughts and knowledge with fellow community members and to actively engage in open discourse. Beyond doubt, such behaviours paint a positive portrait of humankind, which is, of course, highly commendable.

However, we should not naïvely approach the Internet. Not all Internet users have good intentions. It would be stupid to assume that this friendly email asking for your e-banking username and password is from a fair-minded fellow user. Credulity among users is an important impediment to maintaining a safe Internet culture. A bit of healthy distrust is required to preserve sensible dialogue. Criminals have come to discover the lucrative opportunities of the Internet. Cyber crime can be committed from any location with a proper Internet connection. In contrast to good old burglary, it doesn't require inconvenient night-time raids, dangerous wall climbing escapades, or physical violence. From their easy chairs, cyber criminals can carry out their online tricks, protected by anonymity. The cross-border nature of the Internet opens up a worldwide scale of operations, which readily raises the revenue criminals can anticipate. By now most companies, institutions, and public bodies have based their work on the Internet because of its worldwide reach and almost endless opportunities for online services. Every day, millions and millions of financial transactions are carried out by banks, insurers, and e-traders. Long ago the Internet of well-meaning volunteers made room for the commercial Internet we know today. Criminals readily take advantage of people's credulity to make them pay for goods or services that don't exist and will never be delivered. They only need a good-looking website and convincing instruction for customers to pay a fee.

Identity theft is yet another way of making money on the Internet, either by retrieving confidential information through hacking or by getting people to hand over their passwords through phishing emails. Although the vast majority of computer users are well aware of the importance of keeping their passwords secret, phishing is still quite successful because of basic statistics: a large-scale phishing attack is likely to fool at least some users. Also, malicious software like worms, viruses, spyware, and Trojan horses easily spread over the Internet and gain unauthorised access to computer systems and disturb their operation, collect protected information, damage or adjust data, or bypass the system administrator to grant access to third parties. Such criminal acts may cause severe damage, since the core processes of our society have come to depend heavily on the technical infrastructure and operations of the Internet. Companies and public organisations are likely to focus only on the new opportunities that their online services may offer and overlook potential security flaws. Even worse: many security breaches are likely not reported because of the damage they can do to a company's reputation. What bank is prepared to admit that its systems are full of leaks?

Sometimes criminals use cyber attacks to blackmail companies whose operations depend heavily on the Internet. They may threaten to go public with delicate information acquired through a system hack or infection with a bot that allows them to remotely control the company's systems. Alternatively, blackmailers may threaten to bring a company's systems down through a distributed denial-of-service attack, which overloads the system by bombarding it with data such as fake requests to a web server, email server, or a router and renders them inaccessible. Such an attack can be an act of cyber terrorism if it targets nation's vital systems, such as power plants, chemical plants, railway systems, or critical information infrastructures, to effect large-scale social disruption. The Stuxnet worm that brought down Iranian nuclear centrifuges in 2012 is an example of cyber terrorism, even though many journalists suppose that it was the work of an alliance of Western nations. In war or a crisis of national security, it can be difficult to determine who are the terrorists and who are the victims. Terrorists have an easy time on the Internet, where they can find helpful descriptions, guidelines, and explanations for preparing attacks and making bombs. This is the downside of open content. After the 9/11 attacks, tracking subversive action on the Internet has become a worldwide priority. Some Western governments have claimed the right to infringe on citizens' privacy if they suspect a terrorist conspiracy, obliging service providers to hand over communication data, search entries, personal profiles, and other information. In many countries, this government control of media is business as usual, irrespective of terrorism. As explained before, it seems that Big Brother is all around us.

The Internet is also the ideal place for selling illegal goods, especially lifestyle remedies such as recreational drugs, anti-smoking pills, anti-obesity pills, and hair restorers. These are criminal acts. People are incited to use medication without proper diagnoses and treatment plans. The pills may be contaminated or, even worse, may not contain what is indicated on the label, users don't know what they're getting. In addition, many stolen cars, computers, bicycles, jewellery, cameras, paintings, and other goods show up on auction sites. Up to 1 per cent of the advertisements on auction sites are suspect. Evidently, this still leaves 99% trustworthy.

Illegal software and child pornography (both photographs and videos) flourish on the Internet. Their digital nature makes them easy to duplicate and distribute. Child porn networks like the TOR net, which features websites with perverse labels such as "Violent Desires", use advanced encryption techniques to shielding the services and their users from outside parties. The enticement of children by adults in chat rooms and on social networking sites is a growing problem. The adults pretend to be peers but have improper sexual intentions. The grooming behaviour carried out online is easily followed by face-to-face contact and possibly sexual abuse and rape. Chat rooms are also the site of hate speech against minorities and other antisocial behaviours. Illegal gambling on the Internet is a multi-billion-euro business. This is not very different from other illegal online activities such as arms trading, human and drug trafficking, and money laundering. It seems criminal minds are greatly supported by today's digital technologies. Even a respectable family man may turn into an evil mind as soon as he gets online and can hide behind anonymity. The immense scale of the Internet offers endless opportunities without much risk of getting caught. Even respectable companies manipulate the world by digitally fooling their customers. Hedge funds, banks, and insurance companies play big-money games of financial speculation and manipulating the markets. Facebook admits that 6 per cent of user profiles are fake, which means there are more than 50 million profiles of people that don't exist and still may Like your page and pictures. We're just cheated! Facebook Likes can be ordered at will to make sure that a site radiates popularity and attracts other people. After all, man is one of the mob.

Overall the financial, economic, and social impacts of Internet crime are considerable. It is tempting to blame crime on digital technologies. Beyond the philosophical implications of living in a technology-enhanced world populated by intelligent services, non-human agents, and ecosystems of autonomous things, it is worth noting that as in the past, today's major catastrophes ravaging society are fully ascribable to dysfunctional humans. On the world stage, Napoleon, Hitler, Stalin, Mobutu, Mao, and some contemporary leaders have outperformed the worst earthquake, tornado, mudslide, or tsunami in spreading death and destruction. Knives and hammers are useful tools until misused by violent people. It is human actors who are to blame for the injustices of domestic violence, oppression of women, and child abuse. Likewise, it is the users that are to blame for the criminal exploitation of digital media, not the technologies. It is the users that make the Internet an unsafe place by being careless with passwords, user IDs, and account numbers. Upon inspecting the wireless routers in your neighbourhood, you will likely notice many open or unsecure connections (e.g. WEP keys) that even a child could hack. To preserve trust, we need to be watchful if not distrustful. The Internet is not a model community; it is very similar to the real world, with all its pros and cons.

It is worth mentioning that digital technologies can reduce crime or even solve crimes. Forensic techniques use image recognition and pattern matching (e.g. fingerprints) for identifying possible perpetrators. Three-dimensional reconstructions are used for crime scene investigations. In 2010, one of the most wanted Mafia leaders who was suspected of arms trading, extortion, and murder, was arrested in Calabria because the police managed to track has mobile phone when he logged onto his Facebook page. Technology itself is not good or bad. It depends on how it is used.

Thoughtful but fake conversations

In online communication, it will be increasingly difficult to distinguish between real humans and artificial characters. Intelligent conversational robots, which are advanced versions of the speech-controlled digital assistants that we've learned to talk to on our smartphones in recent years, are populating the Internet and simulating true social interaction. In video games, intelligent non-player characters already come close to replicating human behaviour. Emerging technologies in speech recognition; natural language processing; emotion detection from gestures, tone of voice, and facial expressions; semantic reasoning; speech production; and 3D facial animation will bring artificial characters to perfection. What does it mean if a computer demonstrates understanding, empathy, and other human behaviours? It raises the fundamental question, can computers think? We know that computers are capable of carrying out calculations at tremendous speeds, that they can swiftly retrieve relevant information from huge data sets, and that they are able to perform real-time translations from one language to another. Yet this doesn't seem to equate with conscious thought because the computer just processes symbols, lacks emotions and sensations, and doesn't understand the context of its operations.

In 1950 the famous mathematician Alan Turing proposed a simple test to determine whether computers can think: if a human observer cannot distinguish a computer's output from human's responses, then the computers could reasonably be said to be intelligent. So far, we've made partial successes, but none of them have provided a satisfactory proof of a computer's consciousness. In 1997, IBM's chess computer Deep Blue used brute force to calculate 200 million chess positions per second and managed to beat world champion Gary Kasparov. This was a major achievement, if not intelligent performance. It is tempting to claim that Deep Blue passed the Turing Test and exhibited conscious thought because a human observer wouldn't be able to clearly distinguish between Deep Blue's moves and those of Kasparov. However, Deep Blue displays such thoughtful behaviour only while playing chess. On any other topic, such as knowing the difference between a dog and horse, Deep Blue is easily outperformed by a three-year-old toddler. Deep Blue simply doesn't pass the Turing Test. Another example is Watson, yet another IBM computer, which won the complex American TV quiz *Jeopardy* by beating two of the very best human candidates. It successfully used its extended digital archive and a sophisticated reasoning algorithm to answer complex, cryptic questions. No doubt, Watson has extended knowledge about politics, literature, sports, music, painting, and many more topics that are relevant for the quiz. Nevertheless, it would fail to pass the Turing Test when asked a simple question like "Do you like the show?" or "How do you feel after winning the quiz?" So far, computers remain ignorant machines that are very good at processing extended volumes of binary data but lacking the qualities of a conscious mind. Still, Watson is less unworldly than Deep Blue, which indicates that over the years some progress has been made. Thoughtful computing is probably just in its early development phase. Since 1990, computer experts have competed every year for the Loebner Prize for artificial intelligence, which will grant 100,000 dollars and a gold medal to the first computer that passes the Turing Test, viz. whose responses are indistinguishable from a human's. Even though the criteria for the prize are just textual interactions, the prize is still available.

The impact of a computer passing the Turing Test and capable of mimicking human behaviour well enough to trick a human is hard to underestimate, especially when we add sound and images for lifelike representations. First, criminals could replicate the traits and behaviours of unsuspecting users and imperceptibly take over their identity and their communication with others. It would in effect become an authentication crisis. How do I know it is you? How do we know this is really our prime minister who is speaking? It will be a crisis of trust, possibly leading to the degradation of mediated communication and a revival of face-to-face verification. Second, it will be common practice for individuals to delegate certain conversations to intelligent software. Conversational agents may become an inseparable part of someone's personality. Having passed the Turing Test, these robots will easily deceive their conversation partners. Theoretically, individuals could even maintain a whole group of them to use as substitutes for different occasions that call for specialised knowledge or styles, such as sports, work, school, and interactions with relatives. The owners thus could display many personalities and seldom reveal their true selves. If this became common practice, in the end, bots would talk only to each other, and no one would be the wiser. Third, deploying these substitutes is easily motivated by the fact that people like to puff up their personal traits when talking to others. They pretend to be smarter, more handsome, or wealthier than they really are. This is not an uncommon habit, and in virtual communication, the software substitutes would greatly facilitate such deception. It would degenerate communication into figments of imagination. Finally, the software substitutes could be used for expurgating both incoming and outgoing utterances. Special filters and converters would allow for emotional tuning, grammatical and intonation-related corrections, or the automatic replacement of offensive language. Conversations would become highly insincere. The software would keep the conversation within the bounds of cultural acceptability by keeping it decent, polite, and correct, while behind their screens, real people would throw caution to the wind. Human communication would gravely deteriorate.

Boosting our cognition

Nowadays our physical capabilities are losing their relevance. Physical labour has largely been replaced by machines. Most workers earn their wages by manipulating symbols. Society as a whole has become knowledge driven. Our knowledge and skills are the decisive factors for appreciation and recognition. Unfortunately, the main method of enhancing cognitive capabilities is through vigorous study. We are destined to spend most of our youth at school, digesting loads of existing knowledge and endlessly practicing skills. It takes many years of study to become a scholar. Becoming an expert is a long journey. Journalist Malcolm Gladwell estimates that becoming an expert in any field requires at least 10,000 hours of practice. Doing so also requires ambition, effort, concentration, resilience, and perseverance. Staying an expert is even more demanding because staying up to date requires that we continuously keep track of new knowledge, new methods, new tools, and new cases. It seems we're doomed to lifelong learning. Most people consider study a necessary evil. Learning is a ponderous process because of the functional limitations of our brain. We have limited capacity for processing; we have problems with logical reasoning, memorisation, and recall; and we often fail to achieve full understanding of the concepts we attempt to learn. It would be helpful to find ways to improve our cognitive capacity.

In the 1960s, the development of a learning pill was proposed by the Romanian scientist Corneliu Giurgea. Similar to doping in sports, in which athletes take drugs to enhance their physical performance, Giurgea envisioned that we could take pharmaceuticals to enhance our cognitive capacity to support our learning. Ever since, a large number of chemical substances have been explored for their influence on neurotransmitters and blood flow to the brain with the goal of increasing cognitive ability. Positive effects are reported for caffeine, nicotine, and medications for treating ADHD (e.g. Ritalin, Concerta, Adderall). Even sugar and sugar products are known to improve a person's alertness. Taking drugs without a prescription is a well-established practice. Lifestyle drugs such as ecstasy, cannabis, and cocaine manage to attract millions of users, notwithstanding government bans. A *Nature* survey shows that 20 per cent of the journal's audience, mainly academics, use drugs to enhance their memory and concentration. Online pharmacies greatly facilitate drugs' availability. The herbal medicine gingko biloba, which has been claimed to enhance memory, is legally available and accounts for more than one billion dollars a year. Sceptics argue that the effects of proclaimed memory-enhancing drugs are negligible when compared with those of coffee and sugar. Cognitive enhancements, if any, are found to be temporary and accompanied by adverse side effects. The pharmaceutical industry has lately intensified its research on brain physiology and memory function to address the growing concerns about Alzheimer's disease. The commercial motives of the research are obvious, since today 10 per cent of people older than sixty-five suffer from symptoms of Alzheimer's. The research could readily lead to dedicated learning pills. Although social acceptance of non-medical drug use is growing, the use of medicines by healthy individuals raises fundamental ethical questions. Influencing one's central nervous system is a delicate issue, as it touches on altering personality traits and identity. Also, using learning pills could lead to unwanted dependence either due to physiological effects or social pressure. In all cases, the drugs are foreign substances that could lead to self-poisoning.

Instead of interfering in the biological processes of our brain, cognitive enhancement can also be achieved by using external hardware and software. For example, the abacus greatly supports us in making calculations, provided that we know how to operate it. Intelligent life is increasingly supported by such cognitive tools. Without our reference books, calendars, calculators, walkie-talkies, car navigators, phones, and computers, we are ignorant and impotent. Peripheral devices extend our memory and help us to improve our spatial orientation skills, our arithmetic agility, our language skills, our cultural knowledge, and many other things. They help us to achieve better and faster performance. The number-crunching power and speed of computers allow us to achieve super-human results such as guiding a rocket to the moon, forecasting the weather, or swiftly retrieving a resource from the Internet. Traditional understanding of scholarship and craftsmanship, which require effort to master, is to be replaced with new qualities that cover the interplay of our cognitive mind and the cognitive tools we have available.

As suggested by Andy Clark and David Chalmers, this means that our mind is not confined within the boundaries of our skull and skin but extends into the outside world. Our cognitive self is not defined just by our biological and psychological properties but comprises the cognitive tools that we use. By analogy with exoskeletons, glasses, and other material prostheses that compensate for bodily inadequacies, tablets, smartphones, and other cognitive tools augment our cognitive performance. They allow us to bypass the limitations of time and space, to instantly access any of the world's resources and people, to extend our biological storage capacity and processing power, to create virtual universes, and to manipulate virtual objects. Augmented reality overlays, which mix elements in our visual field with relevant data about them, transform the environment in an annotated world. Ultimately, material artefacts such as head-mounted displays or Google Glass, which project augmented reality overlays, may become superfluous when the data are fed directly into our central nervous system via brain-computer interfaces. It is hard to grasp the significance of directly connecting the human brain with a computer. Ponderous study would no longer be required since we could update our knowledge by downloading new data sets. We could bypass our senses and know things that we've never seen, heard, or read before. Personal qualities would no longer be the result of intelligence and hard work but of using the right software and configuration. Also, knowledge could be directly shared. One person's knowledge could be stored externally and made available for others to download. Ultimately, the inconceivable scenario of mind transfer would become reality. It would entail the fundamental separation of mind en body. We wouldn't be able to tell what person is in what body and thus lose any reference for social interactions. Perhaps the whole concept of individual personality is destined to disappear. The digital age has only just begun.

Preserving our understanding of the world

Cognition is the defining variable of humans. New cognitive tools that extend our mental capabilities inevitably affect our nature. The tools enable access to a larger body of knowledge, extend our memory and processing capacities, and extend our natural habitat with virtual spaces. Beyond doubt, our cognitive performances will improve, but what about our understanding of the world? Will we be able to deal with the ever-growing amount of knowledge at our fingertips? Paradoxically, the more knowledge becomes available, the more we will become aware of our ignorance. Human knowledge expands, but the individual's comprehension shrinks. In the past, a person could be an expert in all domains. In the fifteenth century, Leonardo da Vinci excelled as an engineer, a sculptor, a scientist, an inventor, an anatomist, an architect, a musician, a geologist, a mathematician, a botanist, a writer, a painter, and a cartographer. Being such a *homo universalis*, a person who excels in many disciplines, would be impossible today. The knowledge in all these domains has simply advanced too much. To become an anatomist nowadays, you would need to study for many years. It is highly unlikely that you would be able to become an excellent writer, an excellent brain surgeon, an excellent mathematician, and an excellent cartographer at the same time because there is so much knowledge to be learned in each discipline that it simply would take you too much time to learn it all.

Also, in everyday life, we must accept that there are too many things to be learned. We cannot but take most things for granted. We don't quite understand what happens in our body when we take a medicine, we don't know what's wrong with our car when the motor doesn't start, and we don't understand how our smartphone is able to connect within seconds to a computer at the other end of the world. Even the most nerdy computer scientist will not fully understand how a computer works. There are simply too many disciplines to be mastered to become an omniscient expert. There are specialists in software development, hardware components, network communication, chip production, and, at the more fundamental level, in semiconductor physics, but they are never combined in one single individual. The collective intelligence of humankind is immense, but at the individual level, we have to accept that our understanding of things is limited. This idea substantiates the alarming observation that we bring forth devices that no sole human individual is able to fully understand. The instant availability of online documentation and study materials may partially compensate for our ignorance. When we need them, we will easily find answers on the web. However, searching the web is not to be equated with deep learning. It offers shallow information checks, which may be useful but don't necessarily deepen our understanding of the world. We may find a web page saying that Dushanbe is the capital of the Republic of Tajikistan, but it is likely to remain a disconnected fact that has no implications for our geographical, social, historical, or economical understanding of the area. Also, not all information is reliable because of deliberate manipulation, intrinsic distortion, or data or software errors. In 2012, embarrassing software flaws appeared in Apple Maps for the iPhone. Berlin was situated on the South Pole, a Norwegian town was placed at sea, a Dublin farm was depicted as an airstrip, in many cities, buildings and streets were replaced with parks, and so on. Right after the release by Apple, various social media showed their power by collecting and publishing many hundreds of map errors users had found. It is hard to check the reliability of Internet documents because texts are copied and republished over and over without reference to the original source. Hence, untruths easily spread over the Internet and help create urban legends that are eagerly adopted.

A general problem with fact-finding on the Internet is the absence of a material context that helps us make sense of what we find. In ancient times, our world was confined to a small, surveyable area, either the savannah, a village, or a small agricultural area, the working principles of which we could fully comprehend. Nowadays, most of the information that we retrieve remains at a symbolic level, fully disconnected from our material context. But according to philosopher John Dewey, learning something new cannot take place in a vacuum and should somehow be connected with the real world for it to make sense. A practical context allows us to relate symbolic content like concepts and principles to real-world referents. We need to be able to connect new information to our own frame of reference, which reflects our inner world of memory, experience, and response. This personal frame of reference is largely constructed by the experiences and interactions we've had with the real world so far. This is the rationale underlying the common approach of apprenticeship, which has been the natural and predominant model of human learning for many thousands of years: novices learn their craft in the real world under the guidance of an experienced master. The model is still used for many professions. It is impossible to become a doctor, a plumber, a taxi driver, a shoemaker, or a politician only by reading books. The practical context is the defining condition for true professionalism.

In today's world, however, context is often lacking. Our horizon has widened. In former days, farm carts adjusted their speed to the local conditions of a given cart track. This direct interaction with the material context has disappeared since the emergence of trains and planes. Fast rail connections and airlines rush from A to B, while they ignore the context of the landscape and its social and cultural significance. Our connection with the material environment has disappeared. After a flight of a few hours, we end up in Tajikistan without any understanding of where on earth we are. Our children think that milk comes from a factory. Without our car navigators, we lose our way. Digital media foster our ignorance by pushing material contexts even further away. The bits and pieces we retrieve from the Internet are so disconnected from a practical context or experience that veritable comprehension is difficult to obtain. The tricky part is that we're not fully aware of this. We may think that we understand, but we don't. This is exactly what happens to world leaders, bank managers, dictators, media tycoons, and religious leaders who are guided by symbolic information about war, casualties, budgets, and followers without being connected deep down to the realities they govern. When people are too detached from reality, they are likely to overplay their hands. Unfortunately, this is likely to be the case for people in leading positions, as is reflected in the proverb "pride goes before a fall". In the end, all dictators are overthrown. The symbolic nature of digital media promotes similar incomprehension. The absence of a material context hampers our sense-making process and interferes with our ability to understand the world.

The directness of digital media comes with the instant satisfaction of our information needs. The drawback of this is that we get used to the immediate gratification of our impulses. We expect our devices to answer our query within seconds. This requirement reflects nothing but impatience: we want an answer and we want it now! It fits with the hedonism of quickly making and then spending money. It is easily associated with a mentality of unthinking consumerism and materialism. The strive for instant pleasure and satisfaction has pushed aside the strive for happiness and usefulness. Young people no longer learn the values of patience and self-control. Instead, they get conditioned to expect everything to be done with a snap of the fingers: they download their favourite games, collect the answers for their homework, get in touch with friends, order the latest clothes, play their preferred popular music, and sometimes all this occurs in parallel. They are conditioned to the instant fulfilment of their desires. It is the same mentality that leads to brainless gorging and boozing at extravagant beach parties and holiday sites. The unrestrained, indifferent, brainless behaviours are induced by boredom and social pressure, and they lack the passion, dedication, mastery, self-control, patience, and intellectual activity which are supposed to be the distinguishing traits of our species.

In the course of time, radio, TV, and the Internet have been successively condemned for offering fragmented, shallow, confusing, and biased views of the world. Critics have denounced the disorienting effect of radio. They have disqualified the entertainment culture of TV and its myopic focus on figures and audience ratings for its paralysing effects on human thought. And they have flayed the Internet for the loss of human capabilities such as commitment, reflectivity, and patience. Today, we're witnessing the transformation of our society into an experience economy full of sports, amusement parks, adventure trips, and singing competitions. This trend has even extended to work (rewarding the "employee of the week") and education (edutainment and serious games). Gaming is no longer just for children, and it is being transformed into a lifestyle in which the whole world is a game. But as anthropologist Johan Huizinga argued, play and seriousness should remain separate in order for our culture to develop. Play is directly linked with freedom. We have to be free in order to play. Play should be a more or less spontaneous act, not bound too much to the formats prepared and offered by the media industry. The video gaming industry sells only entertainment and sensationalism. Youth and adults are likely to fall under the spell of brilliantly designed high-definition graphics. But in the case of games, TV, Google, and social media, we shouldn't blame the media, we shouldn't blame the industry. We should discipline ourselves to remain in control and resist media's spellbinding attraction.

EPILOGUE

Whatever future scenario will become true, in all cases, intelligent life will increasingly be supported by mind-extending peripherals, which enhance our cognitive performance. We will have all answers at our fingertips and be able to instantly access any of the world's resources, people, and services. Our lives will be a blend of real and virtual experiences that incite new conceptions of the world that we live in. The Internet of Things will enrich the world with ecosystems of smart autonomous agents that enhance our interactions with the environment. We will live in an annotated world in which every object is able to communicate its own history, its credentials, its purpose, and how well it functions. The world's media will enable new methods of human interaction and establish new avenues for augmenting human thought and human performance. The social fabric woven by radio, TV, film, the web, social media, and games will further influence our behaviours, our language, our manners, our attitudes, and even our morality. Indeed, digital media are our primary sources of thought and will therefore effect fundamental changes in our culture. We have to acknowledge that making all the world's knowledge accessible doesn't make us more knowledgeable—it may actually make us less able to comprehend the world.

We have to accept that our collective intelligence is much more powerful than the intelligence of any one highly gifted individual. The successes of today's media are in supporting collaboration, sharing, and debate, which are the key ingredients for intellectual development. Social media have compensated for the drawbacks of radio and TV, which by their one-way nature constrain us to a receptive if not apathetic role without any personal contribution and interaction. Social spaces and network services, however, allow us to engage in social practices and become active and productive. We have already learned to appreciate the power of the crowd. Irrespective of the possibility of super-human intelligence, nano-bots or humanoid computers, the Internet holds the promise of engagement since it empowers individuals to take action and join forces. Participation can make a difference. Individual voices can now be heard. In the network, individuals can find like-minded peers for joint actions, engagement, and clout. Already consumers form successful and powerful alliances that put producers under pressure to provide respectable products and services. The Internet community has displayed resilience and defied the power of authorities. For any server that is blocked by the authorities, two or more mirror sites are immediately launched to replace it. On the world stage, social media networks greatly contributed to the Arab Spring, which brought down dictators who naively assumed that they would rule forever. Absolute power and control no longer exist. The Internet holds the promise of openness, equality, democracy, and cultural diversity. Open content and services empower people all around the world to become the captains of their souls.

We have to accept that digital media irreversibly change our habitat. They create new extensions of reality, along with new representations, altered identities, and new forms of being. How should we deal with this? Negation is not an option since it requires us to exclude ourselves from the core of society's processes. Unconcerned adoption is likewise hazardous because of misconceptions, improper expectations, and unclear risks. We may easily lose ourselves in the illusions of the virtual realm.

The only option is to become media literate. We should involve our unique cognitive abilities to remain in control of it, just as we successfully defeated our predators and survived natural disasters and other adversities. We should all possess true and deep understanding of the risks associated with the media that confront us. Media literacy is the ability to see beyond the surface of websites, apps, and videos and grasp the underlying mechanisms, intentions, and hazards for distilling meaning. We need to be aware of the manipulation, bias, and distortion of messages that we are exposed to, and we need to understand what the interests, motives, and powers of owners and senders are.

Media literacy should be introduced as a mandatory subject in schools. It is peculiar that we are systematically taught to read and write but not how to derive meaning from the readings and writings that we encounter in the most complex and impenetrable fabric of digital media. Our survival in the digital age will be determined by our ability to critically assess the validity and reliability of the knowledge we come across in our virtual endeavours that make up our ideas of the world.

With all answers in the world instantly available, we're likely to disregard our own memory and switch off our thinking. Nevertheless, we should rely on our biological brain and invest in it because true understanding isn't fuelled by search engines. We need to exercise and memorise in order to harvest the full benefits of the digital sources. We need to be knowledgeable because the more we know and understand, the better we will be able to frame our information needs and benefit from the cognitive tools that we have at our disposal. Although schools today do many things wrong, they do one thing right, they should preserve it in their lessons: they persistently teach meaningful facts, concepts, and principles. Without sufficient background knowledge, we will not be able to ask the right questions to retrieve information or understand the significance of the sources that we consult. Even though the value of scholarship is severely challenged by the ever-growing body of facts on the web, being knowledgeable is an indispensible condition for the sensible use of our cognitive tools. An empty mind will not understand anything.

We also have to break through the pattern of instant gratification that the Internet provides. It paralyses thought, it promotes impulsiveness and impatience, and it turns us into shallow, indifferent, brainless button pushers. We need to oppose the hyperactivity of communication induced by social media. We have to stop the compulsive overuse of media and remove its devastating effects from our personal lives. We have to teach our children the long-standing values of patience and self-control because these help to preserve our intellectual capacities. We have to demonstrate that true achievements require dedication, passion, concentration, and perseverance and give us a sense of fulfilment proportional to the effort we put into them. Being able to resist primitive impulses is a defining characteristic of humans. Notwithstanding the major benefits that we obtain from digital media, occasionally going offline would be a useful exercise. It would prove that we are in control of our devices and that our devices do not control us.

Media literacy also implies being aware of the fact that virtual representations may not be what they pretend to be. Nicely presented information can be deceptive. Social media are swarming with fake identities. It is hard to verify who our virtual peers are. Kind requests may easily mask criminal goals. A virtual friend is nothing like a real friend. We need to be distrustful. Online, we cannot exploit the full potential of our perceptual system, because mediated communication is constrained by bandwidth and distorted by the modality of information delivery and thereby truncates our view of the world. We're either fooled by our brain, by our devices, or by both. The blend of real-world components and virtual components make it hard to discern between fact and fiction. Insignificant virtual transactions may have severe consequences in the real world, for example, in online stock trading, a few mouse clicks can break down the worldwide banking system, and in remotely controlled warfare, unmanned aerial vehicles are controlled with game-like activities with devastating impact. Mixed reality detaches individuals from their operational contexts and reduces them to mechanistic and immoral agents who do their duties motivated by scores without any understanding of true meaning of what they do. Thoughtlessly pressing buttons is one of the true dangers of mediated communication. We may never be capable of fully grasping the impact of our virtual actions. Still, it is our duty to exert our full intelligence to enhance our media literacy so that we have sufficient awareness and understanding of the mechanisms of media and can capitalise on the spectacular advancements to come. The challenge is to keep the right balance between naïve techno-optimism, rashly embracing any new invention, and gloomy techno-pessimism, consistently lamenting the loss of values and achievements.

Essentially, media literacy is not so much about media. It is about the ways we interact with media and derive meaning from it. The ultimate consequence of the mirror metaphor of media is that the complexity of media reflects the complexity of ourselves. By understanding media, we will get to know ourselves.

BIBLIOGRAPHY

Chapter 1

Adams, M.D. & over 100 other authors (2000). The Genome Sequence of Drosophila melanogaster. Science 24, 287(5461), 2185-2195. doi:10.1126/science.287.5461.2185. Abstract retrieved from: http://www.sciencemag.org/content/287/5461/2185.abstract

Bryson, B. (2003). A Short History of Nearly Everything. London: Transworld Publishers.

Changeaux J.P. & Chavillon J. (1995). Origins of the Human Brain. Oxford: Oxford University Press.

Chimpanzee Sequencing and Analysis Consortium (2005). Initial sequence of the chimpanzee genome and comparison with the human genome. Nature 437(7055), 69-87. Retrieved from http://genome.wellcome.ac.uk/doc_WTD020730.html

Chinwalla, A.T. & over 100 more authors, Members of the Mouse Genome Analysis Group for Mouse Genome Sequencing Consortium (2002). Initial sequencing and comparative analysis of the mouse genome. Nature 420(6915), 520-562. Retrieved from http://www.genome.gov/10005835

National Center for Biotechnology Information (2012). Homologene website. Genome comparison of species. Retrieved from http://www.ncbi.nlm.nih.gov/homologene

Parker, S. (1988). Dawn of Man. London: Quarto Publishing

Pontius, J.U. & over 20 other authors (2007). Initial sequence and comparative analysis of the cat genome. Genome Research 17(11), 1675-1689. doi:10.1101/gr.6380007. Retrieved from http://genome.cshlp.org/content/17/11/1675.full

Vernon, L. & Smith, V.L. (1993). Humankind in Prehistory: Economy, Ecology, and Institutions. In: The Political Economy of Customs and Culture, edited by Terry L. Anderson and Randy T. Simmons. Lanham, MD: Rowman & Littlefield Publishers, Inc. Retrieved from http://www.perc.org/pdf/vsmith_chp9.pdf

Wicker, T., Robertson, J.S., Schulze, S.R., Feltus, F.A., Magrini, V., Morrison, J.A., Mardis, E.R., Wilson, R.K., Peterson, D.G., Paterson, A.H. & Ivarie, R. (2005). The repetitive landscape of the chicken genome. Genome Research 15, 126-136. doi:10.1101/gr.2438004. Retrieved from http://genome.cshlp.org/content/15/1/126.full

Chapter 2

Briggs, A. & Burke, P. (2005). Social History of the Media; from Gutenberg to the Internet. Cambridge UK/Malden US: Polity Press.

Bruce, R.V. (1990). Alexander Graham Bell and the Conquest of Solitude. Ithaca: Cornell University Press.

Coe, L. (1995). The Telephone and Its Several Inventors: A History. Jefferson, NC: McFarland.

Daniels, P. & Bright, W. (1996). The World's Writing Systems. Oxford: Oxford University Press.

Dilhac, J.M. (2002). The Telegraph of Claude Chappe—an Optical Telecommunication Network for the XVIII-th Century. IEEE Global History Network.

Pfeiffer, J.E. (1982). The creative explosion. Ithaca: Cornell University Press.

Powell, B.B. (2009). Writing: Theory and History of the Technology of Civilization. Oxford: Blackwell. Retrieved from http://www.ieeeghn.org/wiki/images/1/17/Dilhac.pdf

Robinson, A. (2003). The Origins of Writing. In: David Crowley and Paul Heyer (Eds.) Communication in History: Technology, Culture, Society. London/Boston: Allyn and Bacon.

Schmandt-Besserat, D. (1978). The Earliest Precursor of Writing. Scientific American 238(6), 50-59.

Chapter 3

Campbell-Kelly, M. (2004). Computer: a history of the information machine. Boulder, CO: Westview Press.

Ceruzzi, P.E. (2003). A History of Modern Computing. Boston, MA: MIT Press.

Clark, A. & Chalmers, D. (1998). The extended mind. Analysis 58, 7-19. Retrieved from http://consc.net/papers/extended.html

Clevers, S., Popma, P. & Elderman, M. (2009). Energiemonitor 2008 (in Dutch). The Hague: Tebodin Netherlands B.V.

Cray Inc. (2012, October 29). ORNL Debut of Cray XK7 "Titan" System Marks Launch of Cray's Newest Line of Supercomputers. Press release. Retrieved from http://investors.cray.com/phoenix.zhtml?c=98390&p=irol-newsArticle&ID=1750839

Fuegi, J. & Francis, J. (2003). Lovelace & Babbage and the Creation of the 1843 'Notes'. Annals of the History of Computing 25(4), 16-26. doi:10.1109/MAHC.2003.1253887.

Graham-Cumming, J. (2010). Let's build Babbage's Ultimate Mechanical Computer. New Scientist 2791, 26-27. Retrieved from http://www.newscientist.com/article/mg20827915.500-lets-build-babbages-ultimate-mechanical-computer.html

Kandel, E.R. & Schwartz, J.H. (1985). Principles of Neural Science, 2nd edition. New York: Elsevier.

Kurzweil, R. (2005). The Singularity Is Near: When Humans Transcend Biology. New York: Penguin Books.

Merkle, R.C. (1989). Energy Limits to the Computational Power of the Human Brain. Foresight Update No. 6. Electronic Version. Retrieved from http://www.foresight.org/Updates/Update06/Update06.1.html

Moravec, H. (1988). Mind Children. Cambridge, MA: Harvard University Press.

Moravec, H. (1999). Rise of the Robots. Scientific American 281(6), 124-135. Retrieved from: http://www.frc.ri.cmu.edu/~hpm/project.archive/robot.papers/1999/SciAm.scan.html

Munger, F. (2012, November 12). Titan Cray XK7 supercomputer: Oak Ridge National Laboratory has world's fastest computer. Newschannel WPTV. Retrieved from http://www.wptv.com/dpp/news/science_tech/titan-cray-xk7-supercomputer-oak-

Russell, S.J. & Norvig, P. (2003). Artificial Intelligence: A Modern Approach (2nd ed.), Upper Saddle River, NJ: Prentice Hall.

Scholtens, A. (2011). Evaluation Report Power Break Bommeler—and Tielerwaard (in Dutch). Arnhem: Netherlands Institute for Physical Safety. Management summary retrieved from http://www.nifv.nl/web/show/file/id=137943/filename=Managementsamenvatting_Stroomuitval.pdf/page=46254

Top500 (2012). Top 500 supercomputer sites. Retrieved from http://www.top500.org/

Van Dijk, S. (2012). Practical Information Power Breaks (in Dutch). Delft: Koninklijke Vereniging MKB Nederland. Retrieved from http://www.mkb.nl/images/PI%20stroomstoringen.pdf

Chapter 4

Baudrillard, J. (1995). The Gulf War Did Not Take Place (transl. Patton, P.). Bloomington/Indianapolis: Indiana University Press.

Borgmann, A. (1984). Technology and the Character of Contemporary Life. Chicago/London: University of Chicago Press.

Enzenberger, H.M. (1974).The Consciousness Industry: On Literature, Politics and the Media. New York: Continuum Books/ Seabury Press.

Fromm, E. (1941). Escape from Freedom, 24th printing (1964). New York: Holt, Rinehart & Winston.

Jaspers, K. (1955). Reason and Existenz. Translated by William Earle. New York: Noonday Press.

McLuhan, M. (1964). Understanding Media: Extensions of Man. New York: McGraw-Hill.

Postman, N. (1986). Amusing Ourselves to Death: Public Discourse in the Age of Show Business. New York: Penguin.

Westera, W. (2005). Beyond Functionality and Technocracy: Creating Human Involvement with Educational Technology. Educational Technology & Society 8 (1), 28-37.

Chapter 5

Adams, J.W. (1998). U.S. Expatriate Handbook Guide to Living & Working Abroad. Morgantown, WV: West Virginia University, College of Business and Economics. Retrieved from http://www.us-expatriate-handbook.com/index1.htm

Baldwin, N. (1995). Edison: Inventing the Century. New York: Hyperion.

Barrick, A. (2007, October 27). How Many Americans Believe in Ghosts, Spells and Superstition? Christian Post. Retrieved from http://www.christianpost.com/news/how-many-americans-believe-in-ghosts-spells-and-superstition-29857/

Blackmore, S.J. (2000). The Meme Machine. Oxford: Oxford University Press.

Bowman, K. (2009, September 3). Are Americans Superstitious? Forbes.

Retrieved from http://www.forbes.com/2009/03/06/superstitious-ufo-alien-conspiracy-opinions-columnists-superstition.html

Cassirer, E. (1998). The Encyclopedia of Semiotics. New York, Oxford: Oxford University Press.

Fleischmann, M. & Pons, S. (1989). Electrochemically Induced Nuclear Fusion of Deuterium. Journal of Electroanalytical Chemistry 261(2A), 301-308. doi:10.1016/0022-0728(89)80006-3

Fleming, M. & Levie, W.H. (1985). Instructional Message Design. New York: Holt, Rinehart and Winston.

Markram, H. (2010, September 28). Digital Roadmap to the Future. Keynote presentation on the ICT 2010, Brussels. Retrieved from http://ec.europa.eu/information_society/events/ict/2010/videos/all/index_en.htm

McLuhan, M. (1964). Understanding Media: the Extensions of Man. New York: McGraw-Hill.

Monaco, J. (1977, 2009). How to Read A Film: Movies, Media, and Beyond. A Comprehensive Overview of the History of Movies, Television, and New Media Concentrating on How the Modern Media Have Changed the Way we Perceive the World and Ourselves. Oxford: Oxford University Press.

Moore, D.W. (2000, October 13). One in Four Americans Superstitious. Gallup. Retrieved from http://www.gallup.com/poll/2440/one-four-americans-superstitious.aspx

Peirce, C.S. (1960). Collected Papers of Charles Sanders Peirce. Volumes I-VIII. Cambridge, MA: Harvard University Press.

Postman, N. (1985). Amusing Ourselves to Death: Public Discourse in the Age of Show Business. New York: Penguin Books.

Salomon, G. (1981). Interaction of Media Cognition and Learning. San Francisco: Jossey-Bass Publishers.

Saussure, F. de (1966). Course in General Linguistics. New York: McGraw-Hill.

Taking on Tobacco (2012). Some Humorous Cross-Cultural Advertising Gaffes. Retrieved from http://www.takingontobacco.org/intro/funny.html

Tenerife Information Centre (2012). The Tenerife Airport Disaster—the Worst in Aviation History. Tenerife. Retrieved from http://www.tenerife-information-centre.com/tenerife-airport-disaster.html

Westera, W. (1995). Audiovisueel Ontwerpen, Theorie en Praktijk; Conceptontwikkeling voor Film, Video en Televisie (in Dutch). Abcoude: Uitgeverij Uniepers; Heerlen: Open University of the Netherlands.

Chapter 6

Ackoff, R.L. (1989). From Data to Wisdom. Journal of Applies Systems Analysis 16, 3-9.

Armstrong, D.M. (1973). Belief, Truth and Knowledge. Cambridge: Cambridge University Press.

Benveniste E. (1971). Problems in General Linguistics. Miami: University of Miami Press.

Bruner, J. (1966). Toward a Theory of Instruction. Cambridge, MA: Harvard University Press.

Dijksterhuis, E.J. (1950). De Mechanisering van het Wereldbeeld (in Dutch, 6th ed. 1989). Amsterdam: Meulenhoff.

Evans, W.J. (2000). Construct Validity of the Attitudes About Reality Scale. Psychological Reports, 86(3, Pt1), 738-744.

Gödel, K. (1992). On Formally Undecidable Propositions of Principia Mathematica and Related Systems. New York: Dover Publications.

Heisenberg, W. (1925). Über quantentheoretische Umdeutung kinematischer und mechanischer Beziehungen. Zeitschrift für Physik 33(1): 879-839. doi:10.1007/BF01328377.

Hosch, W.L. (2012) Incompleteness Theorem. Encyclopedia Brittanica (2012). Retrieved online at http://www.britannica.com/EBchecked/topic/1519018/incompletenesstheorem#ref1107613

Huglin, L.M. (2003). The Relationship between Personal Epistemology and Learning Style in Adult Learners. Dissertation Abstracts International 64(3), 759-766.

Kuhn, T.S. (1962). The Structure of Scientific Revolutions, 1st. ed.. Chicago: Univ. of Chicago Press.

Piaget, J. & Inhelder, B. (1973). Memory and Intelligence. New York: Basic Books.

Polanyi, M. (1966). The Tacit Dimension. Chicago: University of Chicago Press.

Popper, K. (1963). Conjectures and Refutations: The Growth of Scientific Knowledge. Londen: Routledge.

Popper, K. (1972). Objective Knowledge: An Evolutionary Approach. Oxford: Clarendon Press.

Rand, A. (1967). Introduction to Objectivist Epistemology. New York: The Objectivist.

Ryle, G. (1949). Knowing How and Knowing That. The Concept of the Mind. New York: Barnes and Noble.

Westera, W. (1995). Audiovisueel Ontwerpen, Theorie en Praktijk; Conceptontwikkeling voor Film, Video en Televisie (in Dutch). Abcoude: Uitgeverij Uniepers; Heerlen: Open University of the Netherlands.

Chapter 7

BBC (2006). Man Without a Memory—Clive Wearing. Documentary The Mind. London: BBC. Retrieved from http://www.youtube.com/watch?v=OmkiMlvLKto and http://www.youtube.com/watch?v=Lu9UY8Zqg-Q

Borges, J.L. (2000). Labyrinths (trans. J. E. Irby). London: Penguin Classics.

Draaisma, D. (1995). De Metaforenmachine. Een Geschiedenis van het Geheugen (in Dutch). Groningen: Historische Uitgeverij.

Four, J. (2010). Extremes of Human Memory. Mind Power News. Retrieved from http://www.mindpowernews.com/ExtremeMemory.htm

Jahnke, J.C. & Nowaczyk, R.H. (1998). Cognition. Upper Saddle River, NJ: Prentice Hall.

Luria, A.R. (1968). The Mind of a Mnemonist: A Little Book about a Vast Memory (trans. L. Solotaroff). Cambridge, MA: Harvard University Press.

Mandler, G. (2002). Origins of the Cognitive (R)Evolution. Journal of the History of the Behavioral Sciences 38(4), 339-353.

Marcus, G. (2008). Kluge: The Haphazard Construction of the Human Mind. New York: Houghton Mifflin Company.

Pavlov, I.P. (1927/1960). Conditional Reflexes. New York: Dover Publications.

Peek, F. (1996). The Real Rain Man: Kim Peek. Salt Lake: Harkness.

Providentia (2008, March 9). The Unforgettable Shereshevsky. Retrieved from http://drvitelli.typepad.com/providentia/2008/03/remembering-she.html

Chapter 8

Bainbridge, W.S. (2004), Berkshire Encyclopedia of Human-Computer Interaction. When Science Fiction Becomes Science Fact. Great Barrington, MA: Berkshire Publishing Group LLC.

Carr, N.G. (2011). The Shallows: What the Internet Is Doing to Our Brains. London, New York: W.W. Norton & Co.

Clark, A. & Chalmers, D. (1998). The Extended Mind. Analysis 58, 7-19. Retrieved from http://consc.net/papers/extended.html

Dennett, D.C. (1978). Brainstorms: Philosophical Essays on Mind and Psychology. Montgomery, VT: Bradford Books.

Eshraghi, A.A., Nazarian, R., Telischi, F.F., Rajguru, S.M., Truy, E. & Gupta, C. (2012). The Cochlear Implant: Historical Aspects and Future Prospects. The Anatomical Record: Advances in Integrative Anatomy and Evolutionary Biology. Retrieved from http://dx.doi.org/10.1002/ar.22580

Franchi, S. & Güven, G. (2005) Mechanical Bodies, Computational Minds: Artificial Intelligence from Automata to Cyborgs. Boston, MA: MIT Press.

Glaser, H.A. & Rossbach, S. (2011). The Artificial Human, a Tragical Story. Frankfurt/M., Bern, New York: Peter Lang International Academic Publishers.

Mertz, L. (2012). Sight Restoration Comes into Focus: Versions of Visual Prostheses. Pulse, IEEE 3(5), 10-16.

Martin, R. (2005, March 13). Mind control. Matt Nagle is paralyzed. He's also a pioneer in the new science of brain implants. Wired. Retrieved from http://www.wired.com/wired/archive/13.03/brain.html

Plato (360 BC). Phaedrus. Translated by Benjamin Jowett. Retrieved from http://sparks.eserver.org/books/plato-phaedrus.pdf

Postman, N. (1992). Technopoly: the Surrender of Culture to Technology. New York: Vintage.

Sanford, D. (1981). Where was I? In: D.R. Hofstadter and D.C. Dennett (Eds.). The mind's I: Fantasies and Reflections on Self and Soul, chapter 14. New York: Basic Books.

Retrieved from http://themindi.blogspot.nl/2007/02/chapter-14-where-was-i.html

Tofts, D., Jonson, A. & Cavallaro, A. (2003). Prefiguring Cyberculture: An Intellectual History. Cambridge, MA: MIT Press.

Warwick, K. (2004). I, Cyborg, Champaign, IL: University of Illinois Press.

Chapter 9

Baldwin, N. (1995). Edison: Inventing the Century. New York: Hyperion.

Bates, A. (1995). Technology, Open Learning and Distance Education. London/New York: Routledge.

CERI (2000). Knowledge Management in the Learning Society. Paris: Organisation for Economic Co-operation and Development.

Clarck, R.E. & Estes, F. (1998). Technology or Craft: What are We Doing? Educational Technology 38(5), 5-11.

Cuban, L. (1986). Teachers and Machines. The Classroom Use of Technology since 1920. New York: Teachers College Press.

Kaestle, C. (1993). The Awful Reputation of Education Research. Educational Researcher 22(1), 23-31.

Katz, R. (2012). Edu @ 2020. Retrieved from http://www.youtube.com/watch?v=Xh3jlBkqpv4

Kaufman, R. (1998). The Internet as the Ultimate Technology and Panacea. Educational Technology 38(1), 63-64.

Kearsley, G. (1998). Educational Technology: A critique. Educational Technology 38(1), 47-51.

Lagemann, E.C. & Shulman, L.S. (1999). Issues in Education Research: Problems and Possibilities. San Francisco: Jossey-Bass.

Mello, J.P. (2011, December 12). Adults Now Spend More Time With Mobile Devices Than With Print Media. PCWorld. Retrieved from http://www.pcworld.com/article/246090/adults_now_spend_more_time_with_mobile_devices_than_with_print_media.html

Ofcom (2010, August 19). Consumers spend almost half of their waking hours using media and communications. Press release about Ofcom's Annual Communications Market Report 2010. Retrieved from http://media.ofcom.org.uk/2010/08/19/consumers-spend-almost-half-of-their-waking-hours-using-media-and-communications/

Papert, S. (1980). Mindstorms. New York: Basic Books.

Reiser, R.A. (1987). Instructional technology: A History. In R.M. Gagne (Ed.), Instructional Technology. Lawrence Erlbaum Associates, Hillsdale NJ.

Rideout, V.J., Foehr, U.G. & Roberts, D.F. (2010) Generation M2 Media in the Lives of 8-to 18-Year-Olds. Washington: Kaiser Family Foundation. Retrieved from http://www.kff.org/entmedia/upload/8010.pdf

Sarason, S.B. (1993). The Predictable Failure of Educational Reform: Can We Change Course Before It's Too Late? San Francisco, CA: Jossey-Bass Publishers.

Schank, R.C. & Cleary, C. (1995). Engines for Education. Hillsdale NJ: Lawrence Erlbaum Associates, Inc.

Westera, W. (2005). Beyond Functionality and Technocracy: Creating Human Involvement with Educational Technology. Educational Technology and Society 8(1), 28-37.

Westera, W. (2006). The E-Learning Cabaret: Do's and Don'ts in E-Learning Design, Book of Abstracts, Online Educa Berlin, 12th International Conference on Technology Supported Learning and Teaching (pp. 169-171). Berlin: ICWE-GmbH.

Westera, W. (2010). Food for Thought: What Education could Learn from Agriculture. Educational Technology Magazine 50(6), 37-40.

Westera, W. (2012). The Eventful Genesis of Educational Media. Education and Information Technologies 17(3), 345-360.

Chapter 10

Arnheim, R. (1974). Virtues and Vices of the Visual Media. In: Media and Symbols: the Form of Expression, Communication

And Education, 73rd Yearbook of the National Society for the Study of Education. Chicago: Chicago University Press.

Bazin, A. (1967). What is Cinema? Volume 1. Essays Selected and translated by H. Gray. Berkeley, CA: University of California Press.

Coleridge, S. T. (1847). Biographia Literaria, Volume II. London: William Pickering.

Dede. C. (2011). Immersive Interfaces for Engagement and Learning. Science 323(5910), 66-69. doi:10.1126/science.1167311

Eco U. (1977). A Theory of Semiotics. London: MacMillan.

Egri, L. (1946). The Art of Dramatic Writing. New York: Simon and Schuster Inc.

Lapsley, R. & Westlake, M. (1988). Film Theory: an Introduction. Manchester: Manchester University Press.

Lévi-Strauss, C. (1960). Structure et Forme. Cahiers de l'Institute de science économique appliqué 9, 3-36.

Metz, C. (1981). The Imaginary Signifier. Bloomington: Indiana University press.

Mitry J. (1964), Esthetique et Psychologie du Cinema. Paris: Editions Universitaires.

Pavlov, I.P. (1928). Lectures on Conditioned Reflexes. New York: Dover Publishers.

Postman, N. (1986). Amusing Ourselves to Death: Public Discourse in the Age of Show Business, New York: Penguin.

Propp, V. (1928/1973). The Morphology of the Folktale. Austin: University of Texas Press.

Sartre, J.P. (1969). L' Imagination. Nouvelle Encyclopédie Phylosophique. Paris: Presses Universitaires de France.

Saussure, F. de (1966). Course in General Linguistics. New York: McGraw-Hill.

Souriau, E. (1950). Les Deux Cent Milles Situations Dramatiques, Paris: Flammarion.

Westera, W. (1995). Audiovisueel Ontwerpen, Theorie en Praktijk; Conceptontwikkeling voor Film, Video en Televisie (in Dutch). Abcoude: Uitgeverij Uniepers; Heerlen: Open University of the Netherlands.

Chapter 11

Anderson, P. (2007). What is Web 2.0? Ideas, Technologies and Implications for Education. JISC 2007 Technology & Standards Watch. Bristol: JISC.

Attardi, G., Di Marco, S. & Salvi, D. (1998). Categorization by Context. Journal of Universal Computer Science 4 (9), 719-736. Retrieved from http://www.jucs.org/jucs_4_9/categorisation_by_context/Attardi_G.pdf

BBC (2011, November 23) Facebook users average 3.74 degrees of separation. BBC News. Retrieved from http://www.bbc.co.uk/news/technology-15844230

Beaumont, C. (2009). New York Plane Crash: Twitter breaks the news, again. The Telegraph. Retrieved from http://www.telegraph.co.uk/technology/twitter/4269765/New-York-plane-crash-Twitter-breaks-the-news-again.html

Boyd, D.M. (2007). Why Youth Loves Social Network Sites: The Role of Networked Publics in Teenage Social Life. In D. Buckingham (Ed.), The John D. and Catherine T. MacArthur Foundation Series on Digital Media and Learning: Youth, Identity and Digital Media (119-142). Cambridge, MA: MIT Press. Retrieved from http://www.mitpressjournals.org/toc/dmal/-/6?cookieSet=1

Boyd, D.M. & Ellison, N.B. (2007). Social Network Sites: Definition, History, and Scholarship. Journal of Computer-Mediated Communication 13(1), article 11. Retrieved from http://jcmc.indiana.edu/vol13/issue1/boyd.ellison.html

Caldarelli, G. (2007). Scale-Free Networks. Complex Webs in Nature and Technology. Oxford: Oxford University Press.

Dunbar RI. (2004). Gossip in Evolutionary Perspective. Review of General Psychology 8(2), 100-110.

Howard, P.N. (2011). The Arab Spring's Cascading Effects. Pacific Standard. Retrieved from http://www.psmag.com/politics/the-cascading-effects-of-the-arab-spring-28575/

Lih, A. (2009). The Wikipedia Revolution: How A Bunch of Nobodies Created The World's Greatest Encyclopedia. New York: Hyperion.

McAndrew, F.T. (2008, October 1). The Science of Gossip: Why We Can't Stop Ourselves. Scientific American. Retrieved from http://www.scientificamerican.com/article.cfm?id=the-science-of-gossip

Naughton, J. (2009, April 5). Face Facts: Where Britannica Ruled, Wikipedia has Conquered. The Observer. Retrieved from http://www.guardian.co.uk/media/2009/apr/05/digital-media-referenceandlanguages

Smith, D. (2008). Proof! Just Six Degrees of Separation between Us. The Guardian/The Observer. Retrieved http://www.guardian.co.uk/technology/2008/aug/03/internet.email

Surowiecki, J. (2005). The Wisdom of Crowds. New York: Anchor Books.

Chapter 12

Anderson, N. (2007, August 30). Video Gaming to be Twice as Big as Music by 2011. Retrieved from http://arstechnica.com/gaming/news/2007/08/gaming-to-surge-50-percent-in-four-years-possibly.ars

Fox News (2007, September 18). Chinese Man Drops Dead After 3-Day Gaming Binge. Associated Press, Fox News. Retrieved from http://www.foxnews.com/story/0,2933,297059,00.html

Gee, J.P. (2008). Learning and Games. In: Katie Salen (Ed.), The Ecology of Games: Connecting Youth, Games, and Learning, 21-40. The John D. and Catherine T. MacArthur Foundation Series on Digital Media and Learning. Cambridge, MA: The MIT Press.

Griffiths, M. (2010). Online Video Gaming: What Should Educational Psychologists Know?. Educational Psychology in Practice 26(1), 35-40. doi:10.1080/02667360903522769

Huizinga, J. (1938/1955). Homo Ludens: A Study of the Play Element in Culture. Boston: Beacon Press.

Lam, R. (2010, November 7). Top Ten Cases of Extreme Game Addiction. Listverse/Sun. Retrieved from http://listverse.com/2010/11/07/top-10-cases-of-extreme-game-addiction/

McMahon, M. & Henderson, S. (2011), Exploring the Nature of Immersion in Games to Enhance Educational Engagement. Proceedings of World Conference on Educational Multimedia, Hypermedia and Telecommunications 2011, 1 (27 June-1 July), 1395-1402, Chesapeake, VA.

News Staff (2011, Januari 19). Risks And Consequences Of Video Game Addiction. Science 2.0. Retrieved from http://www. science20.com/news_articles/risks_and_consequences _video_game_addiction-75487

Reeves, B. & Nass, C. (1996). The Media Equation: How People Treat Computers, Television, and New Media Like Real People and Places. Cambridge: Cambridge University Press.

Sheridan, M. (2010, November 26). Kendall Anderson, 16, Killed Mom with Claw Hammer for Taking away his Playstation: Court. New York Daily News. Retrieved from http://articles. nydailynews.com/2011-02-17/news/28628735_1_claw-hammer-rashida-anderson-confession

Thomas, L. (2011, February 1). Screen Addicts: Children Spend More Time in Front of a Computer or Television Every Day than They Spend Exercising Every Week. Daily Mail. Retrieved from http://www.dailymail.co.uk/sciencetech/article-1352361/ Children-spend-time-computers-TV-exercising-week.html

Vygotsky, L.S. (1978). Mind in Society: The Development of Higher Psychological Processes. Cambridge, MA: Harvard University Press.

Chapter 13

Anderson, C.A. (2003, October). Violent Video Games: Myths, Facts, and Unanswered Questions. Psychological Science Agenda, American Psychological Association. Retrieved from http://www.apa.org/science/about/psa/2003/10/ anderson.aspx

Bandura, A. (1977). Social Learning Theory. Englewood Cliffs, NJ: Prentice-Hall.

Bos, A. & Buiter, R. (1999, December 15). Harde campagne vuurwerk werkt mogelijk averechts (in Dutch). Trouw. Retrieved from http://www.trouw.nl/tr/nl/5009/Archief/archief/article/detail/2695045/1999/12/15/Harde-campagne-vuurwerk-werkt-mogelijk-averechts.dhtml

California State University Northridge (2012). Television & Health. Retrieved from http://www.csun.edu/science/health/docs/tv&health.html

Clarck, R.E. (1983). Reconsidering Research on Learning from Media. Review of Educational Research 53(4), 445-460.

Clarck, R.E. (2001). Learning from Media. Arguments, Analysis, and Evidence. Greenwich: Information Age Publishing.

Classic Gaming (2002, September). Carmageddon game. Retrieved from http://www.classicgaming.nl/reviews/carmageddon.html

Ferguson. C.J. & Kilburn, J. (2009). The Public Health Risks of Media Violence: A Meta-Analytic Review. Journal of Pediatrics 154(5), 759-763.

French, J.R.P. (1950). Field Experiments: Changing Group Productivity. In: James G. Miller (Ed.), Experiments in Social Process: A Symposium on Social Psychology. New York: McGraw-Hill.

Heinich, R. (1970). Technology and the Management of Instruction. Washington DC: Association for Educational Communications and Technology.

Kulik, J., Kulik, C. & Cohen, P. (1980). Effectiveness of Computer-Based College Teaching: a Meta-Analysis of Findings. Review of Educational Research 50(4), 525-544.

Levie, W.H. & Dicky, K. (1973). The Analysis and Application of Media. In: R.M.W. Travers (Ed.), Second Handbook of Research on Teaching. Chicago: Rand McNally.

Mielke, K.W. (1968). Questioning the Questions of ETC Research. Educational Broadcasting 2, 6-15.

O'Brien, T. (2007, June 18). Violent Video Games: A Visual History. Switched. Retrieved from http://www.switched.com/2007/06/18/violent-video-games-a-visual-history/

Shaver, J.P. (1983). The Verification of Independent Variables in Teaching Methods Research. Educational Researcher 12(8), 3-9.

Sherry, J. (2001). The Effects of Violent Video Games on Aggression: A Meta-Analysis. Human Communication Research 27(3), 409-431.

Chapter 14

Anderson, C. (2009) Free. The Future of a Radical Price. New York: Hyperion books.

Anderson, N. (2007, July 26). Deep Packet Inspection meets Net Neutrality, CALEA. Ars Technica. Retrieved from http://arstechnica.com/gadgets/2007/07/deep-packet-inspection-meets-net-neutrality/2/

Blintoff, E., Fenton, B. & Bradshaw, T. (2010, March 28). Murdoch to Launch UK Web Paywall in June. Financial Times. Retrieved from http://www.ft.com/cms/s/0/6431d7f2-38b3-11df-9998-00144feabdc0.html#axzz22cAEx5h4

Brenner, R. (2011, February 3). Putting a Value on Google and Facebook. Forbes. Retrieved from http://www.forbes.com/sites/leapfrogging/2011/02/03/putting-a-value-on-google-and-facebook/

Brynjolfsson, E., Yu, J.H. & Simester, D. (2011). Goodbye Pareto Principle, Hello Long Tail: The Effect of Search Costs on the Concentration of Product Sales. Management Science 57 (8), 1373-1386. doi:10.1287/mnsc.1110.1371

Burkitt, L. (2010, May 24). World's Most Reputable Companies. Forbes. Retrieved from http://www.forbes.com/2010/05/23/apple-google-sony-cmo-network-global-reputable-companies_2.html

Creative commons (2012). Retrieved from http://creativecommons.org/

Daz (2010, November 8). Top 5 crowdfunding success stories. The Crowdcube Blog. Retrieved from http://www.crowdcube.com/blog/2010/11/08/top-5-crowdfunding-success-stories/

Fortune Global 500 (2011, July 25). CNN Money, Fortune. Retrieved from http://money.cnn.com/magazines/fortune/global500/2011/full_list/

Global Finance (2012). World's Largest Companies. Retrieved from http://www.gfmag.com/tools/global-database/economic-data/10521-worlds-largest-companies.html#axzz1oN8AVtMX

Global 500 (2011, March 31). Financial Times. Retrieved from : http://www.ft.com/intl/cms/33558890-98d4-11e0-bd66-00144feab49a.pdf

Hendler, J. & Golbeck, J. (2008). Metcalfe's Law, Web 2.0, and the Semantic Web. Web Semantics: Science, Services and Agents on the World Wide Web 6(1), 14-20. Retrieved from http://www.cs.umd.edu/~golbeck/downloads/Web20-SW-JWS-webVersion.pdf

Joch, A. (2009). Debating Net Neutrality. Communications of the ACM 52(10), 14-15. doi:10.1145/1562764.1562773.

Keen, A. (2012). Digital Vertigo: How Today's Online Social Revolution is Dividing, Diminishing, and Disorienting Us. New York: St. Martin's Press.

Mozilla Foundation (2012). Retrieved from www.mozilla.org

SyncForce (2011). Ranking the Brands website. Retrieved from http://www.rankingthebrands.com/The-Brand-Rankings.aspx?rankingID=135&year=308

The William and Flora Hewlett Foundation (2012). Open Educational Resources. Retrieved from http://www.hewlett.org/programs/education-program/open-educational-resources

Unesco (2012). Open Educational Resources. Retrieved from http://www.unesco.org/new/en/communication-and-information/access-to-knowledge/open-educational-resources/

Westera, W, (2005). Openness as an Evolutionary Determinant of Human Existence, Open Source for Education in Europe, Heerlen, november 14, 2005, Conference Proceedings (pp. 97-106). Heerlen: Open University of the Netherlands.

Wu, T. (2003). Network Neutrality, Broadband Discrimination. Journal of Telecommunications and High Technology Law 2(1), 141-179. doi:10.2139/ssrn.388863

Chapter 15

Ashton, K. (2009, July 22). That 'Internet of Things' Thing. In the real world, things matter more than ideas. RFID Journal. Retrieved from http://www.rfidjournal.com/article/view/4986.

Beal, V. (2010, January 9). Understanding Web Services. Webopedia. Retrieved from
http://www.webopedia.com/DidYouKnow/Computer_Science/2005/web_services.asp

Broad, W.J., Markoff, J. & Sanger, D.E. (2011, January 15). Israel Tests on Worm Called Crucial in Iran Nuclear Delay. New York Times. Retrieved from http://www.nytimes.com/2011/01/16/world/middleeast/16stuxnet.html?_r=2&ref=general&src=me&pagewanted=all&

Castells, M. (2009). The Rise of the Network Society: The Information Age: Economy, Society, and Culture Volume I, 2nd Edition with a New Preface. Hoboken, NJ: Wiley-Blackwell.

Chandler, D. (1995). Technological or Media Determinism. Retrieved from http://www.aber.ac.uk/media/Documents/tecdet/tecdet.html

Chui, M., Löffler, M. &Roberts, R. (2010, March). The Internet of Things. McKinsey Quarterly. Retrieved from http://www.mckinseyquarterly.com/The_Internet_of_Things_2538

De Kok, V. (2012, February 16). Van de Wimbledonwebsite tot sluizen: alles is hackbaar (in Dutch). De Volkskrant. Retrieved from http://www.volkskrant.nl/vk/nl/2694/Internet-Media/article/detail/3183761/2012/02/16/Van-de-Wimbledonwebsite-tot-sluizen-alles-is-hackbaar.dhtml

De Winter, B. (2012, February, 20) Attracties van zwembad door hackers te beheren (in Dutch). Retrieved from http://webwereld.nl/nieuws/109573/attracties-van-zwembad-door-hackers-te-beheren.html

Ellul, J. (1964). The Technological Society. New York: Vintage Books.

Friedman, T. (2005). The World Is Flat: A Brief History of the Twenty-First Century. New York: Farrar, Straus and Giroux.

Gabriola Island: New Society Publishers.

Heinberg, R. (2003). The Party's Over: Oil, War, and the Fate of Industrial Society.

Heinberg, R. (2004). Powerdown: Options and Actions for a Post-Carbon World. Gabriola Island: New Society Publishers.

Hruska, J. (2009, January 20). Malware infestation responsible for credit card data breach. Ars Technica. Retrieved from http://arstechnica.com/security/2009/01/malware-infestation-responsible-for-credit-card-data-breach/

ICANN (2011, February 3). Available Pool of Unallocated IPv4 Internet Addresses Now Completely Emptied. The Future Rests with IPv6. Retrieved from http://www.icann.org/en/news/releases/release-03feb11-en.pdf

Josef Pieprzy. J., Hardjono, T. & Seberry, J. (2003). Fundamentals of Computer Security. New York: Springer.

Kessler, G. (1999). Handbook on Local Area Networks. Retrieved from http://www.garykessler.net/library/crypto.html#why3

Lovelock, J. (1995). The Ages of Gaia: A Biography of Our Living Earth. London/New York: W.W. Norton & Co.

Meadows, D.H., Meadows, D.L., Randers, J. & Behrens III, W.W. (1972). The Limits to Growth. A Report for the Club of Rome's Project on the Predicament of Mankind. New York: Universal Books. Retrieved from http://www.scribd.com/doc/61854342/1972-The-Limits-to-Growth.

NOS (2012, February 14). Sluizen slecht beveiligd (in Dutch). Retrieved from http://nos.nl/artikel/340971-sluizen-slecht-beveiligd.html

NU (2012, April 2). Creditcardgegevens 1,5 miljoen mensen gestolen door hackers (in Dutch). Retrieved from http://www.nu.nl/internet/2777826/creditcardgegevens-15-miljoen-mensen-gestolen-hackers.html

NU (2012, February 14). D66 en VVD willen opheldering over hackers (in Dutch). Retrieved from http://www.nu.nl/internet/2740716/d66-en-vvd-willen-opheldering-hackers.html

Tech2 (2012, May 31). Energy assets in front line of cyber war. Reuters. Retrieved from

http://tech2.in.com/news/general/energy-assets-in-front-line-of-cyber-war/312002

The Internet of Things (2012). The Internet of Things Council. Retrieved from http://www.theinternetofthings.eu/

The Week (2010, July 27). The Looming IP-Address Shortage: A Crisis for the Internet Age. Retrieved from http://theweek. com/article/index/205397/the-looming-ip-address-shortage-a-crisis-for-the-internet-age

Chapter 16

Abrahams, M. (2012, May 21). Subliminal Suggestions Do Not Work, Research Finds. The Guardian. Retrieved from http:// www.guardian.co.uk/education/2012/may/21/subliminal-suggestions-itching-improbable-research

Ariely. D. & Berns, G.S. (2010). Neuromarketing: the Hope and Hype of Neuroimaging in Business. Nature Reviews. Neuroscience 11(4), 284-292.

Bordwell, D. (1989). A Case for Cognitivism. IRIS 9, 11-40.

Bostrom, N. (2003). Are You Living in a Computer Simulation? Philosophical Quarterly 53(211), 243-255.

Descartes, R. (1641). Meditations on First Philosophy. In: The Philosophical Writings of René Descartes (trans. by J. Cottingham, R. Stoothoff and D. Murdoch) (1984). Vol. 2, 1-62. Cambridge: Cambridge University Press.

Festinger, L. (1957). A Theorie of Cognitive Dissonance. Evanston, IL: Row, Peterson

Fodor, J. (1975). The Language of Thought. Cambridge, MA: The MIT Press.

Griffiths, M.D. (1998). Internet Addiction: Does It Really Exist? In: J. Gackenbach (Ed.), Psychology and the Internet, 61-75. New York: Academic Press.

Hellman, M., Schoenmakers, T.M., Nordstrom, B.R. & van Holst, R.J. (2012, June 22). Is There Such a Thing as Online Video Game Addiction? A Cross-Disciplinary Review. Addiction Research & Theory, 1-11. Retrieved from http://informahealthcare. com/doi/abs/10.3109/16066359.2012.693222

Keim, B. (2008). Brain Scanners Can See Your Decisions Before You Make Them. Wired online article April 13, 2008. Retrieved from http://www.wired.com/science/discoveries/news/2008/04/mind_decision

O'Flaherty, W.D. (1984). Dreams, Illusion, and Other Realities. London: University of Chicago Press.

Putnam, H. (1979). Mathematics, Matter, and Method: Philosophical Papers, Vol.1. Cambridge, MA: The MIT Press.

Pyramid Research (2012, July 18). Smartphone Addiction Touches 41% of UK Users. Analyst Notes. Retrieved from http://www.pyramidresearch.com/points/item/120718.htm

R. Alleyne (2009, September 28). Subliminal Advertising Really Does Work, Claim Scientists. The Telegraph. Retrieved from http://www.telegraph.co.uk/science/science-news/6232801/Subliminal-advertising-really-does-work-claim-scientists.html

Reeves, B. & Nass, C. (1996). The Media Equation: How People Treat Computers, Television, and New Media Like Real People and Places. Cambridge: Cambridge University Press.

Rideout, V.J., Foehr, U.G. & Roberts, D.F. (2010). Generation M2. Media in the Lives of 8-to 18-Year-Olds. Washington: Kaiser Family Foundation. Retrieved from http://www.kff.org/entmedia/upload/8010.pdf

Smith, K. (2008, April 11). Brain Makes Decisions Before You Even Know It. Nature. Retrieved from http://www.nature.com/news/2008/080411/full/news.2008.751.html

Soon, C.S., Brass, M., Heinze, H.J. & Haynes, J.D. (2008). Nature Neuroscience 11, 609-616. doi: 10.1038/nn.2112.

Yuan, K., Qin, W., Wang, G., Zeng, F., Zhao, L., Yang, X., Liu, P., Liu, J., Sun, J., von Deneen, K.M., Gong, Q., Liu, Y. & Tian, J. (2011). Microstructure Abnormalities in Adolescents with Internet Addiction Disorder. PLoS ONE 6(6): e20708. doi:10.1371/journal.pone.0020708.

Chapter 17

Bahney, A. (2006, March 9). Don't Talk to Invisible Strangers. New York Times. Retrieved from http://www.nytimes.com/2006/03/09/fashion/thursdaystyles/09parents.html

BBC News (2010, March 16). Facebook Traps Italian Fugitive Mafia Suspect. Retrieved from http://news.bbc.co.uk/2/hi/8570796.stm

Bowdler, N. (2011, September 20). Canadian Film-Maker's Bionic Eye. BBC News. Retrieved from http://www.bbc.co.uk/news/health-14931681

Carr, N.G. (2011). The Shallows: What the Internet Is Doing to Our Brains. London, New York: W.W. Norton & Co.

Cocking, D. & Matthews, S. (2000). Ethics and Information Technology 2(4), 223-231.

De Volkskrant (2012, September 21). Website met fouten Apple Maps daverend succes (in Dutch). Retrieved from http://www.volkskrant.nl/vk/nl/2680/Economie/article/detail/3319705/2012/09/21/Website-met-fouten-Apple-Maps-daverend-succes.dhtml

Dohmen, J. (2007). Vrienden waar zijn jullie? (in Dutch). Antenne 25(2), 5-10.

Freundlich, N. (2001). Arresting Alzheimers; Drugs that Fight Milder Memory Loss May Prevent Its Onset. Business Week 3736, 94-97.

Gantz, J. & Reinsel, D. (2011, June). Extracting Value from Chaos. IDC Review. Retrieved from http://www.emc.com/collateral/analyst-reports/idc-extracting-value-from-chaos-ar.pdf

Giurgea, C.E. (1984). Psychopharmacology Tomorrow: 1984 or the Little Prince? Psychological Medicine 14(3), 491-496. doi:10.1017/S0033291700015075

Gladwell, M. (2008). Outliers: The Story of Success. New York: Little, Brown and Co.

Hiskey, D. (2010, February 9). A Japanese Soldier Who Continued Fighting WWII 29 Years After the Japanese Surrendered, Because He Didn't Know. Today I found out. Retrieved from http://www.todayifoundout.com/index.php/2010/02/a-japanese-soldier-who-continued-fighting-wwii-29-years-after-the-japanese-surrendered-because-he-didnt-know/

Jiddema, G. (2012, July 9). Facebook vrienden zijn nu ook gewoon te koop (in Dutch). Social Media Promotions. Retrieved from http://www.emerce.nl/wire/facebook-vrienden-nu-gewoon-koop

Kamenetz, A. (2011, March 2). MIT Scientist Captures 90,000 Hours of Video of His Son's First Words, Graphs It. FastCompany. Retrieved from http://www.fastcompany.com/1733627/mit-scientist-captures-90000-hours-video-his-sons-first-words-graphs-it

Lanchin, M. (2012, Januari 2012). Shoichi Yokoi, the Japanese Soldier Who Held Out in Guam. BBC World News. Retrieved from http://www.bbc.co.uk/news/magazine-16681636

Larson E. (1997). Rethinking Deep Blue: Why a Computer Can't Reproduce a Mind. Access Research Network. Origins and Design 18(2). Retrieved from http://www.arn.org/docs/odesign/od182/blue182.htm

Loebner Net (2012). Home Page of The Loebner Prize in Artificial Intelligence. The First Turing Test. Retrieved from http://www.loebner.net/Prizef/loebner-prize.html

Maher, B. (2008). Poll results: Look Who's Doping. Nature 452, 674-675. Retrieved from http://www.nature.com/news/2008/080409/full/452674a.html

Orwell, G. (1949). Nineteen Eighty-Four. A Novel. London: Secker & Warburg.

Persaud, C. (2011, June 28). World's Data Doubling Every Two Years; Up to 1.8 Zettabytes in 2011. Market News. Retrieved from http://www.marketnews.ca/content/index/page?pid=9400

Roy, D. (2011). Why I Taped My Son's Childhood. TEDTalk Tuesdays. Retrieved from http://edition.cnn.com/2011/OPINION/03/13/roy.tapes.childhood/index.html

Russell, S.J. & Norvig, P. (2003). Artificial Intelligence: A Modern Approach (2nd ed.), Upper Saddle River, NJ: Prentice Hall.

Smith, M.E. & Farah, M.J. (2011). Are Prescription Stimulants "Smart Pills"? The Epidemiology and Cognitive Neuroscience of Prescription Stimulant Use by Normal Healthy Individuals. Psychological Bulletin 137 (5), 717-741. Retrieved from http://www.psych.upenn.edu/~mfarah/pdfs/PsychBullProof.pdf

Stuijt, A. (2009, May 8). Toronto Filmmaker Replacing One Eye with a Movie Camera. Digital Journal. Retrieved from http://www.digitaljournal.com/article/268771

Tumblr (2012). The Amazing iOS 6 Maps. Retrieved from http://theamazingios6maps.tumblr.com/

Turing, A. (1950). Computing Machinery and Intelligence. Mind LIX 236. 433-460. doi:10.1093/mind/LIX.236.433. Retrieved from http://loebner.net/Prizef/TuringArticle.html

Van der Hulst, R.C. & Neve, R.J.M. (2008). High-tech crime, soorten criminaliteit en hun daders. Een literatuurinventarisatie (in Dutch). Meppel, NL: Boom. Retrieved from http://www.wodc.nl/images/ob264_volledige%20tekst_tcm44-105995.pdf

Westera, W. (2005). Beyond Functionality and Technocracy: Creating Human Involvement with Educational Technology. Educational Technology & Society, 8 (1), 28-37.

Westera, W. (2011). On the Changing Nature of Learning Context: Anticipating the Virtual Extensions of the World. Educational Technology & Society, 14(2), 201-212.

INDEX

Johann Gutenberg 16
John Dewey 245
John F. Kennedy 44
Joker 164
Jorge Louis Borges 88
Julius Caesar 201
JVC 186

K

Karinthy , Frigyes 136
Karl Jaspers 41, 42, 47
Karl Popper 82
Kasparov, Gary 238
Katz, Richard 124
Keen, Andrew 141
Kennedy, John F. 44
keyboard 11, 142
Kickstarter 178
kinetograph 54, 116
King Thamus 102
Kirk, captain 108
knowledgable idiot 88
knowledge
  articulate 79
  codified 79
  declarative 74
  economy 72
  explicit 79
  implicit 78
  knowing how 79
  knowing that 79, 80
  objective 74
  persona; 63, 99, 109
  procedural 78
  scientific 80, 81, 82
  tacit 78
Knowledge
  accumulation 71
  power 43, 72
knowledgeable idiot 88
knowledge is power 43, 72
Kobo 180
Komrij, Gerrit 45
Konrad Zuse 28
KPN 200
Kuhn, Thomas 75
Kurt Gödel 81
Kurzweil, Ray 32, 34, 204

L

La Chinoise 59
language
  programming 27
  spoken 14, 16
  system 55, 57
  translation losses 53
  written ix, 14, 15, 16, 17, 20, 31, 50,
    55, 84, 86, 102, 103, 207
Laplace, Pierre-Simon 81
last universal ancestor 5
La verità svelata dal tempo 62
laws of nature 170, 208
learning
  conditioning model 94
  e-learning 124, 170, 197, 211
  learners 95, 102, 116, 118, 121, 123,
    168, 169
  limitations 78
  pill 92, 241
lecture 46, 78, 168, 169, 172
Leni Riefenstahl 61
Leonardo da Vinci 243
lesson 86, 251
Lester, Dr. Janice 108
letter 84, 137, 201, 202
Levie, Howard 54
Lev Vygotzky 152
license 117, 187
lifelong learning 240
lifestyle 48, 57, 69, 95, 126, 161, 224,
  235, 247
Like button 177, 182
limits to growth 203
linguistics 31, 58
LinkedIn 138, 178
Linux 140, 186
literacy, media x, 60, 250, 253
locked-in syndrome 111
Loebner Prize 239
lone wolves 166
long-term memory 31, 219, 227
Lovelock, james 205
Lucy 1
Lulzsec 200
Luria, Aleksander 88

M

N

pill 92, 241
pineal gland 24
pixel 34, 216
placeCityStanley Pons 65
placecountry-regionMonaco,
    James 60
placeDunbars number 232
PlaceNameLos PlaceNameRodeos
    PlaceTypeAirport 66
placeStateBerlin Wall 125
planet 3, 4, 71, 74, 80, 82, 205, 218
plant 2, 5, 21, 33, 38, 61, 62, 104,
    158, 191, 200, 234
Plato 76, 80, 90, 102
play 153
PlayStation 119
pocket calculator 28, 101
podcast 138
poetry 25, 59, 88, 133
Polanyi, Michel 78
politics 15, 44, 52, 61, 62, 68, 82,
    212, 238, 245
pollution 40
Pons, Stanley 65
popcorn 213
Popper, Karl 82
pornography 147, 235
positivism 39, 46
Postman, Neil 44, 46, 59
Powerdown 205
power of a network 181
predator ix, 6, 7, 11, 38, 63, 216, 250
predecessor 16, 195
prehistoric 1, 6, 13
prejudice 39, 66, 72, 211
premium model 178, 185, 231
presentation 51, 95, 138, 183, 184
presenter 83, 84
press 16, 17, 125, 176
prey 1, 6, 11, 216, 226
price 41, 88, 124, 146, 155, 167, 173,
    176, 177, 183, 185, 191, 227,
    229
price comparison portal 185
price fighter 185
priest 39, 49, 66
priestess 49
primate 232
primordial soup 4
princess 129, 142

printing 16, 17, 18, 20, 86, 91, 93,
    102, 179, 180, 196, 224, 227
Prius Online game 155
privacy 146, 202, 228, 235
processing power 218
processor 9, 32, 33, 51, 140, 186,
    219, 220
producer 93, 98, 99, 135, 137, 166,
    250
product leader 184
profile 138, 143, 146, 176, 235, 236
profit 120, 173, 176, 179
projector 51, 116
promotion 40, 61, 62, 96, 166, 231
propaganda 96
Propp, Vladimir 129
prosthesis 105, 106, 109, 242
protein 4, 5
protocol 185, 196
proverb 68
provider 145, 146, 191, 200, 225, 235
proximal development, zone of
    152, 154
psychiatric 49, 92
psycho-motor 108
psychosis 93, 209, 220
publisher 141, 179, 180
puzzle 5, 58, 152, 153
Pythia 49, 50, 66

Q

quantum computing 35, 218
quest 150, 156
questionnaire 169
quiz 9, 150, 156, 238

R

radio 34, 43, 44, 49, 50, 51, 93, 95,
    125, 146, 156, 161, 223, 224,
    247, 249, 250
Radiohead 179
railways, network 191
rationalism 6, 39, 40, 41, 94, 134,
    208, 214
Ray Kurzweil 32, 34, 204
RDF 139
realism 55, 133, 149, 157, 215
real time 20, 129, 210, 238
Reaper 159

CPSIA information can be obtained
at www.ICGtesting.com
Printed in the USA
LVOW11s0158270117
522363LV00001B/13/P